Religion in Five Minutes

Religion in Five Minutes

Edited by
Aaron W. Hughes and Russell T. McCutcheon

SHEFFIELD UK   BRISTOL CT

Published by Equinox Publishing Ltd.

UK: Office 415, The Workstation, 15 Paternoster Row, Sheffield, South Yorkshire S1 2BX

USA: ISD, 70 Enterprise Drive, Bristol, CT 06010

www.equinoxpub.com

First published 2017

British Library Cataloguing-in-Publication Data

A catalogue record for this book is available from the British Library.

ISBN   978 1 78179 464 7   (hardback)
ISBN   978 1 78179 465 4   (paperback)

Library of Congress Cataloging-in-Publication Data

Names: Hughes, Aaron W., 1968- editor.
Title: Religion in five minutes / edited by Aaron W. Hughes and Russell T. McCutcheon.
Description: Bristol : Equinox Publishing Ltd, 2017. | Includes bibliographical references and index.
Identifiers: LCCN 2017006930 (print) | LCCN 2017036778 (ebook) |
    ISBN 9781781796122 (ePDF) | ISBN 9781781794647 (hb) | ISBN 9781781794654 (pb)
Subjects: LCSH: Religion--Miscellanea.
Classification: LCC BL48 (ebook) | LCC BL48 .R4235 2017 (print) | DDC 200--dc23
LC record available at https://lccn.loc.gov/2017006930

Typeset by JS Typesetting Ltd, Porthcawl, Mid Glamorgan
Printed and bound in Great Britain by Lightning Source UK Ltd., Milton Keynes and Lightning Source Inc., La Vergne, TN

Contents

The religions

The study of religion

The future

Preface

Aaron W. Hughes and Russell T. McCutcheon

We've both had a long and fruitful relationship with Equinox Publishers; so when Janet Joyce gave us a copy of *The Five-Minute Linguist* (2nd edition, 2012) and invited us to think about a comparable book in the study of religion, well, it didn't take us long to agree; for it occurred to us how this opportunity would not only let us address a wide-reading and curious audience but would also allow us to involve a group of newer voices in the study of religion. Given our own relationship with a professional organization known as the North American Association for the Study of Religion (NAASR)—for which we currently serve as vice president and president, respectively—it was natural that we looked to our membership for possible contributors.

But one crucial question remained: what would be the questions?

We both agreed that few things are worse than someone trying to think up what their imagined version of someone else might find interesting. So we decided to invite some novice students to pose their own questions—and so, given that only one of us was involved in introductory courses that semester, we invited a group of undergraduate students at the University of Alabama, all in their first course in the academic study of religion during the Fall 2016 semester, to each submit a question or two about religion that they'd like answered. As you can guess, the questions were diverse and, predictably, told us much about who they were and the kind of news they read. From those submissions we narrowed the list down to a set of questions that it seemed readers elsewhere, in different situations, might also want answered. To this list, we added some questions of our own, to supplement it. The set that we finally arrived at, of course, is hardly exhaustive and in no way authoritative. So we make no claim to it being encyclopedic and have no illusions that it somehow comes with no interests or assumptions—we're all situated somewhere, of course—most (but not all) of our authors, and all of our questioners, are in the US, for example. This self-awareness on the part of our authors, we trust, is why you'll find that many of the answers eventually work their way around to suggesting that the question itself is worth mulling over, inasmuch as the questions we ask tell us more about ourselves, and how we see the world, than we might at first realize. So even if the book doesn't have the specific question you'd like to pose it may imbue this attitude and thereby help you to become more curious about your curiosities.

As you'll see by the table of contents, it struck us that the questions could be arranged in terms of three broad areas, so we sorted them that way:

- questions about religion as a phenomenon (often signified in the field by referring to religion in the singular);
- questions about details concerning this or that specific religion (generally denoted by religions, in the plural); and
- those that deal with how to go about studying religion.

These are followed by our own concluding thoughts on where religion—as well as the very category of religion—might go from here. All of the answers, in their various ways, suggest that studying religion is a scholarly activity that examines religion as a human phenomenon, as opposed to how members of any specific religion, whether liberal or conservative, might wish to talk about themselves or others. For the academic study of religion—variously known, depending what part of the world you're in, as comparative religion, the science of religion, the history of religions, or, as it is in many schools, religious studies—has a long history (dating to the late-nineteenth century in Europe, when many of today's academic disciplines were first established or disentangled from one another). The trouble, as we see it, is that many members of the reading public only think of theology—articulate, and rational insider discourses on the meaning and value of 'the faith'—when they think about studying religion (as opposed to just being religious). The problem with such an approach is that it fails to understand that non-confessional but rigorously descriptive and cross-culturally comparative scholars have been studying myths, rituals, symbols, and institutions for well over a century—producing insightful, even provocative studies that help us to understand why we, as human beings, do some of the things that we do. So we're hoping that this little book, with short, easily tackled essays (each with some suggested further readings on the topic), might help to turn that tide, at least a little—whether read by someone for leisure or, perhaps, as a requirement in an introductory class somewhere—by demonstrating that scholars of religion have something interesting (and maybe even useful) to say to those who are curious about these things that we all so commonly know as religions.

Religion

1
Is everyone religious?

Russell T. McCutcheon

Historically speaking, we'd have to answer that by saying a resounding no, not at all; for the word *religion* was once applied rather narrowly (some still do this today, of course). That is, 'they' might have been seen by 'us' as being idolatrous heathens, superstitious savages, or practicing magic, while 'we' were cultured, civilized, and, yes, pious, religious, or even saved. But then, it's not difficult at all to trace the manner in which this designation—labeling something as a religion or something or someone as religious— was gradually expanded, such as in the so-called age of discovery. For people newly encountered seemed to be doing things rather like what 'we' were doing (that is what those earlier European explorers, sailors, missionaries, soldiers, traders, and bureaucrats understood themselves to be doing), yet how could they be like us, uncivilized as they were (and all that came with how 'we' once saw 'them'). Sure, we may all have been using water in rituals, or telling creation tales, but ...

But now, unlike past replies, we'd probably offer a resounding yes, of course they are. Google 'world religions map,' for example, and there's a good chance that you'll come across a variety of maps of the globe in which every inch of territory is colored red or blue or green, or whatever color the map's key associates with each of the world's religions. For today, inasmuch as you are a human being, many of us now tend to think that you're necessarily religious (much as today everyone must claim a nationality and own a passport if they expect to move around the globe—but it wasn't always that way, right?); even people who now claim *not to have a religion*—people who might call themselves agnostics (claiming not to know if there is a god or not), as well as those who see themselves to be atheists (disbelieving in the existence of a god)—are studied today by scholars of religion, which implies that they must have something in common with religious people, given that scholars trained in this one specialty seem to think they have something worthwhile to say about them. In fact, the modern popularity of seeing religion as either a belief system, ideology or worldview—as a way that people make their worlds habitable and meaningful (thereby defining these words in rather particular ways)—implies that inasmuch as everyone could be said to have a point of view then, voila, they're all religious as well. 'The religion of secularism ...' is something people on the religious right now like to talk about when, for instance, making a case for why creationism (or what some now instead call Intelligent Design) ought to be taught in public schools alongside evolutionary theory. Or, again, consider the current fashion of assuming religion to name some deeply human yearning or experience—such as those who see it as synonymous with belief or faith—something that is woven into our very fabric (or, for some biologists and cognitive scientists, we could say our very genes); this means that we can't conceive of 'the human' without at the same time understanding people all to be *homo religiosus*.

So yes, everyone is religious—at least that's what we'd now say.

What should be evident is that answering this question requires one to use a contested term—as other chapters will make evident, there is currently hot debate among scholars around where the word comes from and the limits of its use—that can be defined in so many different ways that the answer tells you more about the one doing the answering than the thing the answer is supposedly about. Case in point: recalling a point made above, consider David Chidester's important book, *Savage Systems: Colonialism and Comparative Religion in Southern Africa* (1996), in which the author charts the progressive intellectual moves that, over time, enabled Europeans who at first maintained that the newly encountered peoples, on the colonial frontier, had no religion to slowly, but eventually, come to see that, well, they were indeed religious, not unlike us. Chidester, like a variety of other scholars in his academic tradition, therefore makes plain that this word religion is a comparative category used in moments of contact— something we talk about inasmuch as we see certain resemblances (or not) across different settings and among different peoples. Should, for example, belief in a creator god rise to the top of your criteria (as it does for many but not all who use the term), then only those systems that satisfy this one requirement may all strike you as looking sufficiently alike to all be called religious. This means that the identification of something *as* religious depends not just on criteria (and, thus, the one determining them) but on how we, as observers of the world, use those criteria to manage what counts as a similarity as opposed to a difference. After all, there are all sorts of things different between, say, Judaism and Shinto, yet if you pick up any world religions textbook you'll find a chapter on each. So the judgment that they're both religions—that people claiming to be each, following customs and making claims associated with each, are religious, as opposed to something else (such as Judaism known as an ethnic identity, at least according to others)—is indicative of a social actors making sense of their world, putting each in their place, so as to manage all that information that comes at us daily. In fact, with that world religions textbook in mind, it's pretty fascinating to look at how it has grown over the years, continually expanding to the degree that, much like the above-mentioned map, virtually every human being alive today is somehow addressed between its two covers.

And it's the malleability of this term, religion, that today strikes some scholars as so interesting. For if that textbook contained only those systems that, as just suggested, claim a creator god to exist, then it would be an awfully thin book. (The apparent absence of a creator god in what we know as Buddhism was among the reasons scholars for so many years—as some do to this day—insisted that it's a philosophy and *not* a religion.) That is, the topics included in such books' chapters all depend on varying degrees of overlap, since none of these things are all identical (despite so many today still using Christianity as the role model for what gets to count as religious). So it's this move from a strict definition that excludes most of the people on the planet to what we have today—an extremely plastic, even totalizing, definition that encompasses virtually everything—that strikes some of us as the far more interesting issue to study.

So while I hope it doesn't read as what we used to call a cop-out, and thus or an attempt to side-step a tough query, answering this seemingly straightforward question depends on what you mean by religion. For if, as the Rev. Thwackum (a character in Henry Fielding's comic novel of 1749, *The History of Tom Jones*—who, like some to this day, maintained that 'there are various sects and heresies in the world') famously reported: 'When I mention religion, I mean the Christian religion; and not only the Christian religion, but the Protestant religion; and not only the Protestant religion, but the Church of England' (vol 1, book III.3), then you can imagine an answer far different than one offered by a cognitive scientist who studies religion as but one instance of an evolutionarily hardwired tendency to project the notion of agency onto the world around ourselves, as if the universe is alive and does things—one of which is to either love or punish us.

About the author

Russell T. McCutcheon is professor and chair of the Department of Religious Studies at the University of Alabama; his work is on the theories of religion, approaches to the study of myth, as well as focusing on the history of the study of religion and the practical effects of classification systems.

Suggestions for further reading

In this book

See also Chapters 2 (origins of the word religion), 3 (classifying religion), 4 (sports as religion), 7 (religions v. cults), 8 (belief in a higher power), 14 (spiritual but not religious), and 15 (atheism or secularism as religion).

Elsewhere

Chidester, David. *Savage Systems: Colonialism and Comparative Religion in Southern Africa.* Charlottesville, VA: University of Virginia Press, 1996.

Smart, Ninian. *Worldviews: Cross-Cultural Explorations in Human Beliefs* (3rd edition). New York: Pearson, 1999.

2
Where does the word religion come from?

David McConeghy

The modern English word 'religion' has ancient origins. The Latin term *religio*, which began to be used around the 1st century BCE, may have roots in two different verbs: *religare* or 'to bind fast' and *relegere* meaning 'to consider carefully.' The use of these terms is complex, but *religio* first appears in discussions by the Roman philosophers Cicero and Lucretius about the ceremonial duties humans owe to the gods to avoid the wrath of forces beyond our control.

Today, tracing 'religion' to *religare* in the sense of bind or connect is more common, but in the fourth century Christians were comfortable using both meanings. *Religio* meant a person's scruples (or second thoughts) as well as described the proper worship that brought humans closer to each other and god(s). The notable theologian Augustine, for instance, argued it was important for religion's worship to be focused on the correct object (i.e., God as opposed to statues). If you were going to bind yourself to god to avoid damnation then you had better consider your options and choose wisely.

Augustine and many others that followed him wrote about Christianity and Judaism using terms from other languages that were not direct synonyms for *religio*. Latin was the primary language of Christian scholars for hundreds of years, but the Bible was translated from Greek and Hebrew. The Greek word *threskeia* dealt more directly with ritual worship, but there were also Hebrew terms that had cultural significance like *ioudaismos*, referring to the Judeans or Jews. After the middle of the seventh century it was necessary to have a serious discussion regarding Islam and what Muslims meant when they used the Arabic word *din* or creed. In all these issue of translation, religion became a lens for cross-cultural understanding. Did Christians and Jews both have religion? What about Romans rituals? Religion emerged as an analytical tool for description, identification, comparison, and classification. This process continued for hundreds of years with growing contributions beyond the Mediterranean.

By the colonial and modern era beginning in the nineteenth century, 'religion' was emerging as the catch-all term for those in Europe and America to describe Buddhism, Christianity, Hinduism, Islam, Judaism, Taoism, and more. Definitions of religion struggled to identify the core of the term that mattered when comparing these traditions. Did it mean belief in one God? Was action or belief primary? Translation continued as in the use of 'Hindu' for Indian followers of Sanatana Dharma or the eternal law. For many in Asia using a more generic western term offered a trade-off: a reduction in the meaning(s) of expansive and complex native terms in favor of cohesion and recognition as 'world religions' alongside Judaism, Christianity, and Islam.

That trade-off is unresolved, so what religion is or what counts as religious varies. The word's primary use remains as a tool of classification to describe an incredibly diverse class of objects, ideas, practices, and institutions. Definitions that have modeled themselves on the legacy of *religio*'s use by early Christianity have been attacked for coercing non-Christians to use a term developed to elevate Christianity and even to denigrate the beliefs and practices of other cultures. These challenges have been exacerbated not only by the legacy of religion's connection to colonial governance, but also because control of the term's scope and meaning influence a range of issues such as the extent of legal protections for religious freedom. The self-evidence of many claims about religion (i.e., 'I know it when I see it') remain a fundamental hurdle for the term's ongoing development. If it once described what Romans did to appease their gods, then today it is is a battleground over identity: can what seems self-evident to one group about what defines religion be used by others who see the world differently? Appropriately, the fight over term's use connects us. We must all carefully consider how cross-cultural translation offers more than synonyms for foreign words. Thus, the word religion's origins remind us that definition and translation are extraordinary powers that shape our connections to others.

About the author

David McConeghy is an independent researcher and writer living in the Greater Boston area. He holds a PhD in religious studies from the University of California, Santa Barbara and has taught religious ethics and world religions at Chapman University in Orange, California.

Suggestions for further reading

In this book

See also Chapters 3 (classifying religion), 5 religion v. mythology), and 6 (religion v. philosophy).

Elsewhere

Masuzawa, Tomoko. *The Invention of World Religions: How European Universalism was Preserved in the Language of Pluralism.* Chicago, IL: University of Chicago Press, 2005.

Nongbri, Brent. *Before Religion: A History of a Modern Concept.* New Haven, CT: Yale University Press, 2013.

3

What does it take for something to be classified as a 'religion'?

Robyn Faith Walsh

Although there isn't a firm consensus, most scholars agree that for something to be classified as a religion, it must demonstrate a concern with or acceptance of some kind of supernatural being or force. Whether described in terms of anthropomorphized gods, elements of nature, deceased ancestors, or unseen agents, these supernatural phenomena are understood to have influence over the natural world. Activities are called 'religious' when these phenomena are acknowledged by some form of ritual or practice such as groups gathering in order to communicate with gods or spirits, ritual meals, or individuals producing specialized kinds of writing or artwork that acknowledge the existence of immaterial forces in the attempt to explain their origins and purpose.

Classifying religion this way allows scholars to identify, describe, and compare certain circumscribed practices and discourses for the purposes of scholarly inquiry. But, this perceived flexibility is also a source of controversy, with critics noting that it imposes what is essentially a modern Western, folk classification onto a set of dynamic practices not so easily set apart from other aspects of social life. To understand this, we must first realize that religion does not exist as a special set of ideas or practices that are universal to all people across time and culture. When any of us speaks of 'religion,' we are not referring to something that is self-evident or a real thing-in-the-world. Instead, 'religion' is one of many terms invented by humans to describe certain aspects of social life. In the West, religion has come to possess strong associations with Western values and culture, and such associations should prevent us from taking its definition for granted.

The concept of religion as it is employed today has had a relatively short lifespan. The word derives from the Latin root *religio* meaning something along the lines of 'duty,' but the ancient Mediterranean authors who first used it intended it to mean everything from 'showing integrity,' to 'practices in recognition of the gods,' to the simple idea of 'rules.' While different groups saw different supernatural powers as authoritative (and this could certainly cause conflict!), they recognized such differences as intertwined with other forms of identification, like ethnicity. Thus, 'religion' maintained its tight association with other aspects of social life and was not easily distinguished from politics, medicine, science, economics and so on.

It is not until the Inquisition in Europe that 'religion' begins to be correlated with private belief. Further associations between 'religion' and coherent systems of faith and practice, sacred texts, institutional leaders, and so forth emerged during the fifteenth century onward, notably during the centuries of European colonialism. As the largely Christian political powers of Europe extended their reach into the continents of Asia, Africa, and what would later be known as the Americas, colonists applied their version of 'religion' in observing indigenous populations who shared certain practices or discourses. These indigenous customs were re-named by colonialists with terms like 'Buddhism' or 'Hinduism,' and many indigenous groups eventually adopted this imposed classification as a means of self-description.

In the US, people often talk about religion as interior or private, using phrases like 'personal belief' or asserting claims such as, 'I'm spiritual, not religious.' Interestingly, those who make such claims continue to engage in established practices (e.g., prayer, meditation) or acknowledge supernatural forces commonly associated with 'religions' (e.g., a creator god) even if they don't explicitly accept such ideas themselves. Relatedly, neither the Congress nor the Supreme Court in the US has ever concretely defined religion, choosing instead to speak in terms of a 'Supreme Being,' 'deeply and sincerely held' morals and ethics, or simply naming various representative categories (e.g., Christianity, Taoism, even Secular Humanism). On one hand, this resistance to classification suggests a certain fidelity to the First Amendment. On the other hand, this failure to define religion, despite repeated calls to do so, demonstrates how difficult it is to isolate it from the larger fabric of everyday social life.

About the author
Robyn Faith Walsh is assistant professor of New Testament and early Christianity at the University of Miami (Florida). Her research interests include the letters of Paul, the history of the interpretation of the synoptic problem, and Greco-Roman archaeology.

Suggestions for further reading

In this book
See also Chapters 1 (ubiquity of religion), 4 (sports as religion), 5 (religion v. mythology), and 6 (religion v. philosophy).

Elsewhere
Arnal, William E. and Russell T. McCutcheon. *The Sacred is the Profane: The Political Nature of 'Religion.'* New York: Oxford University Press, 2013.

Smith, Jonathan Z. *Relating Religion: Essays in the Study of Religion.* Chicago, IL: University of Chicago Press, 2014.

Stowers, Stanley. 'The Ontology of Religion.' In *Introducing Religion*, edited by Willi Braun and Russell T. McCutcheon, 434–449. Sheffield: Equinox, 2008.

4
Can sports be a religion?

Russell T. McCutcheon

The simple answer is: Sure, why not?

Although a more complicated (and thus misleadingly brief) answer would be: It all depends.

On what? By this point in the book the answer might already be obvious: the definition of religion you use, of course—which means that it all depends to whom you're posing the question.

Broadly speaking, there are two types of definitions that people commonly use to define something as religion: substantive and functionalist. While the former identifies what someone might take to be key or necessary features that one would expect to find when looking at a religion, such as belief in a god (the feature most people presume to be essential when it comes to seeing something as religious), the later focuses on the wider role something plays, the purpose it serves, or the effect that it has. While the former approach may have a commonsense ring to it, and thus is often favored in popular discourses on religion (from people chatting in shops to news magazine headlines) the latter approach tends to be more prominent in scholarship; so, for example, while going to a baseball game might not strike someone attending church as being very religious, someone affectionately talking about 'the church of base-ball'—as one of the lead characters in *Bull Durham* (1988) phrases it in the film's opening—might make a lot of sense to a scholar interested in the function such events play in wider social life.

Classically speaking, there were social functionalists and psychological functionalists—Émile Durkheim, a French scholar from the late nineteenth and early twentieth century, comes to mind as an example of the former while Sigmund Freud, from roughly the same era, certainly counts as an instance of the latter. While I wouldn't want to limit functionalism to just these two examples, these at least help us think through the question, since the seemingly obvious, even intuitive, boundary between what is and what isn't religion is not as clear when they're our guides. For although, let's say, football matches in Europe, or that other game called football in North America, obviously are not religion—at least when judged from a substantive point of view that, for instance, expects to see belief in a powerful, moral, and timeless being who loves us and controls the universe—following Durkheim's or Freud's lead means that we won't be so quick to dismiss the crowds, the chants, the players, the mascots, and the rules and traditions associated with the game, when it comes to asking if they're religious. For if the function of religion is to unite a disparate collection of people into a coherent group by means of their participation in a system of interconnected beliefs and practices that are focused on a basic distinction between things that are safe, allowed, and thus sanctioned, from those that are dangerous, disallowed, and thus illegitimate (which is just a slight tweak on how Durkheim famously wrote about the sacred/profane distinction that we commonly associated with things religious), then the opening question isn't so easily answered in the negative—as some might be inclined to answer it, at least on first glance. Or, again, if we understand religion as a culturally accepted social convention that individuals each use to vent and thereby express (always in a strategically coded, and thus disguised, fashion) their own natural, individual desires that, at least in everyday life, are usually thwarted, or in the least, managed, by the larger groups of which they're members (which is pretty much how Freud understood the role played by religion, among such other things as dreams or what we call Freudian slips), then fans clutching their hot dogs and jeering an opponent can be seen in a rather new light. For in both cases (that is, adopting either Durkheim's social theory or Freud's psychoanalytic approach) the simple phrase 'We won!' is evidence of significant social and psychological work being done, whereby not just ideas of us/them and win/lose have been created and reinforced during the match but the curious identification of fans with the members of the team has been solidified; for although only the latter actually played the game the former feels equally victorious—and it is the creation and expression of this feeling, this internalization of victory and superiority (at least when your team wins; surprisingly deep depression and anger often greet a loss) that prompts some scholars of religion to find in sport features that strike them as very familiar from their studies of religion. And so it's not just when fans might pray for their team to win or when players engage in little rituals and lucky charms to ensure a good performance; for the very institution of sports, as an site that plays a crucial role in our larger society, could be argued to accomplish precisely what mosques, synagogues, churches, and temples do as discrete institutions at yet other social sites—all being places where group members form lasting identifications with each other, address and moderate individual idiosyncrasies that potentially undermine larger group interests, reinforce a set of rules that allow them to distinguish good from bad and acceptable from unacceptable, all of which makes it possible to distinguish themselves in seemingly stark terms from those who follow other rules, identify with other totems, and thus those who are seen as crosstown rivals.

So can sports be a religion? You tell me the next time you see the wave start up at a stadium filled with thousands of people who are otherwise complete strangers or a fan clad in the team's emblems crying in joy after a nail-biting big win.

About the author

Russell T. McCutcheon is professor and chair of the Department of Religious Studies at the University of Alabama; his work is on the theories of religion, approaches to the study of myth, as well as focusing on the history of the study of religion and the practical effects of classification systems.

Suggestions for further reading

In this book
See also Chapters 1 (ubiquity of religion), 3 (classifying religion), 12 (function of religion), and 14 (spiritual but not religious).

Elsewhere
Bain-Selbo, Eric. *Game Day and God: Football and Politics in the American South*. Macon, GA: Mercer University Press, 2012.

Bain-Selbo, Eric and D. Gregory Sapp. *Understanding Sports as a Religious Phenomenon*. London: Bloomsbury, 2016.

Chidester, David. *Authentic Fakes: Religion and American Popular Culture*. Oakland, CA: University of California Press, 2005.

5

What is the difference between religion and mythology?

Russell T. McCutcheon

One of the challenges of being a scholar is employing technical categories, to go about your work, that also happen to appear in your native tongue—that is, the task is to distinguish a popular or folk usage of a term from a technical one. Among the more challenging terms to use in our field, then, is this word, myth, inasmuch as it is widely used in the English language but to ends that likely different markedly from how a scholar might use the term. In fact, not unlike the word cult, it is a term that some scholars drop entirely from their vocabularies, recognizing their inability to retool it from its now widespread and almost commonsense uses—whereas some retain it *but redefine it significantly*, so it does rather different work for them.

After all, just because you drink water does not make you an expert on H_2O—the two designations actually refer to different things: a substance you drink as opposed to a molecule studied by chemists or physicists. It makes sense, then, that scientists, though they may quench their thirst with water, study the structure and bonds of H_2O.

This distinction between technical and folk uses is also of crucial importance when it comes to this equally familiar myth.

Like many English words, 'myth' comes to us from ancient Greece, where it was one of at least two words for, well, word. *Mythos* and *logos* were used in different settings, for different purposes, to refer to words and their speakers; classically, we would distinguish between rational sets of words, that made arguments using various forms of reasoning, on the one hand, and fanciful tales on the other; this is why, today, the suffix *-ology*, based on the Greek *logos*, is affixed to many disciplinary names, such as biology (the rational discourse on the *bios*, what we could translate as life) or psychology (the rational discourse on the *psykhe*, what once might have meant breath or spirit, but by which today signifies the mind). Contrary to such discourses—or so the story goes—there is a wide body of tales likened more to storytelling, and thus we see the work done by this word myth for most people today. Usually used to name false tales or untruths (in opposition to the presumed truth of rational discourse), it sometimes is also used to name childish approaches to a topic (i.e., simplistic approaches that run counter to a more technical and complex account; this familiar tale of the word's ancient Greek origins was nicely rethought by Bruce Lincoln when he proposed that types of speech named by the two terms instead named alternative discourses that were in contest with one another, vying for an audience's attention).

Predictably, though, such normative uses of the term (i.e., to name falsehoods versus truths) are not all that helpful to a modern scholar of religion aiming to be rigorously descriptive and cross-culturally comparative. As suggested above, such scholars might drop the word entirely from their lexicon inasmuch as it is a tool that undermines their efforts not to take sides among the people being studied. But some continue to use it, meaning by it, for example, that large body of creation tales (also known as cosmogonies—stories of the origins of the universe, for example) that we find in use across cultures. Others will distinguish between legends, fairy tales, and myths, based on different elements of the tale, their structure, or which group tells it and for what purposes. Yet others, influenced by recent French traditions of critical thought (dating to such mid-twentieth-century writers as Roland

Barthes), will retool the word entirely, using it now to name the process by which historical events or artifacts are portrayed as non-historical—that is, the way contingent items are represented by us as necessary and inevitable. For Barthes, a mythology was therefore a technique of language, a way in which something that could have been otherwise (the outcome of an election, for example, or the style of a car) is imagined as inevitably this and only this. Myth therefore has something to do with language and power.

If we understand myth only or mainly to signify creation tales, then it makes sense that scholars of religion have often used the term, inasmuch as those things we know as religions seem often to include tales of how the universe—or, more broadly, a variety of systems of order—came into being. But given a prominent normative streak that runs throughout the history of the field—whereby some scholars, sooner or later, seem to feel the need to make judgment calls on, say, whether this form of Buddhism is more authentic than some other, or this version of religion being more beneficial than that—it is not difficult to find scholars juxtaposing religion to myth, inasmuch as the latter is seen as what an earlier generation of scholars might have termed more primitive and unsophisticated. It is not difficult, in fact, to find late-nineteenth-century scholars who posited a sequential, developmental track along which human history moved: first from myth (fanciful tales to explain the world), to religion (more unified belief systems revolving around a creator god), and then finally to a scientific worldview. While there are no doubt some today who still subscribe to this pattern, others would instead see such terms as myth and religion as rhetorical devices groups use to arm wrestle among themselves, thereby naming the unknown and the unfamiliar as somehow inferior, fleeting, and derivative whereas the family and the known are somehow more valuable and permanent.

So while some scholars continue to see utility in the term myth, to help them name a subset of narratives that are distinctive and in need of study, there are certainly those in the academic study of religion who don't study myths as much as study the people who call certain things myths.

About the author

Russell T. McCutcheon is professor and chair of the Department of Religious Studies at the University of Alabama; his work is on the theories of religion, approaches to the study of myth, as well as focusing on the history of the study of religion and the practical effects of classification systems.

Suggestions for further reading

In this book

See also Chapters 6 (religion v. philosophy) and 7 (religions v. cults).

Elsewhere

Barthes, Roland. *Mythologies* (translated by Annette Lavers). New York: Wang & Hill, 1972.

Lincoln, Bruce. *Theorizing Myth: Narrative, Ideology, and Scholarship*. Chicago, IL: University of Chicago Press, 1999.

McCutcheon, Russell T. 'Myth.' In *Guide to the Study of Religion*, edited by Willi Braun and Russell T. McCutcheon, 190–208. London: Cassell, 2000.

6

What is the difference between religion and philosophy?

Nathan Eric Dickman

In forging a difference between philosophy and religion, generalizations are unavoidable. A helpful question for resisting hasty ones is: Which? If someone asks, 'What do Hindus do or believe?' Ask, 'Which Hindus?' And if someone asks, 'What do atheists believe?' It's still, 'Which atheists?' Distinguishing variations of people who practice a religion helps us get specific. We *could* ask, 'Which religion, and which philosophy?' This might lead to a provocative difference, like Nietzsche's poke at Christianity as just Platonism for the people.

Let's instead approach the difference in terms of which *notion* of religion (such as the numinous, infantile neurosis, etc.), rather than which religion (Shin Buddhism, Vodun, etc.). And instead of which philosophical school (Averroism, Stoicism, etc.), let's couch it as which *approach* to philosophizing (concept analysis, phenomenology, etc.). Both can be seen as different ways of speaking or language games. We can use 'religion' to name ways people try to *express* in deed or word what's of ultimate concern for them, to represent what's most important. We can use 'philosophy' to name ways people try to *understand* what's most universal for them, to describe and act by what's real as fittingly as possible. Key in these stipulations are 'expressing' and 'understanding.' Religions express our striving for ideals and our deepest sufferings. Our most comprehensive understanding of being occurs in philosophy.

People ordinarily express themselves in expletives, hyperboles, images and more. But with regard to what's most important, religious expression happens in 'symbols.' It's through symbols that people express religious striving and suffering. Symbols hanging together in institutionally sanctioned narrative wholes are 'myths.' Further genres of religious expression include rituals, laments, laws, and creeds. But these revolve around a tradition's definitive symbols and myths. People typically understand things via distinctions, reasons, models and more. But with regard to what *is*, philosophical understanding happens in 'concepts.' It's in concepts that we understand, grasping together diverse phenomena in predicates by which we build up knowledge within disciplines of inquiry. Concepts hanging together in intelligible wholes are 'judgments' or, more comprehensively, 'theories.' Further genres of philosophical understanding include analysis, genealogy, and dialectic. And these consolidate around a field's definitive concepts and principles.

In this light, religious expression is always a first-order language, or—in semantic terms—an object language. Philosophical understanding, though, is always a second-order language, or a meta-language about object languages. (This is why a PhD in a field means you're licensed to philosophize about its contents.) Symbols spring from immediate experience, but concepts constitute reflection. So symbols don't really help us understand. Rather, they purport to give us something to understand, such as a revelation. It takes concepts to interpret the revelation or to explain it isn't what it purported to be, such as a delusion or an effect of economic struggle. Similar to a joke—you laugh if you get it; but laughing isn't explaining it and explaining it doesn't mean you'll laugh. Just because someone lifts up a symbol and a community coordinates institutions around it, that doesn't mean they understand it.

If this difference seems disturbing, it may help to know it isn't new or radical. For example, in medieval Western philosophy, Ibn Rushd, Maimonides, and even Aquinas agreed it takes philosophical interpretation of symbols to understand what's expressed. This difference isn't only Western either. In interpreting the historical Buddha's sutras (sermons), early Buddhist disciples developed the Abhidharma basket of explanatory works.

This difference between expressing and understanding helps explain why we rarely find converts to or from a religion due to reasoned argument alone. Consider the trope spread through popular media of the religious student defeating the apparently atheist philosophy professor by 'proving' a god's existence. The protagonist uses apologetics (philosophical defense) to exonerate their religious commitment. They argue it's at least not irrational to believe in a god. Religious apologetics deploys philosophy to vindicate a preferred symbol. But this won't work because it mixes up language games. Except to interpret it, philosophical conceptualization isn't particularly for or against religious symbolization, just like softball isn't for or against volleyball directly. Someone can define what a god is, and even argue it's at least not irrational to believe *that* such a god exists. But don't confuse argument with worship of, or even believing *in*, that god.

To wax poetic: insofar as religious symbols express immediate ultimate concern, we could call them unquestionable answers. And insofar as philosophical concepts frame reflective striving to know more about what is, we could call them unanswerable questions.

About the author
Nathan Eric Dickman earned his doctorate in religious studies from the University of Iowa, specializing in modern religious thought. He is an Assistant Professor of Philosophy and Religious Studies, and serves as Chair of the Department of Religion and Philosophy at Young Harris College. His research and publications focus on philosophical hermeneutics, philosophy of language, and comparative questions.

Suggestions for further reading

In this book
See also Chapters 5 (religion v. mythology), 9 (sacred books), and 10 (miracles).

Elsewhere

Anderson, Pamela Sue. *Feminist Philosophy of Religion: Rationality and Myths of Religious Belief.* Oxford: Blackwell, 1998.

Averroes (Ibn Rushd). *On the Harmony of Religion and Philosophy* (translated by G. Hourani). Cambridge: Gibb Memorial Trust, 2012.

Schilbrack, Kevin. *Philosophy and the Study of Religions: A Manifesto.* Chichester: Wiley Blackwell, 2014.

Tillich, Paul. *Dynamics of Faith.* New York: HarperOne, 2001.

7

What is the difference between a religion and a cult?

Jason N. Blum

Once upon a time, 'cult' was a legitimate term in the academic study of religion. Originally it referred to the rituals or the organized system of worship within a religion, and as such was perfectly acceptable. These days, however, the term has fallen largely out of use, and with good reason. By the end of the nineteenth century, the term 'cult' began to be applied to a number of diverse, new groups appearing in the landscape of American religions. This trend of the development of new religions continued through the twentieth century, reaching something of a crescendo during the 1960s and 1970s, partially due to the increasing presence of other, 'Eastern' religions such as Hinduism and Buddhism (during roughly the same period, Japan also witnessed a profusion of new religions).

Because these groups—such as the Transcendental Meditation movement, Wicca, the International Society for Krishna Consciousness ('Hare Krishnas'), and the Unification Church— were new, unfamiliar, and stood outside the cultural mainstream of the United States, they were often viewed with varying degrees of suspicion and fear. The presumption that these groups (many of which could be seen as part of the 1960s counterculture) were somehow dangerous was exacerbated by the disapproval of parents who saw their children adopting unusual customs, clothing, and beliefs when they joined. A number of 'cult awareness' groups formed, sometimes supported by law enforcement officials and psychologists who also viewed these groups as suspect (much of the psychological research that labelled such groups as dangerous has since been discredited). And the media, of course, tended to focus on those groups—such as Jim Jones's People's Temple and Aum Shinrikyo in Japan—that actually did engage in violence. These factors coalesced, resulting in a wide array of innocent groups and individuals being tarnished through association with the minority of 'cults' that actually were dangerous.

It was under these circumstances that the term 'cult' came be associated in the public imagination with a negative stereotype: that of a small, relatively unknown religious group that was some-how illegitimate (i.e., not a 'real religion') or dangerous. A variety of specific negative associations came to be connected with the word 'cult': the image of a nefarious and manipulative charismatic leader; the 'brainwashing' of members whose individual will and sense of personal identity were erased; illicit sexual and/or finan-cial practices; ominous predictions of an imminent 'doomsday,' etc.

Although some of these groups were involved in illicit prac-tices or sometimes even horrific acts of violence, the majority of 'cults' were harmless; they simply looked 'weird' to non-members because they were marginal or unfamiliar. 'Cult' came to be a four-letter word in more than the literal sense; it was a term of judgment and disapproval, marking a group as at least suspicious and at worst dangerous, while also implying that the group was not a 'real' or 'legitimate' religion. It is because of this negative ste-reotype that the term has been abandoned by scholars of religion. Scholars of religion study religions as historical phenomena; we do not make judgments about their 'legitimacy' (it is entirely unclear how such judgments could be made, anyway).

Further, consider some of the traits typically associated with 'cults' in the public consciousness: they are often new (although typically drawing on existing religions in multiple ways) and relatively small in terms of membership; they are socially marginal (i.e., they look 'weird' or 'unusual' from the perspective of mainstream society and established religions); they are led by charismatic individuals who claim some sort of special religious authority or knowledge; they offer a different way of life to their members. Described thus, Christianity, Islam, and Buddhism all arguably began as 'cults.' The only difference between today's mainstream religions and those groups that used to be called cults is their relative age, size, and familiarity. Given sufficient time, yesterday's 'cult' could be tomorrow's run-of-the-mill mainstream religion.

Scholars today prefer terms such as 'new religious movement' (NRMs) or 'alternative religious movement' to describe small, new or marginal religions, as they are not freighted with the negative stereotypes attached to the term 'cult.' NRMs are studied with the same techniques and research methods used to study larger, more familiar religions, and scholars do not view NRMs as essentially different in kind from other religions; NRMs are merely smaller and/or newer versions of the same phenomenon.

About the author

Jason N. Blum teaches at Davidson College. His research focuses on theory and method in religious studies, and topics at the intersection of philosophy and religion, particularly the relationship between science and religion, religious experience, and religion, society and ethics.

Suggestions for further reading

In this book
See also Chapters 1 (ubiquity of religion) and 4 (sports as religion).

Elsewhere
Barker, Eileen. *Revisionism and Diversification in New Religious Movement*. Abingdon: Routledge, 2014.

Bromley, David G. and J. Gordon Melton (editors). *Cults, Religion, and Violence*. Cambridge: Cambridge University Press, 2002.

Dawson, Lorne L. *Comprehending Cults: The Sociology of New Religious Movements* (2nd edition). New York: Oxford University Press, 2006.

8

Do all religious adherents believe in the concept of a higher power?

Steven Ramey

Sometimes people define religion as a tradition that includes belief in a higher power. If that is the operative definition of religion, then to be a 'religious adherent' would involve, by definition, belief in a higher power. However, defining religion by such belief, or more particularly theism (belief in a divine being, a god or goddess) is highly contested. European Christianity has been central to the development of common notions of religion that often follow a Protestant model, which emphasizes the individual's acceptance of particular beliefs, beginning with theism. Until the nineteenth century, the main recognized religions from a European perspective were Judaism, Christianity, and Islam, all of which emphasized a belief in a single higher power (monotheism). Thus the singular nature of the phrase 'a higher power' in the question reflects the European origins of 'religion.'

In contrast, some collections or beliefs and practices that many people label religions have followers who complicate the emphasis on a singular higher power. Some communities emphasize a range of divine beings (polytheism), often in a hierarchy, which differs clearly from a belief in a singular higher power. Moreover, some collections of beliefs do not recognize a higher power, as such. For example, followers of Advaita Vedanta, one of several philosophical conceptions commonly related to Hinduism, emphasize the unity of the individual with the cosmos or universal spirit. Any assertion that a higher power is separate from the individual hinders an individual's ability to recognize this monistic nature of the cosmos. Advaita Vedanta, therefore, challenges the common understanding of a belief in a higher power, since that belief typically incorporates a separation between the human (along with the rest of the world) and that higher power.

The teachings associated with Kongzi (Confucius) become identified as a religion in some contexts (Confucianism) and similarly do not focus on belief in a higher power. The Mandate of Heaven comes close to a higher power idea, as the ruler must maintain the Mandate of Heaven to rule legitimately, but a notion of worship of a higher power or even belief in that higher power more generally is absent. This absence becomes one argument that Confucianism is not a religion, something that has been debated in scholarly circles and in Chinese society repeatedly. Of course, excluding Confucianism because it does not have a higher power simply accepts the definition of religion as involving such a belief, making the question itself circular.

People who identify as Buddhist maintain a range of views on the issue of theistic belief. While many devotees pray to the Buddha and other divine figures, the classical understanding of Theravada Buddhism, most common in Sri Lanka and Southeast Asia, does not emphasize belief in a higher power. Those who accept this interpretation argue that Siddhartha Gautama, the historical Buddha, taught that questions of divine beings and a power at creation were not important to the quest for enlightenment. The Buddha is not divine but human, and his teachings become an aid to reaching enlightenment, without divine intervention. Thus, some Theravada monks, whom we often identify as religious adherents, do not acknowledge a divine power.

A different complication involves the tension between the ideal assertion of what a religious adherent believes and the ways individuals construct their own understandings. Alongside a Theravada monk who maintains this non-theistic conception are many participants in theistic traditions who themselves do not believe in a higher power. For example, some who maintain devout practices as Jews simultaneously identify as atheist, much as some Unitarian Universalist congregations explicitly welcome congregants who do not adhere to a belief in a higher power. By many measures, these participants could be identified as 'religious adherents' even though they do not accept the theism commonly presented in their community. Thus, the answer to the question depends on how you define 'religion,' 'religious,' and 'higher power.' If you limit religions to those sets of beliefs that emphasize a higher power in a theistic sense, then you have eliminated these counter-examples from that category by definition. If you take a broad notion of religion and of higher power that does not require worship or much emphasis, then you can find something beyond the immediate perception of an individual in many communities commonly defined as religious (though not necessarily recognized by every participant in those communities). The answer to this question depends on whatever approach and definition you choose, making the answer about your construction, not just a straightforward observation of the world.

About the author

Steven Ramey is professor in the department of religious studies at the University of Alabama, where his research and teaching has focused on contested identifications and practices in contemporary India and the United States. He is the author of *Hindu, Sufi, or Sikh* (Palgrave, 2008) and editor of *Writing Religion* (University of Alabama Press, 2015), and he has an edited volume, *Fabricating Difference*, (Equinox, 2017).

Suggestions for further reading

In this book
See also Chapters 9 (sacred books) and 10 (miracles).

Elsewhere

Nongbri, Brent. *Before Religion: A History of a Modern Concept*. New Haven, CT: Yale University Press, 2013.

Sun, Anna. *Confucianism as a World Religion: Contested Histories and Contemporary Realities*. Princeton, NJ: Princeton University Press, 2013.

9

Do all religions have sacred books?

Russell T. McCutcheon

Do all religions have sacred books? Well, yes and no—which is the sort of (perhaps frustrating) answer that many chapters in this book seem to be giving to its various questions. The reason for this apparent equivocation is that such a question contains a number of key terms that sometimes, for scholars, contain little landmines; for, given this or that way of talking about such a technical term 'sacred,' not to mention 'book,' we might answer the question in rather different ways. No doubt many readers are familiar with the bible, and its place in Christianity, or maybe the role of the Hebrew scripture in Judaism and the Qur'an in Islam—these are therefore probably prototypes for such readers, who work under the assumption that if 'we' have books of consequence here then we presumably will find the same thing over there, when we start doing our cross-cultural comparisons.

So if the question translates as 'What do they call their bible?' then anyone posing such a questions will have to take a step back and reconsider a few things.

First off, in many cases we do indeed find written texts (which might not necessarily be what some readers mean by books) in many of those systems that we commonly know as religions—though, before we go any further, the longstanding distinction between written and oral literature is important to think about. For the ease with which we today take reading and writing to be self-evident things that we just naturally do is part of the problem; in fact, there's a large body of work on the history of literacy and, for example, how the invention of alphabets and writing may have impacted the way we not only organize ourselves socially but also the way in which we actually think about and perceive/interact with the world. So if we instead take seriously that such things as reading and writing have a history (i.e., humans haven't always done it and how we do it changes over time), we'll have to pause and consider that, before human beings developed systematized ways to represent information in public symbol systems, outside of their own brains, they had little choice but to talk to each other, perhaps in a rhythmic, ritual manner (in which their actions and gestures were no less important), so as to increase the memorability of what they were saying—for both the speakers and the listeners. What's more, it would be an error to assume orality was a mark of just ancient human beings—for it's not difficult to find examples in the scholarly literature of small scale societies which have only fairly recently encountered those of us who take writing for granted. Anthropologists in such situations, working on an ethnography of the people, have been known to transcribe the tales they're told, once they've learned the language, thereby producing texts that, over time, may actually come to be authoritative sources not just for scholars *but for the people themselves*—ensuring that we understand the cultural encounter of insider and outsider, that takes place during fieldwork, as having the structure of a feedback loop, whereby a group's onetime oral literature ends up being transformed by the curious observer into a group's own written texts—thereby inventing, in an unintended way, perhaps, their so-called sacred book.

So granting that, sooner or later, groups generally codify the stories they tell, we also have to consider that the items that we find in such texts are hardly all similar—that is, it might not even be accurate to call them all stories. Most simply, a story (or more technically, a narrative) is sometimes defined in a rather minimal fashion as a tale with a beginning, middle, and end (thus having a narrative arc and thereby some kind of climax or resolution). In the study of religion, parts of the bible come to mind as a useful example, notably from the Hebrew text (known as the Old Testament by Christians or Tanakh in Judaism—an acronym from the Hebrew words for 'teachings', 'prophets', and 'writings'), inasmuch as what scholars once called a 'salvation history' is narrated across different texts and a variety of ancient authors (the theological assumption of it all being a divinely inspired text or the Word of God notwithstanding, of course): the tale of a chosen people's calling and destiny. Or consider the narrative that we find in the gospels of the New Testament, notably the first three (called the synoptic gospels since they—unlike the text known as John—all seem to presume a shared viewpoint): the tale of the birth, teachings, and persecution of Jesus. Although not all agreeing or sharing the same details, the texts of Matthew, Mark, and Luke all seem concerned with telling the story (though possibly for widely different audiences, such as those more intimately familiar with the Judaism of the period and those not). But then there are parts of especially the Old Testament that seem more concerned not with telling a story but, instead, with listing and thereby communicating *the proper way* to carry out what we'd today call rituals—a significant difference in texts that, once recognized, opens the door to a large, alternative body of texts that we find all throughout the study of religion. Calling these 'books' might therefore not be all that accurate, inasmuch as they could more accurately be understood as collections of rules, formulas, and ritual instructions, used primarily (sometimes even exclusively) by ritual specialists and almost never even read by laypeople.

Thus, if it is indeed the bible that's being used as the model to poses a question about other religions' books, we quickly land in the middle of some problems, inasmuch as you would never expect to see texts written by and for ritual specialists to be, let's just say, in the bedside table of a motel—for while some may be read for inspiration or consolation (such as a recent radio story I heard about a man in the US who wrote out the bible by hand and testified to the strength the activity gave to him when his partner died) others are more akin either to philosophical treatises, thought to contain the wisdom of the ancient, or to instruction manuals on how specially trained people might maintain order in the universe. Even within Christianity itself we see this tension: think back to the so-called Reformation and the first translation of the bible (published in stages between 1522 and 1534) into the common tongue (i.e., vernacular) of lay Germans; prior to that it was used as if meant only for ritual specialists (for who among the laity even read Hebrew and ancient Greek?), making it hardly seen then as a book containing what later generations would call 'the greatest story ever told.' Thus, although there may be a variety of texts across world religions, in talking about them all as a coherent grouping of so-called sacred books (as late-nineteenth-century scholars did, when translating many of them into English, French, and German for the first time) we need to keep in mind the challenge of holding within one and the same idea, on the one hand, a Brahmin ritual specialist in Hinduism, being watched perhaps by a small circle of local villagers who do not speak or read the language in which his ancient texts are written and which he recites (that is, Sanskrit), performing his ritual gestures over a small fire and, on the other, a small child learning all about the exploits of, say, King David by means of bible stories in Hebrew School.

About the author

Russell T. McCutcheon is professor and chair of the Department of Religious Studies at the University of Alabama; his work is on the theories of religion, approaches to the study of myth, as well as focusing on the history of the study of religion and the practical effects of classification systems.

Suggestions for further reading

In this book
See also Chapters 8 (belief in a higher power) and 10 (miracles).

Elsewhere
Cantwell Smith, Wilfred. *What is Scripture? A Comparative Approach.* Minneapolis, MN: Fortress Press, 1994.

10
Do all religions have miracles?

Russell T. McCutcheon

If we suspend, for the moment, debates over what should (and should not) be called religion, and thereby just accept the commonsense or folk definition that seems rather popular today, then answering this question is still not as simple as saying 'Of course they do.'

As with many of the questions in this volume, this one is likely based on the assumption that something with which questioners are familiar functions for them as an ideal type (or, more recently, we could term it a prototype). The familiar thereby becomes the standard by which the strange is understood: 'We believe in a someone who raised the dead and turned water into wine—do they have miracles too?' I point this out not to criticize this commonplace cognitive strategy, but simply to identify how it is that human beings usually come to know something new about their world—by generalizing from something we already know and thereby using this as a map when charting alien territory. It's inevitable but, at least for scholars, likely requires us to hold onto our maps lightly, prepared for the moment when they fail to adequately make sense of some new situation, rather than holding onto them so tightly that we force the unknown to fit our anticipations. For whatever else a scientific and scholarly attitude might be characterized as being, it is at least the stance of being prepared for your assumptions to be demonstrated to be inadequate when confronted with a previously unknown situation.

So, with that being said, it's fair to say that, while on the one hand, not all religions presuppose the existence of miracles, on the other, they all sort of do. But what do I mean by seemingly talking out of both sides of my mouth?

Well, if we start with the following definition, famously (at least in the European philosophical tradition) offered by the eighteenth-century Scottish philosopher David Hume: a miracle is 'a transgression of a law of nature by a particular volition of the Deity, or by the interposition of some invisible agent' (see §10 of his influential book, *An Inquiry Concerning Human Understanding*), then only those religions whose members posit the existence of a god (or gods, of course)—who, in turn, are assumed to be interact with the world as we know it—could be said to involve miracles. Picking up any world religions textbook—a genre whose content, over the years, has increased dramatically, such that today we have far more things in the world called 'world religions' than back in the late nineteenth century when German theologians first coined the term to name just Christianity and Buddhism (all other religions they called national or ethic religions, under the assumption that they hadn't successfully moved beyond their original kin groups)—you'd soon notice that it's just as easy to find chapters where deities are said to interact with history as it is to find those where they don't. To rephrase, there are plenty of religions that don't even posit the existence of deities—let alone those, like what was once known as deism (prominent between the seventeenth and the nineteenth centuries), where a deity is presumed simply to be some sort of creator, or first mover, who just left the whole system to run on its own after having got it started. So, much as the term revelation doesn't make much sense for a deist (who would, instead, presume that we can rely on our own reasoning to infer the existence of a creator, such as by observing what they'd conclude to be the design of the natural world), it would be unhelpful to go looking for miracles in, say, those parts of Buddhism, Shinto, or Taoism where the existence of a powerful, immortal being, who is involved in our affairs, is not really an issue.

It would also not make much sense to assume people understood certain events as what we might now term miracles if they lacked our own assumptions about what Hume termed laws of nature (such as gravity, to name but one). For seeing something of mass simply hang in the air, or ever float upward, likely isn't such a big deal if you don't presume that, by the strictest definition, all objects when released necessarily ought to fall downward at a regular rate. The point here is that it would not be difficult to argue that only with the rise of a modern, scientific worldview does this notion of miracle even make much sense—for only now are events that we classify as miracles seen as being so anomalous as to require a designation all their own. Case in point: the Greek of the New Testament uses a term—δυναμισ (*dunamis*)—that we often translate today as 'miracle' but which might simply have meant power or, related to this, to have the ability to do something—something out of the ordinary, perhaps, but hardly something that defied Hume's laws of nature, inasmuch as we don't seem to have what we understand to be the laws of nature operating in the minds of these ancient authors.

So miracles presuppose features of religions that just are not universal—which means that not all religions (or religious people) presume their existence.

But, if we think a little wider than Hume's definition and, perhaps, define miracle in keeping with the words own history—coming, as it does, from Latin, for wonderment or astonishment—we can then juxtapose it with those who presume that all we have is the mundane, historical world itself; we might now conclude that it is on this notion of miracles that the very idea of religion pivots. In other words, if we adopted the definition of religion proposed by the University of Chicago's Bruce Lincoln—'Religion, I submit, is that discourse whose defining characteristic is its desire to speak of things eternal and transcendent with an authority equally transcendent and eternal'—then what we have are social systems that presuppose the existence of non-historical (that is, eternal), and thus supernatural situations and authorities. So, contrary to those who talk of the world as if some all-knowing narrator's position can be obtained, thereby allowing one to float outside the world and talk about such things as the origin and meaning of existence as well as its direction and ultimate destination, Lincoln describes what he terms an historical approach, in which history, 'in the sharpest possible contrast, is that discourse which speaks of things temporal and terrestrial in a human and fallible voice, while staking its claim to authority on rigorous critical practice' (see his 'Theses on Method,' number 2). Now, this notion of miraculous, or supernatural, can be used to distinguish between those ways of talking about the world that presume speakers to be limited by their situation or viewpoint (that is, history), on the one hand, and, on the other, those who claim to be able to escape their situation and comment on, say, the world *as it really is*, as if they are able to exist outside their own specific setting. Now, with this distinction between mundane and astonishing in place, we can see that despite not positing the existence of a being who intermittently intervenes in historical affairs—to, say, answer a prayer and thereby change the course daily life—we could still identify certain ways people talk about the world as presupposing the miraculous, even the magical. So a text like the Tao Te Ching (which likely dates either to a few or perhaps several centuries prior to the Common Era), although not narrating the deeds of a great teacher who, for instance, heals the blind or becomes enlightened, could nonetheless be said to be miraculous (dare we say fantastical?) inasmuch as the text claims to offer the proper and thus definitive way of understanding (and thereby acting in accordance with) reality.

So although we might not find miracles in all things classified as religions, inasmuch as we name somethings *as* religious we likely will still find this notion of miraculous handy, inasmuch as some social systems strike us as presuming the existence of something that defies, goes beyond, or came before and thus outlasts the commonplace, day-to-day life that we routinely seem to observe around us. While not all religions might presume miracles, to even talk about some things being religious (and others not) probably requires us to have something like this idea up and running in our conceptual toolbox.

About the author

Russell T. McCutcheon is professor and chair of the Department of Religious Studies at the University of Alabama; his work is on the theories of religion, approaches to the study of myth, as well as focusing on the history of the study of religion and the practical effects of classification systems.

Suggestions for further reading

In this book

See also Chapters 8 (belief in a higher power) and 9 (sacred books).

Elsewhere

Hume, David. *An Inquiry Concerning Human Understanding* (edited by Charles H. Hendel). New York: Pearson, 1995 [1748].

Lincoln, Bruce. 'Theses on Method.' *Method and Theory in the Study of Religion* 8 (1996): 225–227.

11
How did religion start?

Nickolas P. Roubekas

By origin of religion two things are typically meant. First, the historical origin of religion; that is, when did religion first arise in the history of humanity—in other words, when, where, how, and why the first instance of what was later in human history described as 'religion' occurred. Second, the historical origin of a particular religion; that is, when and why did, say, Egyptian religion first arise. Some theorists of religion, that is, scholars who claim to be able to generalize about the category 'religion' across time and space, maintain that they can trace the historical origin of religion and the reason(s) of 'its' emergence. On the contrary, historians of particular religions (e.g., historians of Judaism or Zoroastrianism) are studying the origins of those very traditions without, however, offering a theory of the origin of religion as a phenomenon.

Moreover, origin of religion can refer to two distinct questions: either the historical or the recurrent origin. The latter addresses the questions of when, how, and why religion arises every time it does so; these questions are predicated on the existence of a need, which can vary from longing to come into contact with god(s) to non-religious needs, like for shelter or for explaining the natural world. Theological approaches trace the origin of religion to divine revelations or to an innate divinely given predisposition towards religion, whereas social scientific theories do not usually broach the issue of the truth of religion but rather concentrate on the human conditions that lead people to create religion. In this scheme, theological explanations would reply to the question of how did religion start by resorting to the very existence of a divine power or realm: religion has always existed as has God (or gods). Contrarily, non-theological approaches—usually called social scientific theories as they stem from the social sciences—answer the question by examining the human conditions and motivations that led/lead to the emergence of religion.

Founding figures of the academic study of religion have given diverse replies to the question of how religion started. Sigmund Freud, for example, in *Totem and Taboo* (1913) traced the historical emergence of religion at the dawn of history, as a result of sexual prohibitions and patricide, thus linking the origins of religion to his famous Oedipus complex. Émile Durkheim, on the other hand, in *The Elementary Forms of the Religious Life* (1912) does not broach the question of historical origin—for him, an unscientific question, since it lies outside any empirical access—and concentrates on the recurrent origin, taking as his case study the Australian aborigines and their totemic religion. For Durkheim, the how of origin is a response to a need for social cohesion, hence denying the idea of individual religion. The latter, however, was maintained by Edward B. Tylor in his *Primitive Culture* (1871), who takes religion to be the result of the observation of the natural world; more particularly, the phenomenon of dreams and agency behind the natural physical phenomena, such as rain, thunder, lightning, etc. in the form of spiritual beings. Thus, for Tylor, religion emerges in place of science due to the lack of 'unsophisticated' people to account for their observations scientifically.

Additionally, scholars from archaeology and paleoanthropology have argued that religious practices can be traced back to the Upper Paleolithic period. However, a common mistake often made by scholars from both social and natural sciences is an unreflective utilization of the term 'religion.' Thus, scholars often generalize and classify divergent phenomena as 'religion,' as if the term is a common descriptor for things in the world that can only be described as such rather than, say, as political, ideological, or cultural. In other words, it is scientifically problematic to argue that there was one moment in time, one particular instance and one specific reason for which religion started. Considering the way human cultures evolved in the span of thousands of years, their 'religious' traditions and practices were based on different motivations and rationales. Still, the very term 'religion' is a fairly recent one, which presupposes a certain set of traits that allow for something to be classified as religion. Such anachronistic imposition of a modern term stemming from the Latin language on traditions across time and space creates numerous problems. Hence, the answer to how did religion start is predicated on what is meant as *religion* and according to what particular definition one seeks the *how* of origin of something that is *ex post facto* classified as religion.

About the author
Nickolas P. Roubekas is Assistant Professor of religious studies at the University of Vienna, Austria. He received his PhD from the Aristotle University in Greece, and has held teaching and research positions at the University of South Africa, North-West University (Potchefstroom, South Africa), and the University of Aberdeen, UK.

Suggestions for further reading

In this book
See also Chapters 12 (function of religion) and 17 (oldest religion).

Elsewhere

Durkheim, Émile. *The Elementary Forms of Religious Life* (translated by Karen E. Fields). New York: Free Press, 1995 [1912].

Freud, Sigmund. *Totem and Taboo* (translated by James Strachey). New York: W. W. Norton, 1990 [1913].

McCutcheon, Russell T. (editor). *Fabricating Origins*. Sheffield: Equinox, 2015.

Pals, Daniel L. *Nine Theories of Religion*. Oxford: Oxford University Press, 2014.

Segal, Robert A. 'Theories of Religion.' In *The Routledge Companion to the Study of Religion*, edited by John R. Hinnells, 49–60. Abingdon: Routledge, 2005.

Tylor, Edward B. *Primitive Culture*. London: British Library, 2011 [1871].

12
What is the function of religion?

Rick Moore

There is no simple answer to the question of religion's function, although several common themes emerge. Religion is often thought to be an institution that helps hold society together, producing what sociologists call social solidarity. One way it does this is through creating and fostering shared beliefs, practices and identities. As religion is social—people attend religious institutions together, participate in common religious practices, and communicate with others concerning their faith—it provides opportunities for the kinds of interactions that create a sense of community. Likewise, religion serves as a marker of difference. Not only does it say who belongs in our community, it lets us know who is outside of it, which in turn brings us closer to the people who share our own religious sentiments.

In addition to creating solidarity, religion serves as means of social control and meaning-making. Religions usually tell people what to do, what actions are acceptable in themselves and in others, and what things should be avoided. They also specify rewards and punishments for compliance or non-compliance with these rules, either in this world or in some future context (e.g., heaven, hell, a future life, etc.). In this way, religion is related to the formation of various moralities. This does not mean that one needs to be religious to be moral, but simply that religions are one important source of morality for their adherents, as well as for societies in general. But beyond just telling us what we should and should not do, religion usually gives us an explanation for 'why.' Religions explain not only why we should obey their rules, but why the world is the way that it is, more generally. They give accounts of reality and our place in it that add meaning to events, from everyday interactions, to celebratory occasions like births and weddings, to difficult situations like deaths and national tragedies.

These functions of social control and meaning-making have led some to argue that religion has more 'dysfunctions' than functions; in other words, religion has more negative than positive effects on individuals and society. The nineteenth century philosopher Karl Marx, for example, famously referred to religion as the 'opiate of the masses' because, in his view, its main function was that of propping up an unjust society by numbing people to the inequalities he argued were inherent in the social system. Today, somewhat similar views are held by many of the so-called 'New Atheists,' such as the British biologist Richard Dawkins. These individuals are known for publicly arguing that religion is a harmful institution that has outlived its usefulness, for example, by hindering scientific thought or subjugating women. Most religious people would, however, dismiss the notion that religions' main functions are harmful, even if they might agree that religion can have negative impacts in specific situations.

These differing opinions on what the 'real' purposes of religion are point towards the difficulties inherent in asking questions about religion's function. Religions are extremely diverse and varied. It therefore makes little sense to assume that all religions possess a single set of functions that apply at all times and in all locations. Rather, it is more productive to think about the constellation of functions that individual religions might fulfill, depending on the specific context being examined. Which functions are attributed to religion also vary greatly depending on the perspective of the person making the judgment, as can be seen above.

Besides the social functions, other potential functions of religion include psychological, and what can be called spiritual functions. Psychologically, religion generates a wide range of feelings and emotions. People often take comfort from religion in the face of tragedy or personal difficulties, thus helping them cope with stress. Religion can also create feelings of joy, fulfillment, release from tension and even ecstasy. From the perspective of religious adherents it also provides important spiritual functions. Those who either believe and/or practice their particular faith often understand it as a critical means of communicating with the divine. Religion thus brings them into contact with an aspect of the world that is beyond themselves, fostering experiences of transcendence.

The potential functions of religion are many, as with the functions of any social institution. Depending on the context, other possible functions of religion include: giving people something to do; educating and socializing children; providing employment; and producing societal change, among others. The exact 'functions' of religion depend on the religion being examined, the context, and the perspective of the person asking the question.

About the author

Rick Moore is a doctoral candidate in sociology at the University of Chicago who specializes in the study of religion and secularism in the United States. His research addresses questions of how groups with vastly different perspectives on religion, such as atheists and evangelical Christians, understand what religion is, as well as the political and social implications of their positions.

Suggestions for further reading

In this book
See also Chapters 4 (sport as religion) and 11 (origins of religion).

Elsewhere
Dawkins, Richard. *The God Delusion*. New York: Bantam Books, 2006.

Dennett, Daniel C. *Breaking the Spell: Religion as a Natural Phenomenon*. New York: Viking, 2006.

Durkheim, Émile. *The Elementary Forms of Religious Life*. New York: Free Press, 1995 [1912].

Orsi, Robert A. *The Madonna of 115th Street: Faith and Community in Italian Harlem, 1880–1950*. New Haven, CT: Yale University Press, 1985.

13

What is the difference between rituals and habits?

Russell T. McCutcheon

Classification matters—something that's already probably becoming pretty apparent in this book's answers. For although the difference between a ritual and a mere habit may seem pretty obvious when you first think about it, it doesn't take long before you start to see that the difference may be in the eye of the beholder—or, better put, the classifier.

Right from the start, we'd all probably distinguish the two by referring to this thing we call meaning, as in the assumption that rituals are meaningful—in fact, *deeply* meaningful—whereas habits are not. Rituals, as almost anyone would tell you, are something we think about, a lot, while habits are routine, unthinking, and thus redundant and rather unnecessary. The differences are pretty obvious, then. So while communion in a Roman Catholic church, or making a once-in-a-lifetime pilgrimage to Mecca, are both rituals, brushing your teeth or unthinkingly bouncing your knee are mere habits.

The 'mere' that ends that previous sentence is important—for many people would probably be insulted to elevate (a notion of height, and thus rank and place, is pretty explicit in that very word) so-called bad habits to the level of something they'd call a ritual. In fact, the value-laden distinction between the two is pretty evident in the fact that we're far more likely to understand habits as bad than good—we don't often praise people for having 'good habits,' though, come to think of it, we do encourage a student to develop 'study habits.' Nonetheless, it's probably not by accident that we now consider smoking to be a bad habit.

So let's start here: rituals and habits are different, and the former are desirable or somehow beneficial, and thus important and meaningful—we could go so far as to name them milestones in one's life, even—while the latter are either to be avoided, managed, or are just the inevitable and inconsequential repetitions that some of us ended up doing for whatever reason. So, if we consider brushing our teeth as our example, then comparing that favorably to, say, the bar mitzvah of an adolescent Jewish boy (an occasion to signify to both him and the group his entry to manhood) would sure be seen as a terribly flawed juxtaposition, at least to many people.

But let's take a step back and consider two ritual theorists—Sigmund Freud, a psychologist, and Frits Staal, an anthropologist. Although they hardly studied rituals in the same way, what's interesting for us is that they both approached them in much the same manner: assuming that the acts we call rituals are part of a broad spectrum of behaviors that are united inasmuch as they have the same function or effect (so yes, we'd call them both functionalist). So, instead of deferring to how participants understood their own behaviors—people like you and I doing something we both think are rituals—both assumed that something might be going on in these actions of which the practitioners were not necessarily aware (making both a good example of a scholar of religion keen to study religion, and its assorted elements, as a form of human behavior). Let's start with Freud: simply put, Freud understood those actions that we term rituals as being on the same spectrum—though, yes, at one far end of it, perhaps—as those other actions that we might group together and call obsessive compulsive disorder (OCD, such as excessive handwashing). To rephrase: Freud understood repetitive human behaviors, whether done individually or in social settings of groups, as functioning to channel and express accumulated anxiety, and doing so in a socially safe manner. For his theory of the human psyche, and thus the individual inevitably living in a social setting, was an attempt to understand how the satisfaction of basic and natural needs and desires could be accomplished in groups where members routinely had to forestall or, sometimes, even ignore those desires all together. Anxiety, he concluded, was the inevitable, internalized accumulation that resulted from unfulfilled desires. So, no matter how much you may wish to rise up against an authority figure—say, teenagers and their parents—the terrible consequences for actually doing the act meant teens had to repress those desires, which created anxiety that, sooner or later, was bound to express itself. Ideally, they do not go 'postal' or 'lash out,' as we once used to say, but, instead, channel that anxiety into actions that allow them to symbolically do the deed—perhaps a Freudian slip of the tongue? Or playing violent video games?). Maybe repetitive knee bouncing? Or even the genuflections of devotees repeatedly making the sign of the cross or kissing an Orthodox icon and lighting a candle when entering a church? For all of these, at least to Freud, can be opportunities whereby the natural anxieties associated with individuals who have no choice but to live in society can be expressed, managed, and thereby dealt with, to make room for yet more which are bound to build up tomorrow.

If Freud's theory is persuasive, then the distinction between rituals and habits is not as great as we once thought—in fact, the distinction is merely one that insiders might make, inasmuch as they may be trying to rationale (even prioritize) some of what they do, at the expense of diminishing the significance of something else they do just as frequently and, at least for Freud, for the same purpose.

But many who perform rituals will vehemently reply that these sacred actions are indeed different from those mundane others precisely because only these are meaningful—such as those scholars who once would have considered a seductive or conspiratorial wink being obviously different from an unconscious twitch of the eye. Though they look alike, the winker (and perhaps the winkee) knows the difference—it's all about the intention behind the act, and thus the meaning it conveys.

With this way of distinguishing the two in mind, think now of Staal, who famously studied an elaborate, multi-day Hindu ritual and then wrote about it in a way that prompted him to question the very way in which he had understood it as a ritual in the first place. As he wrote in his article, he interviewed the ritual specialists (known as Brahmin), who performed the ceremony, and despite asking them all sorts of questions, as anthropologists do, concerning the meaning of the ritual (that is, *why* they thought they did it), he came to notice that their answers were always all about *how* they did it—that is, who got to do it, when they did it, where they did it, how long they did this or that, and what material they used and when or where. What he found remarkable, then, is that he realized that his assumption about rituals being deeply meaningful practices was the problem, for that's what drove his questions and, judging by their answered, his questions had missed the mark. And then it occurred to him that rituals are meaningless—that is, they are just rule-governed behavior; and so, in reply to his queries about their meanings, the ritual specialists being interviewed had no choice but to reply about the rules they were following. So if these actions are ever seen as meaningful, by those who do them, then that comes later, upon some sort of hindsight reflection, long after the ritual itself has left the building. For in the doing, in the ritual moment, they are more akin to unconscious habits than we might at first realize.

Although we shouldn't trust ourselves, since we too are now remembering past occasions with the benefit of hindsight (quite possibly reading meaning onto them from our vantage point today, far outside the ritual moment), nonetheless, try to think of an occasion when you were engaged in what you'd likely call a ritual. What was running through your mind at the time? The meaning and deep significance of the occasion? The larger theological context of the action? According to Staal, no. Instead, you were likely focused on *how* you did it, completely preoccupied, even absorbed, by the performance itself. Where do I stand? When do I sit? What do I say? To whom do I say it? Where do I look? How long do I stay seated? What do I say then? And it's not as if this meant that you weren't focused properly, or that you were doing it insincerely—as Protestant Reformers once complained about the so-called empty rituals of Catholicism ('mere popery,' they once called it). No, for, as Staal elaborates, meaning is not in the doing but in the later reflection on it, when the doing can be juxtaposed to other doings, compared, seen as similar or different—a similarity or difference that might prompt us to comment, elaborate, interpret, explain (i.e., *create meaning*). But the action that we call ritual, taking the doer and his or her situation seriously, is an action that comes before meaning has a chance to get off the ground. It's meaningless in a rather technical sense.

Reading this very text you're probably not pondering what it means to read the English language in the early twenty-first century, are you? Instead, you're simply enmeshed in the rules of English grammar, syntax, vocabulary, etc. The meaning comes later.

So what's the difference between rituals and habit? Well, depending to whom you speak about it, the difference could be so minimal as to make it curious that some of us assume the distinction is to be so obvious.

About the author
Russell T. McCutcheon is professor and chair of the Department of Religious Studies at the University of Alabama; his work is on the theories of religion, approaches to the study of myth, as well as focusing on the history of the study of religion and the practical effects of classification systems.

Suggestions for further reading

In this book
See also Chapters 1 (ubiquity of religion) and 3 (classifying religion).

Elsewhere
Freud, Sigmund. 'Obsessive Acts and Religious Practices.' In *The Freud Reader*, edited by Peter Gay, 429–435. New York: W. W. Norton, 1995 [1907].

Grimes, Ronald L. 'Ritual.' In *The Guide to the Study of Religion*, edited by Willi Braun and Russell T. McCutcheon, 259–270. London: Cassell, 2000.

Staal, Frits. 'The Meaninglessness of Ritual.' *Numen* 26 (1979): 2–22.

14
Can I be spiritual but not religious?

Michael Stausberg

If you are from the United States, you would not be alone in saying this about yourself. According to the General Social Survey (GSS) for the year 2012, 38 percent of Americans describe themselves as 'moderately spiritual' and 30.1 percent as 'very spiritual.' Slightly more people self-identified as 'moderately religious' (40.1%), but the number for 'very religious' (18.3%) was much lower. By contrast, the percentage of those opting for 'not religious' (19.7%) was higher than that for not spiritual (10.5%). 7.4 percent described themselves as 'not religious' and 'not spiritual.' Then there are those that self-described as 'not religious' and 'moderately spiritual' (4.2%) or as 'not religious' and 'very spiritual' (3.2%). While these figures are results of cross-tabulations between responses to separate questions, the 2008 survey introduced a new question that gave respondents different options on the combination of 'following a religion' and 'considering myself spiritual.' When asked in this manner, 22.9 percent chose the self-descriptor 'I don't follow a religion, but consider myself to be a spiritual person.' It clearly makes a great difference how questions are posed and answers are constructed in surveys—it is thus important to keep this in mind when dealing with survey data.

Since 1972, a time when the social sciences were expanding, the GSS has created ('gathered') information on contemporary American society. The data constructed and made available by the GSS allows the social sciences to conduct its business. The sociological study of 'American religion' partly relies on surveys and poll data. Note that surveys provide self-reported data. That means we do not know what people really do and think; we only have access to what they report (claim) about themselves as they choose between pre-defined answers to pre-set questions. Surveys reduce communication and complex issues into neatly divided boxes.

The questions 'to what extent do you consider yourself a religious person' and 'to what extent do you consider yourself a spiritual person' were first launched in 1998 and have then been repeated in 2006, 2008, 2010, 2012, and 2014. The decision to include this set of questions probably reflects an awareness of the increased importance of a spirituality discourse, the emergence of which is typically linked to the generation of the so-called 'baby boomers.' The data reveal some changes. From 2010 onwards, the number of those self-identifying as 'not religious' has been higher than the 'very religious.' But self-identification in terms of being 'a spiritual person' has followed a different pattern: the 'very spiritual' self-descriptor has increased from 21.73 percent (1998) to 28.96 percent (2014), while 'not spiritual' has remained relatively stable (11.83% in 1998; 10.56% in 2014).

People mean different things when they call themselves spiritual and we never know what they mean when they tick boxes in surveys. Some typical features include desire for harmony with nature and the universe; search for meaning, self, peace, enlightenment; belief in or intuition of higher powers; emphasis on experience, meditation, worship and holistic practices. The relation to Christianity is ambivalent. Whereas you may belong to those that oppose religion to spirituality ('spiritual-but-not-religious'), for many more spirituality is part of their religion ('Christian spirituality'), while others consider themselves as religious but not spiritual—perhaps because they associate 'spirituality' with New Age, yoga, paganism, 'soft' or 'feminine' versions of religion. The spiritual-but-not-religious discourse tends to operate with a division into two contrasting or opposite entities or realms:

Spirituality	Religion
Experiential	Institutional
Positive	Negative
Innocent	Guilty
Interior	Exterior
Individual	Collective
Egalitarian	Hierarchical
Peaceful	Aggressive

This binary scheme is not a neutral description of an ahistorical given reality, but a rhetorical instrument of critique of 'religion' and self-empowerment as 'spiritual.' Be aware that the notion of 'spirituality'—with different meanings—has been around for a long time, antedating the baby boomers. It is also important to note that the meaning of spirituality varies cross-culturally. Spirituality talk exists not only in English, but in all Western languages. As a result of global interconnectivities, similar notions operate in non-Western languages such as Modern Hebrew, Turkish, Japanese and Chinese, where speakers do all kinds of things with their respective terms.

While psychologists have welcomed the term 'spirituality' to the extent of now routinely speaking of 'the psychology of religion and spirituality,' scholars of religion tend treating 'spirituality' as an insider-term, used by some speakers to make claims in certain contexts. Some scholars seek to account for the success of the discourse in terms of far-reaching sociological theories. Some see it as evidence of modernization and individualization, others as symptomatic for late capitalism and neoliberalism. Some regard these macro-narratives as social-scientific explanations, while others dismiss them as a-historical, ideological or conspiracy theories.

About the author

Michael Stausberg is professor of religion at the University of Bergen, Norway. He has published on a broad variety of topics, including early modern intellectual history, the intersections of religion and tourism, the category of magic, theories of ritual and theories of religion, and Zoroastrianism (a pre-Islamic Central Asian and Iranian religion allegedly founded by Zoroaster).

Suggestions for further reading

In this book
See also Chapter 4 (sports as religion), 12 (function of religion), and 15 (atheism or secularism as religion).

Elsewhere
Data collected by the General Social Survey are freely available at http://gss.norc.org.

Huss, Boaz. 'Spirituality: The Emergence of a New Cultural Category and Its Challenge to the Religious and the Secular.' *Journal of Contemporary Religion* 29(1) (2014): 47–60.

Streib, Heinz and Constantin Klein. 'Religion and Spirituality.' In *The Oxford Handbook for the Study of Religion*, edited by Michael Stausberg and Steven Engler, 73–83. Oxford: Oxford University Press, 2016.

15

Is atheism, or secularism, just another religion?

Craig Martin

This question is difficult to answer, given the fact that the term 'religion' is used in such a wide variety of ways. For those who use the word 'religion' very broadly or loosely (i.e., for any ideology or worldview), then certainly atheism or secularism would count as 'religion.' However, if the term 'religion' is used more narrowly to refer to ideologies that explicitly include a belief in supernatural agents like gods or angels, then atheism or secularism wouldn't be encompassed within the scope of religion. Looking more deeply, then, we must consider why someone might prefer one definition of religion over another.

Two issues are crucial for understanding what's going on in this debate. First is the fact that 'religion' is a loaded term. In some contexts it carries positive associations—such as the claim that religion helps make people moral, upstanding citizens. In other contexts it carries negative associations—such as the claim that religion oppresses people, or that it is fundamentally irrational. The second crucial issue is that this debate almost always follows from someone having insisted upon the negative stereotype that religion is essentially irrational.

When atheists or agnostics criticize 'religious' devotees for being irrational, they're implying that their own view is somehow more rational or reasonable. One obvious response from folks who identify as 'religious' is to counter the claim by insisting that all worldviews or ideologies involve leaps of faith. Practitioners may responds to the claim that religion is irrational by suggesting that scientific theories always have untested hypotheses in them as well, or that the nonexistence of God is just as unprovable as the existence of God. If these claims are received as persuasive, 'religion' and 'atheism' are placed on the same level, and it follows that science and atheism are just as religious as Christianity or Islam. In a sense, this defense amounts to conceding that religion may be in some sense irrational, but following up with the insistence that atheists are in exactly the same boat. Yes, religion is irrational, but atheism is just another religion.

Atheists or secularists who reject religion as irrational, however, are unlikely to want to agree to such a broad definition of religion as any ideology or worldview. In order to distance themselves from the association of 'religion' with 'irrationality,' they are likely to introduce a substantive qualification to the definition of religion. Religion, on their view, is not any worldview but, *more specifically*, a worldview that refers to supernatural beings. This sort of definition places atheism or secularism outside the circle of religion and, more importantly, restricts the application of the negative associations hung on the word religion. In a sense, this defense amounts to denying that all ideologies are equally irrational. Yes, there might be *some* unproven or irrational things about atheism, secularism, or science, but they are not as irrational as the beliefs of those people who believe in gods and angels.

Which definition of religion is most useful to us likely depends upon our particular interests. If we believe in gods, we're probably more likely to prefer the broad definition that says all ideologies are religious and are thus all are on equal footing. If we don't believe in gods, we're probably more likely to prefer the narrower definition that presents supernatural stuff as more irrational than our own views. In summary, there really is no objective answer to this question: any answer will depend on one's identity and sympathies (do you favor the atheists or the theists?), and thus the answer is relative and subjective. This of course makes the question extremely problematic from an academic perspective;

if the answer is contingent upon individuals' likes and dislikes, it probably doesn't rise to the level of objectivity typically required by academic standards.

About the author

Craig Martin is associate professor of religious studies at St. Thomas Aquinas College. His recent books include *Capitalizing Religion: Ideology and the Opiate of the Bourgeoisie* and *A Critical Introduction to the Study of Religion*.

Suggestions for further reading

In this book

See also Chapters 12 (function of religion) and 14 (spiritual but not religious).

Elsewhere

Fitzgerald, Timothy. *Discourse on Civility and Barbarity: A Critical History of Religion and Related Categories*. Oxford: Oxford University Press, 2007.

Fitzgerald, Timothy (editor). *Religion and the Secular: Historical and Colonial Formations*. Sheffield: Equinox Publishing, 2007.

16
Why is religion so often involved in politics?

Ian Alexander Cuthbertson

This question assumes that religion and politics are two clearly delineated and completely separate spheres of human activity. But while it is certainly true that religion and politics tend to be viewed as separate in the context of contemporary Western democracies, this separation is the product of particular historical processes. In other words, the distinction between religion and politics is neither natural nor inevitable. In fact, the idea that religion and politics can (or should) be separate from one another is a relatively recent one that depends upon a particularly modern conception of religion as something that is (or ought to be) apolitical.

Beliefs and practices that typically earn the designation 'religion' have been present in human life and culture for millennia. In many historical contexts, religion and politics were inseparable. In ancient Rome, for instance, emperors such as Julius Caesar were considered to be living gods. The emperor of Japan was likewise considered to be a god until 1948 when he was required by the Allied forces to deny his divinity following World War II. For the ancient Israelites, religious obligations including the worship of Yahweh and circumcision set the Israelites apart as a nation. Likewise, the prophet Muhammad and the Muslim Caliphs who succeeded him were viewed as religious, political, and military leaders.

Religion and politics were viewed somewhat differently in the context of early Christianity. Although the messiah was originally understood to be both a political and religious figure, the New Testament makes a clear distinction between earthly and heavenly kingdoms and explains that Jesus instructed his followers to render to Caesar the things that are Caesar's and to God the things that are God's. The separation of religion and politics within Christianity is therefore itself a religious concept. Yet even with Christianity religion and politics have often been closely linked. James I, King of England and Scotland argued that rulers are God's lieutenants on earth in the early seventeenth century and understood his own rule to be divinely mandated—a view shared by Louis XIV in France. Additionally, political rulers have sometimes also been the leaders of national churches. Following his departure from the Catholic Church in 1543, Henry VIII became the Supreme Governor of the Church of England. Although Queen Elizabeth II has considerably fewer political powers than her predecessors, she remains both the head of state and also the leader of the national church.

The now-widespread idea both that religion should not influence politics and that politics should not influence religion is a modern concept that arose alongside efforts to ensure the separation of Church and State in the late eighteenth century during both the French and American Revolutions. In the French context, the separation of church and state was engineered to prevent religion from unduly influencing the state. In the American context, the official separation of church and state was implied in the First Amendment as a means of protecting religious minorities from the kind of discrimination they faced during British rule.

Yet although religion is often constitutionally, legally, or at least practically separated from politics in Western democracies, religious values and ideas continue to influence public debate. In part, this is because religious issues are not always just religious. While some Christians believe homosexuality is a sin, any attempt to legally limit marriage to heterosexual couples necessarily enters the realms of politics and law. Likewise, political issues are not always just political. Requiring employers to provide health care that includes contraceptives considered by some Christians to constitute abortion has been described as a violation of the employer's rights to religious freedom. While some political philosophers including John Rawls have argued that comprehensive doctrines including religious views ought to be kept separate from political debates, legal scholars such as Steven D. Smith have argued that religious views inevitably affect public discourse—though these are often disguised as neutral or secular arguments. If religion involves deeply held convictions about what is moral then it may always be difficult to separate these views from secular conceptions of what is appropriate in the political sphere.

The modern notion that religion and politics ought to be separate was by no means an inevitable development. Religion is so often involved in politics because it nearly always has been and because for much of human history the line dividing these two seemingly separate spheres has been blurred at best.

About the author
Ian Alexander Cuthbertson is Baker Postdoctoral Fellow and adjunct assistant professor at Queen's University, Kingston. Ian is broadly interested in exploring how the modern category religion is deployed to legitimatize certain beliefs, practices, and institutions while delegitimizing others.

Suggestions for further reading

In this book
See also Chapter 8 (belief in a higher power) and 12 (function of religion).

Elsewhere
Asad, Talal. *Formations of the Secular*. Oxford: Oxford University Press, 2003.

Fox, Jonathan (editor). *Religion, Politics, Society, and the State*. Oxford: Oxford University Press, 2012.

Pellegrini, Ann and Janet R. Jakobsen (editors). *Secularisms*. Durham, NC: Duke University Press, 2008.

Rawls, John. *A Theory of Justice*. Cambridge, MA: Harvard University Press, 2005.

Smith, Steven D. *The Disenchantment of Secular Discourse*. Cambridge, MA: Harvard University Press, 2010.

17
What is the oldest religion?

Vaia Touna

There are many different speculations among scholars regarding
which is the oldest religion. Some would argue, based on archaeological findings, that evidence of religious practices started thousands of years ago when the first humanoids begun to bury their
deceased. Others would see evidence of religious beliefs in the
cave paintings (depicting mostly animals and sometimes hunting
scenes) found in Africa, Europe and western Asia, dating to almost
40,000 years ago. Although these instances are not considered as
organized religions, they can be seen as indications of religious
thought, and scholars have developed an array of words and theories to classify and explain these phenomena; so they often talk
about 'animism,' (as did E. B. Tylor in the late nineteenth century)
or 'anthropomorphism' (as does Steward E. Guthrie in his *Faces
in the Clouds*) or 'shamanism' (such as Mircea Eliade; see David S.
Whitley's *Cave Paintings and The Human Spirit*). When it comes
to judging the oldest among so-called organized religions again
there are different views. Some would argue that Hinduism is the
oldest religion tracing its origins around 3000 BCE, in the civilization that developed in the basins of the Indus river, encompassing
what is today parts of Pakistan, western India, and northeastern
Afghanistan. Archaeological artifacts (e.g., texts, statues, pottery,
etc.) that have been excavated in that area and from that period
have led archaeologists and historians to speculate that they represent religious beliefs. Similarly, scholars will speak of religion
in the Cycladic and Minoan civilization that flourished around

3000 BCE in southern Greece, or Ancient Egyptian religion; in fact, for any ancient civilization some scholars will talk about their religious practices and beliefs.

What is of interest, though, is that there are studies that show that those ancient societies didn't have any concept of what we commonly understand today as 'religion'—which makes it curious, then, as to how can we determine or even locate 'the oldest religion' so far back in time. Despite the fact that we commonly think of religion as a natural, cross-cultural phenomenon that's easily identifiable across the world today, or the ancient world as well, this is hardly the case—which makes this question rather difficult to answer in a straightforward or simple.

Of course one might argue that people in the past had gods and performed rituals in their honor; 'doesn't that constitute a religion?' one might ask. If that is one's definition of religion then yes, but belief in the existence of supernatural beings and the narratives (often known as myths) and practices (often known as rituals) associated with these beliefs could also be explained in terms of political, economic, psychological theories and not necessarily seen as being religious. This suggests that it would not be difficult, when we find historical claims about Zeus, for example, to see not religion in the ancient world but, perhaps, political struggle among competing groups, all of whom used myths and rituals as one way to wage their contests.

Which brings us back to the question: 'What is the oldest religion?'

As should be clear by now, in order to be able to answer this question we will need first to determine what do we mean by 'religion.' There are many definitions of religion, which we can generally divide between common sense definitions and those that are scholarly. So, while commonsense may tell us that religion is an essential element of being human, and as such is an ancient thing, some scholars have suggested that the very term 'religion' is a fairly recently developed system of classification used by people to organize and divide their worlds (that is, calling some things religious and other things secular; see Arnal and McCutcheon's

The Sacred Is the Profane), doing so in order to meet their own interests. Such scholarly definitions of religion are important because they prompt us to decide which objects or behaviors can be grouped under that classification system—not losing sight of the choices people make in organizing their worlds. Since definitions are not fixed in stone they change over time and according to the scholar's research interest, and theoretical questions, which in effect may change the objects and behaviors that will become her/his object of study. To give you a brief example although Hinduism is today considered as a 'world religion,' when scholars in the eighteenth century were trying to determine which religions counted as world religions Hinduism was not listed as such, in fact only Christianity and Buddhism were thought to be world religions (see *The Invention of World Religions* by Masuzawa); yet today we take its membership in this family for granted. In fact world religions textbooks routinely list Hinduism as a world religion; that is not because of some particular characteristic that those religions possess but, instead, because the definition of what makes something a world religion has changed.

Similarly, we can say that to determine which is the oldest religion depends on how scholars define religion. This act of definition on the part of scholars—as with anyone offering a definition of anything—allows them to organize and systematize archaeological artifacts that can be understood *as* religious, or to determine whether something is a religion or not. But this act of definition (or we can say of fabricating identities and meanings of material artifacts) has more to do with the interests that drive those definitions and classifications than with the things being defined and classified as religious or religions.

So, to answer the question, perhaps the oldest religion is Hinduism, or Buddhism, or some other religion—or, perhaps, instead, no religion is any older than our fairly recent habit of calling them religions.

About the author

Vaia Touna is assistant professor at the Department of Religious Studies at the University of Alabama, USA. Her scholarly interests range widely, from looking at specific concepts of religion in the Greco-Roman world to methodological issues concerning the study of religion in general.

Suggestions for further reading

In this book
See also Chapters 12 (function of religion) and 18 (how many religions?).

Elsewhere

Arnal, William E. and Russell T. McCutcheon. *The Sacred Is the Profane: The Political Nature of 'Religion.'* Oxford: Oxford University Press, 2013.

Clottes, Jean. *What is Paleolithic Art? Cave Paintings and the Dawn of Human Creativity* (translated by R. D. Martin). Chicago, IL: University of Chicago Press, 2016.

Geertz, Armin W. *Origins of Religion, Cognition and Culture*. Abingdon: Routledge, 2013.

Guthrie, Steward E. *Faces in the Clouds: A New Theory of Religion*. Oxford: Oxford University Press, 1993.

Masuzawa, Tomoko. *The Invention of World Religions: Or, How European Universalism Was Preserved in the Language of Pluralism*. Chicago, IL: University of Chicago Press, 2005.

McCutcheon, Russell T. *Studying Religion. An Introduction*. Sheffield: Equinox, 2007.

Nongbri, Brent. *Before Religion: A History of a Modern Concept*. New Haven, CT: Yale University Press, 2013.

Smith, Jonathan Z. *Imagining Religion: From Babylon to Jonestown*. Chicago, IL: University of Chicago Press, 1982.

Smith, Wilfred Cantwell. *The Meaning and End of Religion: A New Approach to the Religious Traditions of Mankind*. Minneapolis, MN: Fortress, 1991 [1963].

Tylor, Edward B. *Primitive Culture*. London: British Library, 2011 [1871].

Whitley, David S. *Cave Paintings and The Human Spirit: The Origin of Creativity and Belief.* New York: Prometheus Books, 2009.

18
How many religions are there?

Michael J. Altman

There's an old story about a man walking down a street in Belfast (Northern Ireland) during the height of the Protestant versus Catholic conflicts of the late twentieth century. He's approached by a group of tough-looking young men. 'Are you Catholic or Protestant?' the leader of the youths demands from him. 'I'm Muslim,' he replies. The young man pauses for a moment and looks around at his companions a bit bewildered. 'Well, are you a Catholic Muslim or a Protestant Muslim?' the youth rejoins.

The story of the Belfast Muslim offers one answer to the question of how many religions there are. There are two: 'ours' and 'theirs.' For the young toughs, who are either Catholic or Protestant depending on who tells the story, the idea that there was a third option was unthinkable. Similarly, the modern concept of religion emerged in Europe though two 'us and them' confrontations: the Protestant Reformation and European exploration of the New World. Religious pluralism within Europe and religious encounters beyond Europe increased the number of religions being counted.

In 1667 the English writer Richard Baxter tried to make sense of the proliferation of religion around the world and enumerated the religions he saw in the world at that time. There were four: Christianity, Judaism, Islam, and Heathenism. This four-fold list of religions would hold sway in Europe and America well into the nineteenth century. The four-fold list worked well because it accounted for the three traditions that Europe had been familiar with—Christianity, Judaism, and Islam—while also leaving room for all of the new religions Europeans encountered around the world. The religions of Asia, the Americas, and Africa could all be accounted for with the elastic category: heathenism (or sometimes paganism). Despite the differences between what a person might be doing along the coast of Africa and in the hills of Mexico, from the European perspective it was all heathenism.

As European empires grew during the nineteenth century and produced more and more knowledge of non-European peoples the list of religions expanded. Writers began to describe 'Buddhism' and 'Hinduism' as religions in the late nineteenth century. For example, one American author, James Freeman Clarke, published a book titled *Ten Great Religions* in 1871. His list of ten religions included some less popular on lists today such as 'Brahmanism' (instead of Hinduism), Zoroastrianism, and Scandinavian religion. At the 1893 World's Parliament of Religions, held in Chicago, organizers enumerated a different ten world religions represented: Confucianism, Taoism, Shintoism, Hinduism, Buddhism, Jainism, Zoroastrianism, Judaism, Christianity, and Islam. Comparing these ten religions to the older list of four religions reveals how the old 'heathen' category was transformed into various separate 'isms.'

In the twentieth century, anthropologists and other scholars of religion found the list of world religions incomplete for understanding a number of groups that did not fit into any of the categories. Various cultures and peoples around the world were not part of any 'world religion' and yet, the scholars argued, they did have a religion. This argument led to the use of the phrase 'the religion of ...' For example, anthropologist Godfrey Lienhardt published *Divinity and Experience: The Religion of the Dinka* in 1961. Similarly, another anthropologist, Clifford Geertz, published *The Religion of Java* in 1960. The 'religion of ...' approach meant that the number of religions is limitless. Every society of people, like the Dinka, or place, like Java, can have its own religion.

Each attempt to count up the number of religions in the world serves a specific purpose. Counting 'my religion' and 'your religion' functions to identify that we are not the same or that we are at least in different religious groups. The four-fold count divided Europe from the rest of the 'heathen' world. The innumerable 'religion of' approach allows anthropologists to isolate a given place or group in order to do their work. So, how many religions are there? Well, it all depends on who is counting.

About the author

Michael J. Altman is Assistant Professor of Religious Studies at the University of Alabama where he researches and teaches course on colonialism, Asian religions in America, and critical theory. He holds a PhD in American Religious Cultures from Emory University, an MA in Religion from Duke University, and a B.A. in Religious Studies and English from the College of Charleston.

Suggestions for further reading

In this book
See also Chapters 20 (how many are right?) and 21 (distinctions in religion).

Elsewhere
Baxter, Richard. *The Reasons of the Christian Religion*. London: R. White, 1667.

Clarke, James Freeman. *Ten Great Religions*. Boston, MA: Houghton Mifflin, 1895 [1871].

Geertz, Clifford. *The Religion of Java*. Chicago, IL: University of Chicago Press, 1976 [1960].

Lienhardt, Godfrey. *Divinity and Experience: The Religion of the Dinka*. Oxford: Clarendon Press, 1987 [1961].

Masuzawa, Tomoko. *The Invention of World Religions*. Chicago, IL: University of Chicago Press, 2005.

Sharpe, Eric J. *Comparative Religion: A History*. New York: Charles Scribner's Sons, 1975.

Smith, Wilfred Cantwell. *The Meaning and End of Religion*. San Francisco, CA: Harper & Row, 1978.

19
How does religion spread and what is its appeal?

Sarah E. Dees

In 2015, *Business Insider* published a two-minute video of an animated map depicting the spread of five religions over the course of thousands of years.[1] During the video, five areas with distinct colors—each denoting a different religion—develop, morph, and extend into different regions of the globe. While they offer a basic account of the development of select 'world religions' over time, videos like this may obscure more than they reveal. Among the many questions these types of videos raise, let us consider two. First, when religions move and expand, what is moving and expanding? In other words, what do the colorful areas on the animated map actually represent? Second, what cultural, social, economic, and political forces precipitate these movements?

The 2015 animation is likely meant to trace the growth and movement of *people* who are adherents of the different religions represented on the map. People are ultimately the central subjects in the academic study of religion; hence, scholars' interests in people's movements when considering the spread of religion. Yet a simple map cannot easily convey spaces of religious diversity and contestation. As an example, consider the city of Jerusalem, sacred to Jews, Christians, and Muslims alike. In this region and in

---

1 Retrieved on February 27, 2017 from www.businessinsider.com/map-shows-how-religion-spread-around-the-world-2015-6.

countless areas around the globe, people from different religious communities have fought for physical and social control over specific areas. This contestation requires us to attend to the ways in which naming and claiming specific areas as 'religious' are also social and political projects. People may not always agree whether one area is the primary domain of one religion.

Let us now focus more specifically on the growth and movement of religious adherents. Religions can spread when religious individuals and communities move to different areas; in addition, religious ideas and practices spread when people who were not previously adherents of a particular tradition convert to or join a new tradition. These processes—of migration and conversion—can both be either voluntary or involuntary. Mass migrations have often been involuntary, caused by social or political issues that threaten the livelihood of specific communities. This is the case with members of the European Jewish community who for centuries endured numerous displacements due to anti-Semitic violence. This creates a *diasporic* community in which members of a tradition are spread throughout different regions of the world.

Some religious groups actively seek to convert others to their traditions. *Evangelism* is the process of actively seeking to spread one's religion. While the term is derived from the context of Christian missionization, we may also consider parallel movements in other religious traditions in which members encourage others to join their community or adopt their beliefs and practices. As an example, members of the International Society for Krishna Consciousness have, since the 1960s, sought to share their unique form of Hinduism throughout the world.

Many adherents who are engaged in missionization view their work as positive and see the conversion process as entirely voluntary, stemming from an individual's genuine desire to follow the tradition. Evangelists may present positive aspects of their tradition and hope that others who find it appealing will convert. However, the process of conversion can also be violent. In some instances, ruling forces have required those under their rule to convert to a particular religion. This was the case when European explorers traveled to the Americas. Europeans forced indigenous Americans to renounce previously held beliefs, give up old practices, and adopt new beliefs and lifestyles. It is important to note that these forms of forced conversion of Native Americans, from the fifteenth century to the present day, have often required the rejection of aspects of culture as well as religion. Interestingly, scholars have argued that many Native Americans historically agreed to convert to Christianity because of the medicinal benefits they believed the European Christians could offer.

Finally, it is important to consider the appeal of different aspects of religion when individuals do choose voluntarily to adopt new religious practices. Religious communities promise many benefits—both material and immaterial—to potential converts: a sense of belonging or community, salvation, social status, healing and well-being. Considering the appeal of religions remains a key goal of many scholars of religion. Scholars draw on numerous methodologies—anthropological, sociological, historical, literary—to examine and express the many reasons why aspects related to religion remain compelling sources of individual and social expression.

About the author

Sarah E. Dees (PhD, Indiana University) is a postdoctoral fellow at Northwestern University. Her research focuses on American and Indigenous religions.

Suggestions for further reading

In this book
See also Chapters 1 (ubiquity of religion) and 12 (function of religion).

Elsewhere
Boyarin, Jonathan. *The Unconverted Self: Jews, Indians, and the Identity of Christian Europe.* Chicago, IL: University of Chicago Press, 2009.

Reff, Daniel. *Plagues, Priests, and Demons. Sacred Narratives and the Rise of Christianity in the Old World and the New.* Cambridge: Cambridge University Press, 2005.

Saunders, Jennifer B., Elena Fiddian-Qasmiyeh, and Susanna Snyder (editors). *Intersections of Religion and Migration: Issues at the Global Crossroads.* Basingstoke: Palgrave Macmillan, 2016.

20
Why do so many people believe that only one religion can be right?

Nathan Eric Dickman

Have you noticed people who think only one religion can be right always think it's their own? Wouldn't it be strange to hear a Reformed Christian assert only one is right, but it's Taoism? That only one is right seems based on a logical principle: two contradictory claims can't both be true in the same sense at the same time. But we can detect here an implicit alliance between politics and logic. Religious institutions are in the business of winning hearts and minds (and wallets!). If deploying 'logic' buttresses institutional interests, all the better. Consider this illustration: What year is it? Is it 2017 'AD' or 'CE'? Despite secularizing the era-naming system, we know what year zero really concerns (Christianity). Moreover, for many Buddhists, it's 2560. For Jews, 5777. For some Hindus, 5119. For Muslims, 1438. Some Muslims even object to Greenwich Mean Time as colonialist, advocating for Mecca Time by trying to use 'science' to show Mecca's longitudinal magnetic uniqueness. Only one gets time right?

Confronting the so-called problem of religious diversity, we quickly move into the broader topic of metaphysical truth. A variety of options are worth exploring. And fortunately we don't have to start from scratch since we've inherited five philosophically informed responses. *Exclusivists* hold only one religion is right, and not subscribing to it inhibits one's complete fulfillment. Even atheistic naturalists can be exclusivists, with a notion of fulfillment containing nothing supernatural. *Inclusivists* hold only one religion is correct, but it's so powerful that it supplies fulfillment to people practicing other religions. Some twentieth-century Catholic theologians called moral non-Christians 'anonymous Christians'—they're Christian but don't know it yet. *Pluralists* think most religions are unique perspectives on, but not accurate descriptions of, one ultimate reality. Accuracy is out of place because concepts and symbols are culturally contextual, and so aren't exhaustive universal descriptions of the ultimate. This is often illustrated by the ancient Indian parable of the elephant and the blind monks.

Those three assume there's a unified underlying reality religions accurately, or partially, capture. But, as Shankara explains, utter oneness is paradoxical. *Relativists*, alternatively, seem to hold there are multiple distinct realities—relative to each tradition or to each individual. You've heard people say, 'What's true for me, is true for me; and what's true for you, is true for you.' *Skeptics* are a fifth option going one of two ways: rejecting knowledge about which religion is true in principle since concepts are too limited, or suspending the question for now because although we don't know yet we might one day.

All five responses presuppose one job of religions is to describe reality accurately. Only one (or no) religion can be right *if* religions make conflicting truth-claims. But religious language largely consists of symbols facilitating group identification and empowerment of individuals, such as Zen koans. Perhaps doctrines or creeds lay out descriptive claims? Christianity is peculiar in emphasizing standardized belief-claims—which is why it's called 'orthodoxy' (correct belief) in contrast to other religions focused on 'orthopraxy' (right practice). Nevertheless, it's difficult to find standard doctrines with single interpretations across all sects of even one religion. This is increasingly complicated by digital exchange where more and more people who identify as Christian state they believe in, say, reincarnation—an apparently Hindu notion. Notice people don't call other kinds of descriptions doctrines or dogmas. In physics, we call general descriptions 'theories.' In history, we call specific descriptions 'histories.' When we criticize a physicist or historian for biased descriptions, they're 'indoctrinated.' So exclusivists reduce complex religious phenomena to conflicting descriptive claims (at least inadvertently) when they think their religion is right.

Another reason people practice exclusivism is that single religious belonging seems normal to them. But 'normalcy,' like logic, can serve institutional interests. Single religious belonging is a recent feature of Abrahamic monotheisms. Yet people throughout the world participate in multiple traditions without worry about apparent contradictions. In many Japanese homes, you can find a *kamidana* (Shinto shrine) and a *butsudan* (Buddhist shrine). Even Solomon seemed content practicing both Yahwism and forms of Egyptian religion. This has been called 'ambiguity tolerance,' implying the default is single belonging. So participating in multiple religions apparently means you're intellectually compromised in tolerating ambiguity. But if it's actually normal to participate in multiple religions—perhaps we should call exclusivists 'false dichotomy tolerant'?

Maybe it's true you can't serve two masters. While people may speak as if their exclusivism is merely in the service of logic, they're probably subordinating logic to their religious institution.

About the author

Nathan Eric Dickman earned his doctorate in religious studies from the University of Iowa, specializing in modern religious thought. He is an Assistant Professor of Philosophy and Religious Studies, and serves as Chair of the Department of Religion and Philosophy at Young Harris College. His research and publications focus on philosophical hermeneutics, philosophy of language, and comparative questions.

Suggestions for further reading

In this book
See also Chapters 16 (religion in politics) and 19 (spread of religion).

Elsewhere
Gross, Rita. *Religious Diversity—What's the Problem? Buddhist Advice for Flourishing with Religious Diversity*. Eugene, OR: Cascade Books, 2014.

Hick, John. *An Interpretation of Religion: Human Responses to the Transcendent* (2nd edition). New Haven, CT: Yale University Press, 2004.

Nietzsche, Friedrich. *On the Genealogy of Morals: A Polemic* (translated by D. Smith). Oxford: Oxford University Press, 1996.

Wuthnow, Robert. *America and the Challenges of Religious Diversity*. Princeton, NJ: Princeton University Press, 2005.

21

If everyone worships a god, why are there so many distinctions in religions?

Leslie Dorrough Smith

While believing in a god is not a universal human characteristic (in other words, not everyone *does* worship a god), it is true that the religions of most cultures share in common a deity concept. Rather than presume that the frequency with which a deity appears throughout the world's religions indicates that they are all fundamentally the same (differing only in their details), perhaps we can dig deeper and ask why religions are this way by examining their relationship to culture, since all religions are a product of their cultures.

By *culture*, I am referring to a group's widespread preferences, politics, beliefs, and projects that make it different from other groups; these differences are sometimes quite significant, as anyone who has ever traveled to a country much different from their own can likely attest. The characteristics that make a culture distinct are the product of everything from its geography and natural resources to its media outlets to the history of its political and social movements. Yet for all of the differences that distinguish various cultures from one another, what they share in common is a certain set of social dynamics that regulate their collective relationships. Broadly understood, it is these cultural variations that make religions different from one another, and these social similarities that make them similar.

For instance (and important to our discussion here), virtually all cultures will have some people who are in power and some who are not; the powerful members of that culture will consistently be able to provide explanations for why this arrangement exists (such as their superior intelligence, their hard work, or the will of a deity, for instance). In addition, most cultures will express pride in certain practices or traditions that they believe makes them unique or important. The truth or falsehood of these explanations is not so critical here as is the fact these narratives—which we call *myths*—exist in order to reinforce the identities of those who repeat them. Although we often use the word myth to describe a falsehood, when used as a technical term, myth refers to any narrative portrayal of reality that attempts to make one group's perspective appear to be the only legitimate one. The job of myths is to reinforce those relationships for insiders whose conformity to those proscribed roles is necessary to maintain the social status quo.

Of course, those on the 'losing' end of these myths (that is, those who are disenfranchised or powerless) often do not find them to be as persuasive as do those whom they benefit. If we can think of society as a series of narrative contests (not unlike a political election), then it is possible to see why appealing to a deity would be an exemplary way of 'winning' a contest of myths. Deity stories are almost ubiquitous across cultures because they represent the ultimate power card when used with a group of people who are already religious. Appealing to a deity allows groups to claim support from a transcendent power that cannot be critiqued, and in so doing, to elevate the authority of their claims above others against which they compete. After all, it is much more persuasive it is to hear 'A powerful, supernatural being commands you to obey!' versus 'That guy over there commands you to obey!'

If most cultures have in common their use of religious myths as a mechanism of social regulation, where they differ is in the details and content of those myths. This explains the difference between religions, but also among adherents of the same religion. For instance, a Hindu living in the United States will likely approach Hinduism in a way that is different from a Hindu in India, even if they engage in what appear to be identical rituals or claim similar beliefs. Although these differences may tempt us to ask which is the more correct version of Hinduism, for those of us who critically study religion there is no such thing as a single 'right' version, but only variations on a particular theme that are determined by a particular culture's interpretation of it.

Understanding religion from a wider perspective may therefore help us see that, even though they differ based on a variety of social, historical, and other factors, most cultures will still engage in 'deity talk' because it serves very basic social functions involving the maintenance of power relationships and social norms.

About the author

Leslie Dorrough Smith is associate professor of religious studies, chair of the Department of Religious Studies and Philosophy, and director of the Women's and Gender Studies Program at Avila University. Her research focuses on the impact of conservative Protestantism on sex, gender, and reproduction rhetoric in US public discourse.

Suggestions for further reading

In this book

See also Chapters 18 (how many religion?) and 19 (spread of religion)

Elsewhere

Cotter, Christopher R. and David G. Robertson (editors). *After World Religions: Reconstructing Religious Studies*. New York: Routledge, 2016.

Lincoln, Bruce. *Discourse and the Construction of Society*. New York: Oxford, 1992.

Martin, Craig. *A Critical Introduction to the Study of Religion*. New York: Routledge, 2014.

22
Do people actually believe in their religious practices because they want to, or because of how they were raised?

Nathan Colborne

Why do people have the religious beliefs they have? What are the causes of religious belief and practice? Before dealing with specifics, we may want to ask why people develop religious beliefs at all. What are the social and psychological contexts that make religious belief so common? How would we go about answering this question? If all human capabilities have evolved as humans evolved, then studying human evolution will help us understand the features of religion just as it will help us understand any other human belief. The leaps being made in our understanding of human evolution have helped us understand what kinds of religious beliefs are 'catching' (easily remembered and passed on to others), what are the features of our brains that make these beliefs appear persuasive, why we might have the experiences these beliefs purport to explain, and what might have caused humans to gather in groups that reflect and reinforce these beliefs.

These analytical tools may tell us why religious belief is common but not why a specific person has specific beliefs. For this we must look at the social factors that make up the specific context of the individual or group we're curious about. Unsurprisingly, upbringing is one of the most significant factors in anyone's religious identification though it is not the only factor and it is very difficult to isolate it from other social factors. Over half of the population identifies with the same religious tradition as their parents did. This means, however, that many people don't take on the same religion as their parents. People are also influenced by their peers, their education, and their broader social context, all of which have a strong correlation with religious belief, practice, and identification.

But there is an even more interesting question also being asked. The question contrasts religious beliefs that result from how a person is raised (including their entire social context) with religious beliefs that result from what someone 'really wants' to believe. Is there a cause of religious belief that cannot be reduced to social factors? Are there human desires (such as the desire to believe particular things) that exist before our formation by social factors? Are there 'pure' or 'natural' desires or identities?

Now, on the surface, this appears to be a possibility. When we think about our own beliefs and identities we usually acknowledge the influence of others on these beliefs, including our parents and other family members, peers, mentors, even prominent individuals in our field or celebrities. We also acknowledge the impact of our broader social context on our beliefs and desires. But even if I acknowledge the socially embedded nature of my identity, is there an underlying core identity that is untouched by social factors? Is there, perhaps at the level of my race or gender, or, if such a thing were possible, something deeper underlying these things, a basic, natural identity that is not formed by my social context?

We might ask, however, how I might look into another person, or even into myself, and distinguish those desires and identifications that are 'natural' from those that are a result of social formation? In fact, the deeper we probe to find this 'pure' identity, the further it recedes from our grasp. Even those aspects of my character that reflect my 'taste', which would seem to be the most mysterious and least influenced parts of my personality, the music I respond to, the foods I prefer, the romantic partners I find myself attracted to, correspond very closely to those shared by others in my social and economic position. See also Pierre Bourdieu's work on personal 'taste' as a reflection of social and economic distinction, listed in the further reading section below.

In light of this, the contrast that the question poses between the beliefs a person 'wants' to believe and those that result from the person's upbringing dissolves. This is because what a person wants to believe is formed by social, economic, and political context, namely, by upbringing. If there is some remainder, some aspect of subjectivity that resists social formation, we have no reliable tools that can isolate it and determine its influence. We haven't yet been able to find this 'self' and, despite how strongly I may want to believe in it, it seems impossible to uncover it from all of the influences that drive human behavior.

About the author
Nathan Colborne is associate professor of religions and cultures at Nipissing University in North Bay, Ontario, Canada. His areas of focus are religious and political identity and theories of sacrifice.

Suggestions for further reading

In this book
See also Chapters 1 (ubiquity of religion), 8 (belief in a higher power), 12 (function of religion), and 13 (rituals v. habits).

Elsewhere
Barrett, Justin L. *Why Would Anyone Believe in God?* Walnut Creek, CA: AltaMira, 2004.

Bourdieu, Pierre. *Distinction: A Social Critique of the Judgement of Taste.* Cambridge, MA: Harvard University Press, 1984.

Boyer, Pascal. *Religion Explained: The Evolutionary Origins of Religious Thought.* New York: Basic Books, 2001.

Zuckerman, Phil. *Invitation to the Sociology of Religion.* New York: Routledge, 2003.

23
Can people belong to more than one religion?

Ann Taves

Many people assume that a person can belong only to one religion, because some religions officially forbid people from joining more than one. In practice, however, the situation is much more complicated. Regardless of what traditions officially allow (and they differ on this), many people feel they do belong to more than one religion.

The answers you will get to this question depend on whom you ask and how they interpret 'belonging to more than one religion.' Belonging can mean many things including identifying with, participating in, practicing, and officially joining more than one religion. If you ask official teachers, their answers will depend on the traditions to which they belong. Monotheistic traditions that restrict worship to one deity, such as Judaism, Christianity, and Islam, typically make a sharp distinction between the worship of their deity and the worship of other deities, which they typically view as idolatrous devotion to 'false gods.' Traditions that recognize many deities may prioritize some deities over others and/or view one as ultimate, but they are typically more open to incorporating the deities and practices of others into their tradition. Such traditions, which include ancient Roman religion, the traditional religions of Africa and the Americas, and most religions of South Asia, China, and Japan, do not necessarily make a sharp distinction between 'religions' in our modern sense. Instead, they may distinguish between deities and practices that are appropriate for different occasions, stages of life, or types of people (e.g., lay people, initiates, specialists). For these traditions, the question of whether you can belong to more than one religion may not make much sense.

If we want to answer the question in light of official teachings, we can see what is at stake more clearly if we ask whether a tradition approves of people *worshipping* more than one deity. In the monotheistic traditions the official answer is 'no.' In traditions that recognize multiple deities, the official answer is 'yes.' Some monotheistic traditions, however, look less monotheistic than others. Christians not only worship God; they also worship Jesus. Catholic and Orthodox Christians also are devoted to the Virgin Mary and other saints. Christians claim they are monotheists because they worship one God who manifests as three 'persons'—the Father, the Son (Jesus), and the Holy Spirit. Catholic and Orthodox Christians claim they venerate Mary, but do not worship her. Jews and Muslims reject the Christian claim that Jesus is God and do not worship him or his mother. When Catholic missionaries arrived in China in the sixteenth century, they used these distinctions to figure out if Confucianism was a religion and therefore incompatible with Christianity. The key issue in their minds was whether the Chinese were *worshipping* their deceased ancestors or simply venerating them, as Catholics claimed they venerated Mary and the saints. The Jesuits missionaries argued that the Chinese venerated their ancestors and thus that Confucian practices were compatible with Catholicism. Franciscan missionaries argued that the Chinese worshipped their ancestors and that these practices were therefore incompatible with Catholic teaching. When the pope sided with the Franciscans, he in effect decided that Confucianism was a 'religion' not simply a 'philosophy' as the Jesuits claimed.

In traditions that recognize multiple deities, newly introduced deities are more easily accepted if they can be incorporated into the traditional pantheon. When Chinese missionaries brought Buddhism to Japan, the Japanese incorporated buddhas and bodhisattvas into their traditional pantheon. The Japanese did not officially recognize 'Buddhism' and 'Shintoism' as two separate religions until the nineteenth century. Due to their long history of integration, Japanese typically do not view themselves as 'belonging' to two different religions. This integration of deities and practices, which took place in other parts of Asia and in the Greco-Roman empire as well, made it easy to shift between practices without considering them as part of different 'religions.'

For many traditions, the crucial issue is not so much what you personally believe or even what practices you personally observe but whom you marry and how you raise your children. According to Jewish tradition, the Talmud prohibited intermarriage; it is still controversial today, although less so among the more liberal Jewish denominations. Muslim women are expected to marry Muslim men, although Muslim men may marry Jewish or Christian women. Prior to the Second Vatican Council, non-Catholics who married Catholics were expected to raise their children as Catholics. Although traditional Hindus can chose between different deities and different devotional paths, they traditionally had less choice when it came to marriage. Prohibitions against marriage between members of different castes preserved traditional socio-religious roles within the Hindu way of life.

In the modern globalized world where people of many traditions routinely interact, ordinary people are increasingly claiming multiple religious identities regardless of the official teachings of the traditions with which they identify. Today we see people who characterize themselves as, for example, Jewish Buddhists, Hindu Catholics, or Sufi Christians, and those who eclectically appropriate a wide range of spiritual practices. As people increasingly marry across religious lines, they are finding many ways to relate diverse traditions to create novel family practices. Children raised in such families will surely add to the number of young people who identify with more than one tradition.

About the author
Ann Taves is professor of religious studies at the University of California at Santa Barbara. Her most recent book is *Revelatory Events: Three Case Studies of the Emergence of New Spiritual Paths* (Princeton University Press, 2016).

Suggestions for further reading

In this book
See also Chapters 1 (ubiquity of religion) and 22 (belief in religious practices).

Elsewhere
Cornille, Catherine (editor). *Many Mansions? Multiple Religious Belonging and Christian Identity*. Maryknoll, NY: Orbis, 2002.

Hsia, Ronnie Po-Chia. *Matteo Ricci and the Catholic Mission to China, 1583–1610: A Short History with Documents*. Indianapolis, IN: Hackett, 2016.

Miller, Susan Katz. *Being Both: Embracing Two Religions in One Interfaith Family*. Boston, MA: Beacon Press, 2014.

Rajkumar, Peniel J. R. and Joseph Prabhakar Dayam (editors). *Many Yet One? Multiple Religious Belonging*. Geneva: World Council of Churches, 2016.

Van Bragt, Jan. 'Multiple Religious Belonging of the Japanese people.' In *Many Mansions*, edited by Catherine Cornille, 7–19. Maryknoll, NY: Orbis, 2002.

24
Who are the 'Nones' and why are they so important?

Michael Graziano

In late 2015, the Pew Research Center released an article titled 'Religious "Nones" Are Not only Growing, They're Becoming More Secular.' This headline makes clear the difficulty surrounding interpretations of what Pew terms the 'Nones': those people who do not identify with religious institutions. Simply put, much of the excitement and controversy about the Nones is perhaps better understood as a debate about how to 'measure' religion. There is not a 'Church of None' or 'Grand Mosque of None' on Main Street, USA—the Nones are, instead, an organizational convenience devised by pollsters to describe people who do religious things but do not identify with traditional religious organizations. But is it possible to measure religious identity or belief? What does it mean for a group to be more or less secular than other groups? How we understand the Nones will depend in large part upon why and how we measure religion.

The Nones emerged as an object of study by polling firms in the mid-2000s. The category of 'Nones' originally referred to those polled who claimed no institutional religious affiliation. Respondents were asked to identify the religious group with which they personally identified, from a list of pre-selected groups (that is, are you Muslim, Buddhist, Christian, etc.). Those that answered 'nothing in particular' were lumped together as 'Nones.' As a result, Nones share an avoidance of traditional religious institutions more than any doctrinal belief.

Nones tend to be whiter, younger, and more liberal than the average American. They support same-sex marriage, abortion rights, and environmental regulation by overwhelming margins. However, the Nones are not identical. A third of the Nones earn less than $30,000 in annual income, and an almost equal number earn over $50,000. While almost 40 percent of the Nones have only a high school education, a significant number also possess college and postgraduate degrees.

The debate about the 'Nones' is a debate about how to describe religious identity. The Nones are classified as a religious group in Pew's system, alongside other 'unaffiliated' but 'non-religious' groups like atheists and agnostics. Yet many people who fall into (or more accurately, are placed within) the category of 'Nones' still describe doing things that many people would call 'religious.' For example, according to Pew's 2015 data, half of the Nones claim they are either 'absolutely' or 'fairly' certain that they believe in God. Over a third of the Nones claimed religion was either 'very' or 'somewhat' important in their lives. One-fifth of the Nones pray at least daily. These seeming discrepancies have led to charges of hypocrisy or confusion on the part of the Nones. How can they believe in God, or pray daily, yet claim no religious affiliation?

This confusion offers an opportunity to think about why some see this as hypocritical in the first place. Consider the following: religious belief in the United States (where these polling outfits are located and the 'Nones' polling was conducted) has long been understood through group identity—that is, 'Catholics believe X while Baptists believe Z.' And in the United States, the surest way for a religious group to be recognized as legitimate is to take a corporate form, providing themselves with a distinct legal existence. Much ink has been spilt, and a great deal of legal arguments expended, on what 'counts' as a religion in American society (and thus, which groups get to reap the benefits reserved for groups deemed religious). The presence of the Nones—even as little more than a polling convenience—is a reminder of longstanding disagreements about what religion 'is' in the United States. The seeming incoherence, to some, of the Nones' stated beliefs is perhaps a result of this bureaucratic arrangement which assumes religious identity flows from religious groups down to the individual citizen. Yet while the Nones may offer a challenge to governments interested in monitoring and interacting with distinct religious groups, their stated beliefs have much in common with the American population as a whole.

Looked at another way, the Nones—and the discussion around them—offer an opportunity to see how societies reimagine religion. Their presence may seem confusing precisely because they serve as a reminder that religious identity—and any other claim of identity, for that matter—is malleable, the product of human choice and imagination. The Nones, then, remind us of changing ideas about religion—and the challenges in measuring those changes—in American society.

About the author
Michael Graziano specializes in American religious history. He teaches religious studies at the University of Northern Iowa.

Suggestions for further reading

In this book
See also Chapters 1 (ubiquity of religion), 12 function of religion), 14 (spiritual but not religious), and 23 (belief in multiple religions)

Elsewhere
Bullard, Gabe. 'The World's Newest Major Religion: No Religion.' *National Geographic* (April 22, 2016). Retrieved from http://news.nationalgeographic.com/2016/04/160422-atheism-agnostic-secular-nones-rising-religion.

Flory, Richard. 'What's in a Name? Religious Nones and the American Religious Landscape.' *Religion Dispatches* (July 24, 2015). Retrieved from http://religiondispatches.org/whats-in-a-name-religious-nones-and-the-american-religious-landscape.

Pew Research Center. 'Religious Landscape Study: The Unaffiliated.' Retrieved from www.pewforum.org/religious-landscape-study/religious-tradition/unaffiliated-religious-nones.

Pew Research Center. 'Religious "Nones" Are Not only Growing, They're Becoming More Secular.' Retrieved from www.pewresearch.org/fact-tank/2015/11/11/religious-nones-are-not-only-growing-theyre-becoming-more-secular.

The religions

25

Are there any religions that do not have official leaders?

Jason W. M. Ellsworth

Jorge Mario Bergoglio is the 266th pope (Pope Francis) of the Roman Catholic Church, Tenzin Gyatso is the 14th Dalai Lama, and Thomas Spencer Monson is the current president of the Church of Jesus Christ of Latter-day Saints (LDS). All three hold positions that one could name as the leader to their respective organizations and communities. At the same time one might find a priest in charge at a local Catholic church, an abbot that oversees a Buddhist monastery, or a chapter president of a local church of the LDS. All of these organizations have hierarchal schemes that organize a chain of command in some fashion. But are there religions that do not have leaders?

The mindfulness movement in North America has been characterized by an individualistic self-focused meditative practice that discards many of the other ritualistic practices and organizational aspects commonly associated with Buddhism (as discussed in more depth by scholars such as Jeff Wilson). When examining the mindfulness movement, there is no central organization and thus no 'official leader.' The practice is in part legitimated and viewed as more *authentic* on the premise that it focuses on the essence of what the original historical Buddha taught—a focus purely on the mind and meditation. For some in the mindfulness movement, it is the very lack of an 'organized religion' and 'official leader' that legitimizes the practice.

However, one might ask what is meant by the term 'official'? This should give pause, adding a second question—can a religion have an 'unofficial' leader? By choosing terms such as official and unofficial one makes a subjective claim legitimizing specific people as more of a leader compared to others. Even by removing the term 'official,' one is still left deciding who is a leader and who is not. Instead, we could rework the question to ask who holds the *authority*? Within the mindfulness movement we find many authorities that have great influence across North America such as Jon Kabat-Zinn, who is the founder of mindfulness-based stress reduction programs. Kabat-Zinn may not be a 'leader' in the traditional sense, as he does not hold a specific role, yet it would also be wrong to discount his power.

By moving beyond the term leader and focusing on authority one can deconstruct a set of relationships to better understand where power exists and who benefits from the process. But authority can also come from authoritative *things* and *absent authority figures* as has been discussed by scholar Craig Martin. Things include texts, rituals, practices, buildings, and more. Within the Sikh tradition the Guru Granth Sahib is a scripture that is viewed as the eleventh and final Guru of the tradition. It is housed within the main hall of a Sikh gurdwara and is viewed as the word of God. Like any text or scripture it is open to interpretation by its adherents. At the same time we find absent authority figures such as gods, saints, spirits, other types of supernatural entities or beings who have passed away. This could include those that are considered founders. Whether it is a text or absent figure someone must interpret and reinterpret. One might better ask, who has the authority to interpret or reinterpret a text? Who has the authority to speak to and for a god? Or who has the authority to make decisions for an organization or a community?

This is not to ignore that organizations do name leaders. When someone names a leader we might ask who recognizes and gives the stamp of approval for a leader to be official? Who has the power and privilege to state this? What is at stake for each party involved when naming a leader? It should be noted that claims of leadership are often contested situations. The contested space of two opposing or competing claims of leadership is a place to analyze power, privilege, and knowledge. It is the very process of naming a leader that offers a place of insight into the formation of authority.

About the author

Jason W. M. Ellsworth is a doctoral student in social anthropology at Dalhousie University and a sessional lecturer at the University of Prince Edward Island. Jason received his MA in religion and culture from Wilfrid Laurier University (2010), an honors BA in religious studies from Saint Mary's University (2009), and a BComm in marketing from Saint Mary's University (2003).

Suggestions for further reading

In this book

See also Chapter 9 (sacred books), 10 (miracles), and 29 (differences among religions).

Elsewhere

Martin, Craig. 'How Religion Works: Authority.' In his *A Critical Introduction to The Study of Religion*, 117–144. New York: Routledge, 2014.

Wilson, Jeff. *Mindful America: The Mutual Transformation of Buddhist Meditation and American Culture*. Oxford: Oxford University Press, 2014.

26

Is it true that women play a lesser role in most religions?

Leslie Dorrough Smith

Rather than an institution that is independent from the culture in which it exists, religion is an extension of that culture, and thus, like a mirror, it reflects that culture's dominant priorities and principles. This means that a racist culture will often produce a religion with racist elements; a sexist culture will often produce a religion with sexist elements, and so on. The primary element of sexism is patriarchy, which is a social arrangement wherein men disproportionately lead the culture and control most of its status, wealth, and resources. Since most cultures today are patriarchal, this means that most religious groups are, as well.

So when we consider what role women play cross-culturally in religion, it is correct to say that women are often very poorly represented in the leadership of many groups if they are even represented at all (consider the fact that there has never been a female pope, for instance). On the other hand, women have long constituted the primary membership of many religious groups and have also been responsible for the work that happens behind the scenes to keep religious organizations alive. In this sense, they have often played a very vital role despite their lack of consistent, high-level leadership status.

As with all cultural phenomena, the reasons for this division of labor are hardly random, as they are power moves made in the name of order. In most cultures, one's sex (that is, one's biological

traits) is presumed to indicate one's gender (one's behavioral conformity to standards of masculinity, femininity, or some other
gender norm). While gender norms differ from culture to culture,
gender is usually a very powerful benchmark by which most societies are organized. Scholars who study gender have shown that,
rather than being inborn or natural, gender differences are actually
taught to individuals by their culture through a process of sociali-
zation that starts from birth. The reinforcement of gender norms
through religious stories and texts thus plays an important role in
naturalizing these otherwise social events so that they appear a
matter of divine will or natural order.

We can see some of the classic patriarchal tendencies of religion on display in the ways that many religions depict sex and
gender, which tends to involve the notion that men are naturally
more equipped for religious leadership. Typically, this happens
through stories that depict the god(s), any ideal human archetypes, and/or and the central characters in religious texts as male,
with women appearing as peripheral characters (if they appear at
all). Moreover, women are often portrayed in religious traditions
and texts as weak or morally compromised.

Apart from formal theological statements and scriptures, religious groups also tend to rely heavily on essentialist arguments
to explain gender difference. These arguments claim that men
and women are physically, psychologically, and behaviorally different from one another due to some transcendent design. These
religious narratives about gender are then often reinforced in
the larger culture, even outside of explicitly religious contexts.
For instance, in many countries with large Muslim populations,
women often explain the various body coverings they wear as
something done in the name of modesty and not necessarily as an
explicitly religious act. Nevertheless, this particular interpretation
of modesty comes from passages from the Qur'an and Hadith, two
important Muslim texts.

Some scholars have questioned the narrative that women
are categorically disempowered in religion since women who
are involved in lower leadership positions within religious

organizations are likely enacting subtle influence on the larger contours of the group. And since women tend to be more heavily represented as religious participants, they are probably benefitting from avenues of interpersonal and psychological support (such as a sense of agency, security, and comfort) due to their religious involvement.

Nevertheless, as greater gender equity becomes a reality across the world, many religious groups have been forced to openly account for how they portray gender. More conservative religious groups tend to stand by the claim that traditional gender roles are the unquestionable will of a deity or transcendent order. More progressive groups have chosen to interpret texts and traditions in more historical or metaphorical ways, although this often happens very selectively. The question of the role of women across the world's religions is one that engages a phenomenon of tremendous diversity, and yet certain trends predictably arise due to the largely patriarchal nature of the cultures that produce those religions.

About the author

Leslie Dorrough Smith is associate professor of religious studies, chair of the Department of Religious Studies and Philosophy, and director of the Women's and Gender Studies Program at Avila University. Her research focuses on the impact of conservative Protestantism on sex, gender, and reproduction rhetoric in US public discourse.

Suggestions for further reading

In this book
See also Chapter 27 (women covering themselves).

Elsewhere
Griffith, Marie. *God's Daughters: Evangelical Women and the Power of Submission*. Berkeley, CA: University of California Press, 2000.

Gross, Rita. *Feminism and Religion*. Boston, MA: Beacon Press, 1996.

27

Why do women in some religions cover up their faces, or even their whole bodies?

Leslie Dorrough Smith

While we often think of it as nothing more than a means of physical protection or a mundane habit, the simple act of wearing clothing is also highly symbolic. Not all cultures feel compelled to cover the same body parts, and yet in almost all cultures failing to cover one's body in particular ways is usually considered a moral issue rather than a matter of mere preference or comfort. This indicates that clothing is a way to turn one's body into a walking emblem of a culture's morals and values.

It is important to recognize, however, that the phrase 'morals and values' actually describes how a society both naturalizes and standardizes certain power relations: who may (or may not) be seen, interact with, behave in particular ways, and ally with others. For instance, why is it considered morally inappropriate in many places for women to go topless but perfectly respectable for men to do the same? Rather than reflecting some self-evident moral stance, the answer is rooted in elements of a particular culture's power structures that render certain body parts inappropriate, sexual, or otherwise best hidden when they belong to one sort of person, while others within that same culture with different bodies can boldly display them. Men have certainly been subject to clothing and appearance expectations from religious groups, but controlling the appearance of women has long been a particular focus of religion.

One of religion's major social functions is that it provides a transcendent, and therefore relatively unquestionable, rationale to naturalize the otherwise constructed claims that cultures make. In this context, religious justifications for certain types of clothing are very much about identity and power. Many religions point to scriptures or gender essentialist arguments as their authority for expecting women to cover their bodies more than men. One major reason is to emphasize what many religions perceive to be women's subordinate status. For instance, some conservative Christian groups expect women to cover their heads to acknowledge both their submission to their husbands and to God.

Some other religious people argue that more conservative clothing for women helps promote a more ethically minded society. For example, many Muslim women describe the hijab or burqa as an important assertion of their personal modesty and/or as a barrier to keep men from sexually objectifying them. This line of thinking is also often backed by religious scriptures or gender essentialist arguments that tend to view women as emblems of the society's ethics (and thus expect them to live up to standards that others might not, such as in their dress or sexual practices). Alternatively, the fact that many women are expected to cover themselves so that *other* people (i.e., men) do not break the culture's moral codes reveals how women's bodies have often been interpreted as so dangerously sexual that they are obliged to keep others from viewing it. Since the sexuality of certain body parts is not a self-evident thing (for instance, some cultures consider a woman's hair or shoulders sexual, while others do not), whose bodies get labeled in this way tells a lot about the sanctioned relationships within that culture.

Finally, we cannot overlook the fact that many women wear specific religion-related dress to make a political statement that asserts their allegiance to their religion and/or their rejection of a culture that many alienate them due to that religion. The very same covering that may be taken as a sign of subordination in one circumstance may therefore become a sign of agency when worn in a context where it is otherwise uncommon or taboo.

What should stand out to us regardless of the rationale for restricting women's dress is that such efforts to visibly differentiate people by sex are not illuminating a pre-existing difference as much as they are *manufacturing* that difference. In other words, if men and women were naturally born with the traits that religious groups claim that their clothing communicates, then we could reasonably expect that all men and women across the globe would behave in virtually identical ways due to their biology. Since this is not the case (and very far from it, in fact), this reveals how concepts such as modesty, sexuality, and subordination, while seemingly self-evident to the culture that embraces them, are actually concepts that specific cultures invent to reinforce the power relationships that define them. Religion is the tool used to lend authority to those relationships.

About the author

Leslie Dorrough Smith is associate professor of religious studies, chair of the Department of Religious Studies and Philosophy, and director of the Women's and Gender Studies Program at Avila University. Her research focuses on the impact of conservative Protestantism on sex, gender, and reproduction rhetoric in US public discourse.

Suggestions for further reading

In this book
See also Chapter 26 (role of women).

Elsewhere
Abu-Lughod, Lila. 'Do Muslim Women Really Need Saving? Anthropological Reflections on Cultural Relativism and Its Others.' *American Anthropologist* 104(3) (2002): 783–790.

Gross, Rita. *Feminism and Religion*. Boston, MA: Beacon Press, 1996.

28

Why do people fight so much over their religious beliefs?

Craig Martin

This sort of question probably assumes that there is something problematic about fighting over religious beliefs; perhaps those asking the question think that religious beliefs should be private and inconsequential—that is, perhaps they literally don't matter socially—so why would anyone fight over them? It's clear that we often have stated beliefs that we don't fight over. If I believe the best rock band is Pink Floyd and you think it is AC/DC, it's unlikely we'll come to blows over it—one's favorite rock band is simply too inconsequential to necessitate a fight. If I believe in Jesus but you believe in Allah, what difference does it make when we clock in at work? Why would we fight over competing beliefs that have no real consequences in our daily lives?

What people clearly more often fight over is competing interests rather than mere competing beliefs. If you state different beliefs than me, I may not care, but if you show up on my property with a gun and try to seize my house—well, in that situation you're infringing on my material interests, which I'm liable to fight to defend. Arguably, people never fight over their stated religious beliefs *except when* those beliefs become tied to material interests.

The crusades are often brought up as examples of people fighting over religious beliefs. However, if we look more closely at the details, a fuller picture shows that a lot of the European Christians who invaded Arab lands sought to gain wealth and prestige by conquering them. The Muslims who lived there responded with violence not because of their religious beliefs, but because their land was being invaded by foreigners. In retrospect, it appears that the Christian beliefs people appealed to during the crusades were largely justifications for the theft of land.

Similarly, Al-Qaeda is often criticized for attacking the United States on September 11, 2001 for religious reasons. However, if we look at Osama bin Laden's writings, we can see that he lists a number of material grievances. He accuses the US as having previously invading and attacking the Middle East, he accuses the US of stealing oil from the Middle East, and he accuses the US of supporting Israel—and accuses Israel of using American funds to buy weapons of war that have been used to crush Arabs in Palestine. Now, these claims are partly true and partly false, but what matters for our purposes is that it is clear that Al-Qaeda was not attacking the US merely for having different religious beliefs; Osama bin Laden explicitly cited a number of material interests at stake.

These sorts of conflicts of interests are exacerbated when religious identities are aligned with national or regional identities. For instance, following the Protestant Reformation there were several wars between Protestants and Catholics. At the time, European kings believed there should be only one ideology for the entire state. As Louis XIV put it, 'One king, one law, one faith.' Because the church's identity was aligned with the state's identity, the presence of competing churches was tantamount to sedition or treason. For early modern Europeans, claiming allegiance to a different church was almost like claiming allegiance to a different country. Having Protestants reciting their creeds in a Catholic nation would be like Russians reciting the US's pledge of allegiance.

Last, it is worth noting that despite the common view that people fight more violently about their religious beliefs, it is clear that most of our conflicts these days are not over religion. As James W. Laine says in *Meta-Religion*:

The twentieth century was the bloodiest on record. If we moderns are not fighting about religion, and we often are, we are still fighting about something. And most often, we still prosecute our wars with a rather religious conviction.

In summary, people seem to fight over competing interests more than they fight over mere beliefs, although when competing religious identities are aligned with competing group interests, dissension is more likely to invite conflict. And, despite the stereotype that religion produces the most conflict, in the twentieth century most wars were between first world nation-states, not religious groups.

About the author

Craig Martin is associate professor of religious studies at St. Thomas Aquinas College. His recent books include *Capitalizing Religion: Ideology and the Opiate of the Bourgeoisie* and *A Critical Introduction to the Study of Religion*.

Suggestions for further reading

In this book

See also Chapters12 (function of religion) and 16 (religion in politics).

Elsewhere

Cavanaugh, William T. *The Myth of Religious Violence*. Oxford: Oxford University Press, 2009.

Fitzgerald, Timothy. 'Radical, Religious and Violent.' In his *Religion and Politics in International Relations: The Modern Myth*, 115–156. London: Continuum, 2011.

Laine, James W. *Meta-Religion: Religion and Power in World History*. Berkeley, CA: University of California Press, 2014.

29

Is there a large difference between the main religions or do they just have minor variations on the same overall idea?

Steven Ramey

People respond to this question in a variety of ways. The rhetoric of leaders in many communities often emphasizes the distinctiveness, even the superiority, of their understanding of the universe and the position of humans within it, thus distinguishing their beliefs and practices from those of their neighbors. In contrast, some people emphasize the commonalities that they identify among all religions. Ironically, even those who argue for the commonality describe it in different ways.

One conception that is often identified with Hinduism suggests that all religions are different paths leading to the same ultimate goal (although not everyone who identifies as Hindu espouses this idea). A different assertion comes from some communities that identify as Bahá'í, who often emphasize that the divine has sent messengers to all people, and those messengers explain the similar moral ideas found in many cultures, such as the notion that people should treat others like they want to be treated. Of course, these two ideas (similar path and similar messages from the singular divine) are not limited to adherents who identify with Hinduism or Bahá'í, as a wide variety of people assert ideas that resemble these two general points. Some who identify with Islam, for example, have asserted that figures such as Krishna and Hanuman, who are commonly identified as Hindu deities, were messengers whom God sent to the people of the region we now identify as India; therefore, revering these figures as prophets is acceptable. Moreover, many times the people who assert these ideas draw clear distinctions between their communities and communities that emphasize differences. So the assertion that religions have significant commonalities itself becomes a means to assert the superiority of their true religion versus the distortions of those communities who emphasize major differences.

Moving beyond these doctrinal debates, some identify similarities among these practices, institutions, and beliefs that we commonly label religions in their social functions. They identify the commonality as constructing community, making meaning in the confusing world, and providing a moral framework for living, among other social functions. Of course, others point out how institutions and practices that we do not normally identify as religion also serve similar functions. Beyond that critique, some note that the assertions of general similarity overlook differences beyond the names for divine beings and variations on practices, as the conceptions of the universe and the end goal of human life and practices, even the moral frameworks, do not line up as simply as the assertion of commonality implies.

The differences between these assertions of commonality can be identified as only minor differences or as significant, large differences. The designation of what counts as a large or minor difference depends on perspective. While people who identify as Presbyterian or Methodist may consider the differences that distinguish these Protestant denominations from each other significant, from a broader perspective, the differences seem minor in comparison to the differences with groups labeled Roman Catholic, Mormon, or Orthodox Christian. Similarly, the differences between any of these denominations that many identify with Christianity appear minor if compared to those who do not recognize Jesus as divine and salvific. And to continue on this vein, differences between adherents who identify themselves as Jewish, Christian, and Muslim appear to be quite large among themselves, but minor in comparison to religions that do not recognize the significance of figures like Moses, Abraham, and David (which all three groups generally do).

Therefore, a definitive answer to the question about these differences being significant or minor is impossible, as it depends on the starting point and perspective of whomever makes the judgment. Often, people on both sides of the debate reference the same authoritative texts, emphasizing different parts of those texts to develop the opposing interpretations. Clearly, those who assert that the differences are only minor, only a matter of semantics and names, accept a notion of broad acceptance and common humanity that often gets labeled as a liberal ideology. Those who emphasize the significance of differences often present a more narrow interpretation of particular texts that becomes the basis for mobilizing a specific community. This type of position people frequently label conservative or traditional. As with any act of comparison, the assertion of difference or similarity reflects the conceptions of the person making the comparison more than the elements being compared.

About the author

Steven Ramey is professor in the department of religious studies at the University of Alabama, where his research and teaching has focused on contested identifications and practices in contemporary India and the United States. He is the author of *Hindu, Sufi, or Sikh* (Palgrave, 2008) and editor of *Writing Religion* (University of Alabama Press, 2015), and he has an edited volume, *Fabricating Difference* (Equinox, 2017).

Suggestions for further reading

In this book
See also Chapters 18 (how many religions?), 21 (distinctions in religion), and 36 (Christian differences).

Elsewhere
Paden, William. *Religious Worlds: The Comparative Study of Religion.* Boston, MA: Beacon Press, 1994.

Sharpe, Eric. *Comparative Religion: A History* (2nd edition). London: Duckworth & Co., 1986.

30
Is voodoo a religion?

Emily D. Crews

In the 1987 film *Angel Heart*, a private detective named Harry Angel travels from New York City to New Orleans in search of a missing person. In what might be the film's most lurid scene, Angel, crouched behind a thicket of bushes, spies on a young woman as she participates in a 'voodoo' ritual. Clad in only a thin white shift, she dances suggestively to the heavy beat of drums, a white chicken clutched in her hands. As the music reaches a fever pitch, the woman slices the throat of the chicken with a straight razor, bathing her face and bare breasts in its blood as she dances. She falls in a passionate heap at the base of a candlelit altar of bottles and offerings, gyrating against the body of the bleeding chicken, her face grinding into the white Louisiana dirt. Through Angel's gaze, the woman and her fellow practitioners are sources of dangerous, aberrant allure, evoking simultaneous arousal and disgust.

The type of scene described above is likely familiar to many readers of this essay. From movies like *Skeleton Key* and *The Princess and the Frog* to *Major League* and *Eve's Bayou*, Hollywood has made millions by trading on images of curse dolls, ecstatic dances, and gruesome animal sacrifices. But what *is* 'voodoo' and is it accurately portrayed in these films? Is voodoo a religion? And what is at stake in how we answer these questions?

The first accounts of something called 'voodoo' can be traced to the late eighteenth century, when European travelers encountered the complex societies of South America and the Caribbean, and most especially Haiti. As citizens of colonial powers engaged in the wholesale exploitation of those regions, many such travelers were already predisposed to imagine the cultures they encountered to be inferior, if not also strange or deviant. The letters and reports they sent back to Europe told sensational tales of the horrific dances and sacrifices they (supposedly) witnessed. Later accounts followed similar patterns to these early stories—and were often based on equally little evidence—and provided the basis for those to come, including films like *Angel Heart*. In all of these accounts the life-worlds of racially and economically oppressed peoples became objects of white desire and disgust, foils against which the reader/viewer is able to set himself, priding himself on his own civilized, rational cultural practices.

The accounts of a thing called voodoo mentioned above are not entirely based in fiction. There are, of course, religions in Haiti and the broader Atlantic world that resemble those we see on the page and the screen. For many of their practitioners, however, these are rational forms of engagement with a spirit realm that is entirely real and extremely relevant to the human world. Many scholars thus distinguish between voodoo (the phenomenon invented out of racist fantasy about African peoples) and Voodoo or Vodun (the actual system of beliefs and practices that emerged out of the interaction of African, Native American, and European religions in the Caribbean and the United States). It is precisely this disjuncture that has led to debates about whether or not spirit-related cultural practices of the African diaspora are religions. White European (and later American) culture advances a model in which religion is primarily monotheistic, text-based, strongly personal, often private, and broadly benevolent. African diasporic traditions diverge from many of these characteristics. They are typically polytheistic, communal, performative, and often ecstatic, with symbols and deities that are largely understood to be morally ambiguous. They thus seem, to many white eyes and minds, not a religion at all but something else—magic, superstition, even evil.

In the case of 'voodoo,' Vodun, and anything between and beyond, I would argue that it is not the job of scholars to adjudicate the question of a whether or not something is or is not a religion. Rather, it is more important to consider how people have answered this question at various moments in history, what evidence they have used to arrive at their conclusions, and what those conclusions might convey about their own assumptions and motivations. To put it differently, we might say that the seemingly simple act of classification—this thing is this, this thing is another thing, these things are similar, these are different—is a political act undertaken by people, groups, and institutions that each have their own goals and biases. For those who have claimed that 'voodoo,' Voodoo, and/or Vodun are or are not religions, the question we must ask is: to what end?

About the author

Emily D. Crews is a PhD candidate at the University of Chicago Divinity School. Her dissertation investigates the role of religion (in its many forms) in Nigerian immigrant communities in the United States.

Suggestions for further reading

In this book

See also Chapters 1 (ubiquity of religion), 3 (classifying religion), and 7 (religions v. cults).

Elsewhere

Kenny, Kevin. *Diaspora: A Short Introduction*. Oxford: Oxford University Press, 2013.

Murphy, Joseph M. 'Black Religon and "Black Magic": Prejudice and Protection in Images of African-Derived Religions.' *Religion* 20 (1990): 323–337.

31

Why did Romans basically copy the Ancient Greek religion?

Roger Beck

Short answer: basically, they didn't. What the Romans copied—the 'cultured' elite Romans, that is—was Greek mythology instantiated in works of literature. Likewise, the representation of the gods in the visual arts, especially sculpture. Not infrequently, statues of the gods in Rome were all too literally expropriated from their Greek subjects.

Writing in the middle of the first century BCE, the Roman aristocrat and intellectual Marcus Terentius Varro distinguished three kinds of theology: the mythical, the physical, and the civil. (Varro's original work, *Antiquities Human and Divine*, is lost, but much of it is summarized in Book 6 of Augustine's *City of God*.) Mythical theology, said Varro, was to be found in poetry and on the stage. Most of it was undeniably Greek or of Greek origin, as the Romans freely acknowledged. The same was true for 'physical theology,' by which Varro meant philosophical speculation about the nature of the gods.

Varro (as quoted in *City of God* 6.5) defined his third kind of theology, the civil, as 'that which in cities the citizens, and especially the priests, ought to know and to practice. It comprises what gods are to be publicly worshiped, and what sacred rites and sacrifices each person is to perform.' Clearly, Varro's 'civil theology' is the core of what the Romans understood as 'religion.' Clearly, too, when one examines it in any detail, it is Roman, not Greek. The Romans in fact gloried in its indigenous nature.

Rome's religious calendar was full of traditional festivals without Greek counterparts, except in the very broadest sense, let alone Greek origins. Consider, for example, the Lupercalia. At this festival, held on February 15, men of an aristocratic fraternity, the Luperci, ran a set course in the city center naked except for belts made of the skins of newly sacrificed goats. As they ran, they lashed bystanders of both sexes with thongs from the same goatskins. The Lupercal itself was the cave in which a she-wolf (*lupa*) was said to have nurtured Romulus, Rome's founder, and his brother Remus as infants. The Lupercalia is the most obviously indigenous of Rome's festivals, but there is a host of other examples. In the generation after Varro, the major poet Ovid composed a whole book about them, the *Fasti* (or, as we might translate the title, *The Calendar*). These festivals comprised the 'what,' 'when,' and 'where' of Roman religion, the 'who' being on the human side the idiosyncratic Roman priesthoods and on the divine the Roman gods, sometimes equated with Greek divinities, sometimes not.

The blending of the Roman and the Greek in Roman religious thought can be best appreciated in Rome's national epic, Virgil's *Aeneid*. (Virgil, the creative jewel of the age of Rome's first emperor, Augustus, wrote in the late first century BCE, roughly between Varro and Ovid.) His epic tells the story of Aeneas, a refugee from the fall of Troy, who eventually found safety in Italy, establishing the community which would develop into Rome itself. The *Aeneid* is modeled on Homer's two great Greek epics, in that it tells of both warfare, like the *Iliad*, and wandering, like the *Odyssey*. Moreover, the same quarrelsome gods help and hinder humans, though in Virgil less arbitrarily than in Homer. In sum, Roman gravitas is imposed on Greek ebullience.

About the author

Roger Beck, an Emeritus Professor at the University of Toronto, is among the world's foremost authorities on such ancient Roman mystery cults as Mithraism.

Suggestions for further reading

In this book

See also Chapters 21 (distinctions in religions), 29 (differences among religions), and 73 (ancient religion).

Elsewhere

Beard, Mary, John North and Simon Price. *Religions of Rome* (2 vols). Cambridge: Cambridge University Press, 1998.

32
Is Satanism a religion?

Nathaniel J. Morehouse

Yes, or maybe, and most unsatisfyingly, it depends. Historically, within Christian Europe, anything that deviated from mainstream Christianity was lumped together as having been influenced by Satan. Previous Greco-Roman gods were seen as demons. Those who attempted to get Christians to comply with various Roman laws and make sacrifices to the Roman gods were seen by Christians as being influenced by Satan. Jews were frequently associated with Satan throughout much of European history. Witches (or those who were deemed external and problematic to society for one reason or another) were believed to have sold their soul to Satan (and frequently accused of having sexual relations with him as well) and consequently Satanic. In none of these cases would the practitioner of the 'irregular' custom have considered what they did to be Satanic. Romans did not identify with Satan any more than Jews did. In the case of witch hunts in medieval Europe, there is no evidence that anything like the practices described in the *Maleous Malifacarum* ever existed. The things that were labeled as satanic and the practices that women (most frequently) and men were put to death for simply did not exist.

In all of these cases there was/is a power dynamic at play in the labeling of a practice that was deemed problematic with the Satanic. This is true of many things that are considered counter-cultural by those making the claim of Satanism. One has only to think of the association of rock and roll or *Dungeons & Dragons* with Satanism in the second half of the twentieth century. More recently, a very small minority of Christians have maintained that *Pokémon Go* is a tool for recruiting Satanists. Frequently those with the power to do so use the labeling of something as Satanism or satanic as a means of establishing the boundaries of society. Anything outside of those arbitrary boundaries or that threatened the established power of the dominant group within a social unit was seen as dangerous, or satanic. It was something to be shunned or violently stamped out.

This is the Satanism whose religiosity one might call into question, because it does not necessarily exist as a thing in itself, rather it was a label placed upon things (or more often imaginary fears) by the powerful with the intention of eradicating the individuals or practices which threatened their power. There are modern groups, however, who claim the term 'Satanism' or the 'Church of Satan' for themselves, and regarding these groups I would most certainly answer this question in the affirmative.

The Church of Satan was founded in 1966 by Anton Szandor LaVey as an atheistic group which advocated a non-conformist ideology promoting individuality, pride, sex, and rebellion. To this Satan stood as a metaphorical figurehead. Currently the Church of Satan does have a hierarchical priesthood, with Peter Gilmore as High Priest. There have been many offshoots from the Church of Satan, most notably the Temple of Set which was founded in 1975 by Michael Aquino, and which unlike the Church of Satan does have a more traditionally divine component. This is often referred to as Theistic Satanism (although followers of the Temple of Set typically do not claim the name Satanist for themselves; due to their history with the Church of Satan scholars typically include Temple of Set within the general category of Satanism). Regarding this split, and all subsequent splits and disagreements (e.g., The Satanic Temple), the Church of Satan claims exclusive ownership to the name 'Satanist,' and refers to all other groups as 'devil worshipers.' Or as LaVey noted, 'There are no categories of Satanists—there are Satanists and nuts.' Of course this too is an act of power, that is to say there is but one form of Satanism, perhaps an orthodoxy of Satanism.

While the Church of Satan, especially after the death of LaVey, focuses on the individual Satanist rather than on theological concerns, they do practice various rituals or 'Greater Magic.' Officially these hold no spiritual component, but are occasionally necessary for individuals to participate in what they refer to as 'self-transformational psychodrama' rather than appeasing a god. In his text, *The Satanic Rituals*, LaVey outlines his ideas for rituals for large groups. Due to the emphasis on individualism, however, none of these rituals are necessary for one to be a practicing Satanist in the Church of Satan.

In general, for the groups which self-identify as Satanist (whether in the Church of Satan or not) there is no reason to exclude them from the category of religion (if it can be satisfyingly defined). However, groups that have been labeled as Satanic by outsiders should either be known by other nomenclature which does not carry the stigma of 'Satanism'—or they probably never existed in the first place.

About the author

Nathaniel J. Morehouse earned his MA in religious studies from New York University and his PhD in religious studies from the University of Manitoba. He currently lives in Northeast Ohio where he teaches courses in religious studies and philosophy. His first book *Death's Dominion Power, Identity, and Memory at the Fourth-Century Martyr Shrine*, was published in 2016 by Equinox.

Suggestions for further reading

In this book

See also Chapters 1 (ubiquity of religion), 3 (classifying religion), and 7 (religions v. cults).

Elsewhere

Dryendal, Asbiorn, James R. Lewis, and Jesper A. Petersen. *The Invention of Satanism*. New York: Oxford University Press, 2016.

Faxneld, Per and Jesper Aagaard Petersen. *The Devil's Party*. New York: Oxford University Press, 2013.

Frankfurter, David. *Evil Incarnate: Rumors of Demonic Conspiracy and Satanic Abuse in History*. Princeton, NJ: Princeton University Press, 2006.

33
Who wrote the Bible?

Stephen L. Young

Lurking in the shadows of the question 'Who wrote the Bible?' is the very idea that the Bible is a book. This is why it seems so obvious to ask who wrote it. But one crucial task of scholarship is asking whether what seems obvious may, in fact, be misleading. So, what happens when we critically examine the idea that the Bible is a book? The ways we label or classify things shape our expectations of them. When we think of the Bible as a book, we expect it to be unified. We expect it to have an author who created or arranged each part so it could be part of the whole. But the classification of book can mislead when it comes to thinking about the Bible. It is instead a collection of numerous writings, many of which are themselves complex collages of earlier texts.

A more fruitful way to think about the Bible may be as a set of books on a library shelf. The books on a shelf in the Russian literature section of a library were written by many people over many years, and they did not write their books for the purpose of existing on a library shelf. We would not expect these books to have any inherent relationship to each other. In fact, the current situation of all these books residing together on a Russian literature shelf tells us more about the interests of the people who arranged the library and created the category of Russian literature, and less about the individual books on the shelf. We would thus not expect all of these books to agree with or even necessarily show awareness of each other. To the extent that some were written with knowledge of or in response to others, the nature of that response varies. One book may selectively allude to, agree with, contest, or creatively develop one or more of the others. Among the things we can say about these books: All somehow pertain to Russian literature, at least as the curators of the library imagine the category. All may creatively draw from a reservoir of stories, characters, themes, and settings prominent in Russian literature. All were written by people with the interests and literacy skills necessary for composing something that could eventually make its way to a Russian literature shelf.

This analogy reframes the question, 'Who wrote the Bible?' If the Bible resembles a library shelf more than a book, this changes our expectations. Many different writers and editors produced its writings over the course of perhaps a thousand years (spanning the first millennium BCE through the second century CE). They did not compose their writings for the purpose of being part of the Bible any more than Fyodor Dostoevsky wrote *Crime and Punishment* to be on a library's Russian literature shelf. Some writings of the Bible were written with knowledge of or in response to others, but not because an author wove a single, organically unfolding story.

Biblical writings originated in the ancient Mediterranean world. This was a setting wherein a tiny minority of people had the resources, skills, and interests necessary to compose the writings of the Bible. And these people were almost always men. A smaller group within this tiny minority would have been interested in creating writings that routinely feature the Israelites, Jews, and their high God. This small group of male writers was thus associated with Israelite and Jewish culture. They continually drew from and refilled an evolving reservoir of stories, characters, themes, settings, events, and cultural imagination in their writings. Sometimes these writers would creatively develop, allude to, contest, combine, disassemble, appropriate, or rewrite portions of other writings that drew from the same reservoir. Additionally, these biblical writers or editors composed their works for the same reasons others have written throughout history. They wrote to tell stories, to promote a specific temple or royal house as the legitimate one, to encourage people to give money to one group and not another, to entertain, to construct a national history, to explain how to live a virtuous or wise life, or any combination of these or other purposes. And eventually a handful of these writings made their way onto the library shelf we know as the Bible.

So, who wrote the Bible? Rather than simply repeating the question, scholars of religion prefer to examine the ideas that drive it. We can thus not only find new answers, but also reimagine the question altogether. If the Bible is more like a library shelf than a book, then the question of who wrote it gives way to different questions. What do we know about the diverse books on the shelf? Why did people write them, and to whose benefit? How do these books actually relate to each other—if at all? And what were the social and historical processes that resulted in the creation of the library shelf of the Bible?

About the author

Stephen L. Young has a PhD in religions of the ancient Mediterranean from Brown University and teaches in the Department of Philosophy and Religion at Appalachian State University. He researches myth, textuality, and discourses about deities in the ancient Mediterranean.

Suggestions for further reading

In this book

See also Chapters 9 (sacred books), 11 (origins of religion), and 37 (St. Paul).

Elsewhere

Haines-Eitzen, Kim. *Guardians of Letters: Literacy, Power, and the Transmitters of Early Christian Literature*. New York: Oxford University Press, 2000.

Mroczek, Eva. *The Literary Imagination in Jewish Antiquity*. New York: Oxford University Press, 2016.

Schniedewind, William. *How the Bible Became a Book*. New York: Cambridge University Press, 2004.

34

Do Jews believe in the afterlife?

Aaron W. Hughes

On one level, this question is very simple to answer: yes, of course. Since all religions posit some sort of afterlife or world to come, and Judaism is a religion, it stands to reason that it possess a concept of the afterlife. However, traditional Judaism, unlike Christianity is a religion of orthopraxy ('correct practice') as opposed to orthodoxy ('correct belief'). I suspect, as will be discussed below, that this distinction is somehow behind this question.

Religious Jews who recite the daily morning liturgy refer to God as 'he who revives the dead' (*m'chayeh ha-meitim*). Explicit in this locution is that people will be resurrected and live again, offering further evidence that, of course, Jews believe in an afterlife. The question becomes trickier, however, when one inquires into the contours of what such afterlife might look like. Since Judaism is primarily focused on life here and now, and on actions (e.g., not mixing meat with dairy, linen with wool, determining what one can and cannot do on the Sabbath, and so on) as opposed to beliefs, rabbinic tradition does not speculate a great deal on the afterlife—which in Hebrew is referred to as *olam ha-ba*, literally 'the world to come'—and leaves a tremendous amount of space for personal opinion.

Despite this, the messianic ideal has played a fundamental role in the history of Judaism. Implicit in this ideal is that the world is imperfect on account of human imperfection and sin, and that at some future point in time there will come a Messiah who will, depending on the interpreter, either radically transform (e.g., as found in some of the Dead Sea Scrolls) the world or give Jews political independence (e.g., the twelfth-century thinker known as Maimonides). Given the problems that some so-called messianic figures have created for Jews in history (e.g., Bar Kokhba in the second century; Shabbatai Zvi in the seventeenth), such speculation now tends to be rather quiescent.

There also exists some debate as to what the Hebrew term *m'chayeh ha-meitim* refers to. In traditional (i.e., orthodox) Judaism, the term is often interpreted to refer to the literal bodily resurrection of the dead at the time when the Messiah comes. Reform Judaism, a more liberal form of the tradition, finds the idea of resurrection anti-modern and unscientific, and has actually changed the phrase *m'chayeh ha-meitim* in its prayer book to *m'chayeh ha-kol*, which means God is 'the one who gives life to all.' Interestingly, however, the Reform Movement has recently re-added *m'chayeh ha-meitim* alongside *m'chayeh ha-kol*, presumably as a way to be more inclusive and 'traditional.'

The more interesting question, however, is why non-Jews, specifically Christians, insist on asking this question and on maintaining the assumption that Jews do not believe in an afterlife. Here a number of factors are at work. The first is literalism. Whereas the New Testament has many verses describing the afterlife and eternal existence with God, the Hebrew Bible (or 'Old Testament') is relatively silent on the matter. If we take a Protestant view of scripture and assume that religions have to be what is literally found in their scripture, we might conclude that Judaism does not talk much about the afterlife. Such a position, however, completely ignores the later commentary tradition in Judaism—a tradition that is as important, if not more so, than the actual Hebrew Bible. In the Talmuds, midrashim (i.e., commentaries), and other works, we see a great deal of mention of the afterlife.

The second feature is the traditional notion of supersessionism that is built into Christianity, and which dates to the time of Paul. Christianity and Christian teaching are now perceived to be the spiritual fulfillment of biblical Judaism. In order to do this Paul made Judaism into a religion of the law and Christianity into one of the spirit. This stark juxtaposition, of course, worked in Christianity's favor and transformed Judaism into a corporeal and legalistic tradition: whereas Judaism circumcised the flesh, for example, Christianity circumcises the spirit; whereas Judaism is fixated on earthly matters such as not mixing meat and dairy or wool and linen, Christianity is concerned with the spiritual world; and, in the case of our question, whereas Christianity is predicated on the afterlife in the eternal, Judaism is not.

As should be clear, however, this is religious polemic and not at all based on the facts of Jewish teaching. What better way, in other words, to show the superiority of one's own religion and the inferiority of one's rivals than to say that the latter does not have the concept of an afterlife?

About the author

Aaron W. Hughes is the Philip S. Bernstein Chair in the Department of Religion and Classics at the University of Rochester.

Suggestions for further reading

In this book

See also Chapters 8 (belief in a higher power) and 35 (Jewish views on the messiah).

Elsewhere

Segal, Eliezer. *Introducing Judaism*. Abingdon: Routledge, 2008.

35

Why don't Jewish people believe that Jesus was the Messiah?

Sheldon Steen

I remember as a child hearing a preacher declare with conviction that only one person had fulfilled all of the messianic prophecies in the Old Testament: Jesus of Nazareth. The natural next question is why anyone, especially a Jew who held these scriptures as sacred, would then fail to recognize Jesus as the Messiah. Not surprisingly, this question is a bit more complicated than it first appears and reveals some of the tensions between Jews and Christians, especially their respective readings of the Hebrew Bible/Old Testament. The question could be approached in any number of ways, but this discussion focuses particular attention on the diversity of Jewish messianic expectation in and around the time of Jesus and how early Christians came to identify Jesus as the Messiah.

A primary issue at stake here is the assumption held by many modern readers that Jewish messianic expectation was/is monolithic and that every Jew believes the same things about the Messiah's identity and role. Yet even a cursory survey of ancient sources, both biblical and extra-biblical, reveals that Jewish messianic expectation has always been variegated. While the discovery of the Dead Sea Scrolls in the late 1940s was a huge boon for our understanding of Judaism in the Second Temple period (*c.*515 BCE–70 CE), it also muddied the waters in significant ways, painting a much more diverse and complicated picture of Judaism(s) during this period. The issue of messianic expectation in the scrolls remains a hotly debated topic, with many even suggesting evidence for expectations of two separate Messiahs. The diversity of messianic expectations largely stems from the various functions messianic figures serve in the Hebrew Bible, the scrolls, and other ancient Jewish texts such as priest, prophet, king, and others. One of the most consistent expectations, however, is that the Messiah will liberate the Jewish people from oppressive regimes and usher in an age characterized by God's justice and peace.

The term 'messiah' itself comes from the Hebrew word *mashiach*, which simply translates to 'anointed one' (the Greek translation is *christos*). Yet, usage of the term *mashiach* in the Hebrew Bible indicates that it should not always be taken to refer to the expectation of a future Messiah. For instance, in one particularly interesting use of the term in Isaiah 45.1 a foreign king, Cyrus the Great, is referred to as God's 'anointed' (*mashiach*). Cyrus, the king of Persia, is famous for issuing a decree that allowed exiled Jews to return home and to rebuild the temple that had previously been destroyed by the Babylonians. Moreover, not all messianic figures are identified by the term *mashiach*. For example, the 'Son of Man' in Daniel 7, with whom Jesus is often associated, is never explicitly called the Messiah, but was identified as a Messianic figure from very early in its interpretation.

As diverse as messianic expectation was, however, one thing remained consistent: the Messiah was not supposed to die. While most modern Christian readers can't help but think of Jesus when they read certain 'messianic' texts like Psalm 22 or the 'Suffering Servant' texts from Isaiah, those texts don't appear to have been connected to messianic expectations until after Jesus. Jesus's death was therefore somewhat of a scandal for early Christians. The famous account of Jesus's appearance to two of his followers on the road to Emmaus in Luke 24 reflects some of the scandal of an executed Messiah when his followers say, not yet realizing that they are speaking to Jesus, 'But we had hoped that he was the one to redeem Israel' (Lk. 24.13).

It is therefore worth asking how early Christians came to identify Jesus as the Messiah given the issues surveyed above. One way to make sense of this is to recall the importance of the belief in the resurrection as vindication of Jesus's messianic identity. The belief that he had been raised from the dead prompted a (re) reading of the Hebrew Bible in light of the one whom they had already identified as the Messiah, and they mined the text for clues to validate his messianic identity. Thus, the narratives they crafted about Jesus were often written to reflect and legitimate their pre-suppositional belief in Jesus as the Messiah. The above discussion also illuminates a deep-seated divide between Jews and Christians that continues even into our contemporary context: to whom do the scriptures belong?

About the author

Sheldon Steen is a PhD student in religions of Western Antiquity at Florida State University. He primarily specializes in early Jewish and Christian apocalyptic literature.

Suggestions for further reading

In this book

See also Chapters 34 (Jews on the afterlife) and 49 (Jewish, Christian, Muslim similarities).

Elsewhere

Collins, John J. *The Scepter and the Star: Messianism in Light of the Dead Sea Scrolls*. Grand Rapids, MI: Eerdmans, 2010.

Levenson, David B. 'Messianic Movements.' In *The Jewish Annotated New Testament*, edited by Amy-Jill Levine and Marc Zvi Brettler, 530–535. New York: Oxford University Press, 2011.

36

What are the main differences between Protestantism, Catholicism, and Greek Orthodoxy?

Vaia Touna

Although at first this seems to be as a very straightforward question there are implications in the way we will try to answer it. If you open any world religions textbook you will certainly find among the major religions 'Christianity.' Christianity is discussed in those books—and sometimes people in general often think of it—as a unified religious system (that can be distinguished from, say Judaism or Buddhism), but like all other religious systems it is also divided internally, into various denominations, each one claiming to follow the proper dogmas, and principles, just as the early Christians would have. One should do well, then, to ask first, which kind of principles are taken to be the most representative of the Christian thought and therefore comprise the essence of Christianity? And so when one is asked to answer this seemingly straightforward question, one faces a similar problem, that is, which of the many Protestant denominations will we take as the representative to then compare it with Roman Catholicism or Orthodoxy (keeping in mind that among and within each of these, there are also many differences).

So in order to be able to answer the question at hand we will have to make some important generalizations and say that the movement known today as Christianity saw two major schisms, or internal conflicts, one in 1054 CE, when a debate between the Church centered in Rome and the Church centered in Constantinople resulted eventually in what we know today as Roman Catholicism in the west and Greek Orthodoxy in the east. A second division later occurred within the Roman Churches, beginning in 1517 CE, which eventually resulted in the creation of what we know today as Protestantism.

The differences or disagreements between the various Christian churches are in regard to the following:

- the nature and essence of the trinity (the manner in which God is described as father, son, and also the holy spirit);
- the role the Virgin Mary or Theotokos (the mother of god) plays in their theology;
- the interpretation of the Bible (whether it is something that can be done individually, as advocated by some Protestant denominations, or only within the church through its patristic traditions and dogmas, such as in Catholicism and Orthodoxy);
- the organization of the churches and the role of its lay members as opposed to the ordained leadership (for example, women cannot become priests in the Roman Catholic and Greek Orthodox Churches);
- differences in the role the icons play in their theology (in Greek Orthodoxy icons, or images of Jesus, Mary, the disciples, etc., play an important role);
- differences also are reflected in the churches' architectural styles (for example, Greek Orthodox churches have a rich iconography in them, but it is unlikely that you will find any statues similar to the ones found in many Roman Catholic churches, while most Protestant churches are symbolically minimalistic in comparison);

- the role of the communion in the worship rituals, or liturgy, and both its content (does one use leavened or unleavened bread in celebrating the Eucharist?) and meaning (does it commemorates the so-called Last Supper Jesus had with his followers?); and also
- the presence of Jesus in the ritual event (whether it is seen as real, as it is for most Orthodox and Catholic Churches, or merely symbolic, as it is for some Protestant Churches).

About the author

Vaia Touna is assistant professor at the Department of Religious Studies at the University of Alabama, USA. Her scholarly interests range widely, from looking at specific concepts of religion in the Greco-Roman world to methodological issues concerning the study of religion in general.

Suggestions for further reading

In this book

See also Chapters 18 (how many religions?) and 29 (differences among religions).

Elsewhere

Anatolios, Khaled and Stephen F. Brown. *Catholicism and Orthodox Christianity* (3rd edition). New York: Chelsea House Publishing, 2009.

Binns, John. *An Introduction to the Christian Orthodox Churches*. Cambridge: Cambridge University Press, 2002.

Cunningham, Mary B. and Elizabeth Theokritoff. *The Cambridge Companion to Orthodox Christian Theology*. Cambridge: Cambridge University Press, 2009.

Ware, Timothy. *The Orthodox Church: An Introduction to Eastern Christianity* (2nd edition). London: Penguin Books, 1993.

37
Why did St. Paul write all those letters?

Patrick Hart

There is no doubt that the apostle Paul pervades much of the New Testament, given that virtually half of its twenty-seven books are associated with him in some form or another. In most modern Christian bibles, Paul first appears as a central character in Acts, a book identified as the second volume of Luke's gospel. Following Acts, one then typically finds thirteen letters—arranged basically from longest (Romans) to shortest (Philemon)—that identify Paul as their putative author.

In contemporary scholarship, however, there is debate over whether Paul actually authored all thirteen letters attributed to him. In New Testament studies, most scholars classify the following seven letters as 'undisputed,' or authentically authored by Paul: Romans, 1 and 2 Corinthians, Galatians, 1 Thessalonians, Philippians, and Philemon. On the other hand, there are some letters that are identified as pseudepigraphic, or falsely attributed to Paul. For example, most scholars agree that Paul did not write 1 and 2 Timothy, as well as Titus, three letters often referred to collectively as the 'Pastoral Epistles.' Unfortunately, there is little consensus when it comes to the remaining three letters (Ephesians, 2 Thessalonians, and Colossians), as some scholars identify one or more of these as authentic while other scholars do not. Given this, the question concerning *why* Paul wrote all those letters first requires one to consider the question of *whether* Paul wrote all those letters.

In one of the undisputed letters, Galatians, we can find some background to Paul's mission, and a general impetus behind his literary activity. Here, Paul acknowledges that he had previously 'persecuted the church of God violently and tried to destroy it' (Gal. 1.13). He then goes on to explain that he received a revelation about God's son, Jesus Christ, noting further that God 'was pleased to reveal his Son to me, in order that I might preach him among the Gentiles' (Gal. 1.16). Following this experience, Paul travelled to various communities in the first-century (CE) Greco-Roman world, evangelizing specifically to Gentiles (or non-Jews). In turn, this led Paul to write letters that in some manner or another related to his missionary activity.

For the most part, Paul's undisputed letters were written to audiences that he had already evangelized to (1 Thessalonians, 1 and 2 Corinthians, Galatians, and Philippians), or intended to evangelize to (Romans). In the case of Philemon, Paul wrote the letter to an individual recipient, Philemon, who Paul identifies as a 'dear friend and fellow worker' (Phil. 1.1). Yet in every case, Paul's letters were written in response to particular circumstances and to particular audiences. As such, it is important to recognize that these letters were not composed with the intention of becoming 'scripture.' Nor were they even assembled as treatises, or written for the purposes of widespread dissemination or publication. Rather, they were generally intended to address specific issues brought to Paul's attention, or to clarify elements of Paul's theology that were unclear to the 'churches' that he had founded. Given this, Paul's letters can by and large be described as instances of ad hoc theologizing.

Paul's letter to the Galatians serves as an example of this ad hoc approach. In this epistle, Paul is clearly enraged with his audience, the Galatians, as he states, 'I am astonished that you are so quickly deserting him who called you in the grace of Christ and turning to a different gospel' (Gal. 1.6). Following from this, Paul goes on to explain to the Galatians that the message, or gospel, that he had originally presented to them is the only authentic gospel. As such, by 'turning to a different gospel,' the Galatians had committed the most egregious of errors, and were in need of correction from Paul. This, in fact, was the very reason that Paul wrote to the Galatians. With that context established, the remainder of the epistle focuses on the authoritative legitimacy of Paul and his gospel, and explicates the theological inconsistency between the 'different gospel' and the one Paul had initially preached to the Galatians.

For the most part, Paul's other undisputed letters can be understood in a similar fashion, as his correspondence was generally written in response to particular situations that came up in the communities that he had a prior relationship with. Consequently, Paul's epistles were ultimately the means by which he attempted to address issues, or respond to questions, that arose among the groups that he had established.

About the author

Patrick Hart is a PhD candidate in religious studies at the University of Alberta in Edmonton, Alberta. His doctoral research focuses on the particular theoretical interests of scholars that underlie various studies on the apostle Paul.

Suggestions for further reading

In this book

See also Chapters 9 (sacred books), 11 (origins of religion), and 33 (Bible's authors).

Elsewhere

Horrell, David G. *An Introduction to the Study of Paul* (3rd edition). London: T. & T. Clark, 2015.

Roetzel, Calvin J. *The Letters of Paul: Conversations in Context* (5th edition). Louisville, KY: Westminster John Knox Press, 2009.

38

Why do some Christians use snakes in their worship?

Brad Stoddard

> And these signs shall follow them that believe; In my name shall they cast out devils; they shall speak with new tongues; *They shall take up serpents*; and if they drink any deadly thing, it shall not hurt them; they shall lay hands on the sick, and they shall recover. (The Gospel of Mark 16.17-18; italics added)

Why do some Christians use snakes in their worship? The short answer is that so-called serpent handlers believe that God wants them to. Why? As quoted above, the Christian Bible contains a brief passage where Jesus allegedly instructed his followers to 'take up serpents.' As self-professed biblical literalists, serpent handlers argue that they have no choice but to handle serpents (serpent handlers typically distinguish serpents, which are poisonous, from snakes, which aren't poisonous). That the practice is illegal in most states doesn't deter them from the practice.

Serpent handlers typically capture their serpents in the wild and later release them after several months, as they don't want the serpents to become tame, docile, or used to interacting with people. Serpent handlers bring the serpents to church in locked boxes, which they place at the head of the church near the pulpit. At various points in the church service, someone who feels 'anointed' by God will remove the serpent and handle it for a brief period of time before passing it to another believer or replacing it in the box and securing the lid. Serpent handlers confine the handling of poisonous serpents to the front of the building, creating a buffer of sorts between children, non-believers, and others who would rather not handle.

Serpents rarely bite their handlers, but on the rare occasion when a handler is bitten, the handler typically refuses medical help under the assumption that God will either heal the handler or will allow him to die. If the handler dies, the community believes it the will of God, as they believe that God allows the occasional death to remind those who are skeptical of the practice that it is dangerous. To date, scholars have documented slightly more than 100 deaths.

Serpent-handling Christians are a relatively small form of conservative Christianity. The movement grew out of the larger Fundamentalist movement, which is a relatively new form of conservative Christianity that developed in the late nineteenth century. Though the self-proclaimed Fundamentalists disagree on various doctrinal and liturgical issues, they agree on certain basics, or fundamentals (hence the term Fundamentalists). Among other things, they reject Catholicism, atheism, evolution, liberal Christianity, and secularity more broadly. Instead, they affirm their commitment to what they believe are traditional forms of Christianity, including a literal interpretation of the Bible. The Fundamentalist movement spread first in America and then beyond. Serpent handlers were but one small branch of the larger movement, separated from other Fundamentalists primarily by their literal interpretation of Mark 16.17-18.

Scholars estimate that there are perhaps fifty serpent-handling churches, with roughly 1,000 Christians who routinely attend these churches. The practice originated in the early twentieth century and spread in various communities in or near the Appalachian Mountains. Though it occasionally spread beyond Appalachia, serpent handling continues to be a regional practice primarily confined to mountain communities in Tennessee, Kentucky, Alabama, and West Virginia.

Christian critics of the practice typically argue that Jesus does not intend for his followers to have a literal interpretation of the serpent-handling clause in the Gospel of Mark. Additionally, New Testament scholars (both Christian and otherwise) commonly agree that verses seventeen and eighteen (in addition to others) were not in the original text, but were added later. Serpent handlers scoff at both of these positions, as they believe the Bible, typically the King James Version, is the literal and inerrant (without error) Word of God. If God did not intend for those verses to be in the Bible, serpent handlers argue, then they wouldn't be there in the first place.

Scholars have offered a variety of insights to help explain the movement. Around the 1950s, the first scholars who studied the group offered psychological explanations, as they argued that serpent handlers have sexual dysfunctions and handle serpents (which resemble the male phallus) as a psychological coping mechanism. Recent scholarship dismisses this interpretation. Though it may apply to some of the handlers, psychologists argue, it does not explain the larger movement. Recent scholarship stresses that we must conceive of serpent handling as a regional form of Appalachian mountain religion that is a peculiar manifestation of local tradition combined with Fundamentalist Christianity.

Regardless of the reason that serpent handlers exist, they are a unique form of American Christianity. Though it remains relatively small, scholars are reluctant to write the movement's obituary.

About the author
Brad Stoddard is an assistant professor of religious studies at McDaniel College in Westminster, Maryland. His research addresses faith-based correctional programs and religion and public policy.

Suggestions for further reading

In this book
See also Chapters 3 (classifying religion), 12 (function of religion), 36 (Christian differences), and 39 (speaking in tongues).

Elsewhere

Covington, Dennis. *Salvation on Sand Mountain: Snake Handling and Redemption in Southern Appalachia*. Reading, MA: Addison-Wesley, 1995.

Hood, Ralph W. and W. Paul Williamson. *Them That Believe: The Power and Meaning of the Christian Serpent-Handling Tradition*. Berkeley, CA: University of California Press, 2008.

Kimbrough, David L. *Taking Up Serpents: Snake Handlers of Eastern Kentucky*. Chapel Hill, NC: University of North Carolina Press, 1995.

39
What is 'speaking in tongues'?

Jennifer Eyl

'Speaking in tongues' is a vocalization practice in which people utter unintelligible sounds that are similar to words, but lack clear meaning or grammar. Practitioners shout and mumble word-like utterances that, to outsiders, sound like gibberish. To insiders, the vocalizations are thought to be the words and sounds channeled directly from a divine source. To some, a divinity temporarily inhabits the human body and controls the practitioner's mouth, while to other practitioners, the sounds are simply divinely inspired. The practice is common among various forms of Pentecostal and charismatic Christianity, but practices like it can be found through history among various cultures. These 'esoteric speech acts' (as scholar Dale Martin calls them) can be found wherever deities are thought to possess the bodies or mouths of people. The practice is also called glossolalia, from the Greek *glôssa* (tongue) and *lalein* (to utter).

Although the sounds are not actual words, they do employ patterns of consonants and vowels, and tend to reflect the types of sound patterns found in the native languages of the practitioners. So, for example, Portuguese speakers will 'speak in tongues' in a way that sounds vaguely Portuguese, while English practitioners will enunciate sounds that vaguely reflect the rhythms and sounds of English. Thus, the practitioner draws on native speech patterns and sounds, even though the sounds are thought to come from an entirely different, and divine, entity. No matter the language of the practitioner, however, the utterances are not actual words or sentences.

Christians trace the practice to the apostle Paul and the earliest evidence for Christianity in the New Testament. In 1 Corinthians 12.4-10, for example, Paul lists a range of 'gifts' bestowed on people through the divine spirit of Christ. These gifts include things like miracle healing and prophecy. They also include various forms of 'tongues' as well as the ability to interpret tongues. It is clear at least in Corinth that some followers of Paul were also uttering unintelligible forms of speech that needed to be interpreted by others. The gifts are arranged hierarchically, though, as he makes clear in 1 Corinthians 14.2-5, when he indicates that prophetic speech is more valuable than speaking in tongues. But even Paul lived in an ancient Mediterranean culture that understood deities to occasionally possess the bodies and mouths of humans; he did not invent the practice whole cloth.

Speaking in tongues presents an interesting quandary, especially among religious groups that adhere to strict reliance on written texts such as the New Testament. The practice eschews written rules, regulations, or commandments. It appears to be spontaneous, impromptu, and unpredictable. This generates a tension between authoritative written commandments and the things that the Holy Spirit makes a person do or say, in the moment. If there is a contradiction (which there often is), between what the conservative texts demands, and what the Holy Spirit moves a person to do or say, which authority ought to be obeyed? Because the practice is simultaneously spontaneous but deeply trusted among some religious groups, the practitioners themselves are permitted to sidestep conventional expectations about behavior, in the face of such contradiction or tension.

For example, many Pentecostal Christian groups hold the conservative belief that women should not speak in church or maintain positions of authority. But because speaking in tongues is thought to come upon a person directly from the Holy Spirit, the women who practice it are able to talk, shout, sing, dance, and utter things in church services that they would otherwise never be permitted to do. Likewise, the practice allows a degree of prestige and social capital to those who would otherwise rarely possess such prestige, as it sidesteps more traditional routes of accruing expertise and legitimacy. One does not need to practice or to become 'accredited' to speak in tongues; a person is simply thought to be visited and moved by the Holy Spirit. In that sense, speaking in tongues is a great democratizer vis-à-vis any system of education, promotion, or authorization. Only some may become preachers, but anyone can speak in tongues.

About the author

Jennifer Eyl is an assistant professor of religion at Tufts University. She works primarily on ancient Christianity.

Suggestions for further reading

In this book

See also Chapters 12 (function of religion), 36 (Christian differences), and 38 (snake-handling Christians).

Elsewhere

Cooper-Rompato, Christine. *The Gift of Tongues: Women's Xenoglossia in the Later Middle Ages*. University Park, PA: Penn State University Press, 2010.

Goodman, Felicitas D. *Speaking in Tongues: A Cross-Cultural Study of Glossolalia*. Chicago, IL: University of Chicago Press, 1972.

Johnson, Lee A. 'Women and Glossolalia in Pauline Communities: The Relationship between Pneumatic Gifts and Authority.' *Biblical Interpretation* 21 (2013): 196–214.

Martin, Dale B. 'Tongues of Angels and other Status Indicators.' *Journal of the American Academy of Religion* 59 (1991): 547–589.

May, L. Carlyle. 'A Survey of Glossolalia and Related Phenomena in Non-Christian Religions.' *American Anthropologist* 58 (1956): 75–96.

Samarin, William J. *Tongues of Men and Angels: The Religious Language of Pentecostalism*. New York: Macmillan, 1972.

40

Is it true that religions outside of Christianity have stories of a virgin mother, crucifixion, etc.?

Robyn Faith Walsh

Yes. Other ancient Mediterranean and Near Eastern religions offered stories of virgin mothers, sons of gods, wise teachers, savior figures, healings, and other miracles.

Myths abound in the ancient Mediterranean of women (and animals) being impregnated by gods or other supernatural forces. Plato, for example, was described as the son of the god Apollo. A similar claim was made about the emperor Augustus by the Roman historian Suetonius, who tells us that Apollo impregnated Augustus' mother by taking on the form of a snake. According to the Greek biographer Plutarch, a snake also appeared at the side of Alexander the Great's mother Olympias and was later revealed to be Zeus-Ammon.

Given these tales and others like them, it would not seem strange to an ancient reader for an extraordinary man to be the son of (a) god. What's more, the notion that the gods could beget mortal children was supported by ancient ideas about the physical world. The Platonists and Stoics, for example, thought that the universe was permeated and held together by an ethereal substance called '*pneuma*' (often poorly translated into English as 'ghost' or 'spirit') that was closely associated with the gods. Because it was always in motion or 'tension' with the material world, *pneuma* also came to be associated with anything that invisibly animates or activates: wind, air, breath, even sperm. By this logic, a god needn't bother taking on a bodily form to get a woman pregnant. All the god had to do was come in contact with her womb by any other (non-sexual) means like breath or wind. Jesus himself claims he is born from *pneuma* in the Gospel of John (3.5). The Gospel of Luke tells us that an angel appeared to Mary and told her a holy *pneuma* would 'overshadow' her and she would conceive a divine child (1.35).

That Mary was a virgin and 'untouched' made her a particularly appealing candidate to carry God's progeny. The idea of a virgin mother existed as far back as the Babylonian period in the form of the virgin-goddess Ishtar. Ancient commentators on the Hebrew Bible, like Philo of Alexandria, often spoke of God's preference for 'undefiled' soil and virgin women whose purity and lack of mortal passion matched his own (see §49 of Philo's *On the Cherubim*).

That Jesus was a divine figure who was killed is also not unusual. Gods routinely died in ancient mythology. The late Bronze Age god Aliyan Baal, the Akkadian god Tammuz, the Egyptian god Osiris, and the Phoenician and (later) Greek god Adonis, the Greek gods Dionysus-Zagreus and Heracles, and the Greek goddess Persephone all found themselves at one point or another killed or otherwise sent to the underworld. While some of these gods were able to communicate with the living, delay their deaths, or find a substitute to replace them, none were able to defeat death fully.

Where the story of Jesus differs from others is in that God fully resurrects him. Not only is Jesus able to come back from the dead, but the apostle Paul tells us that he will eventually defeat all earthly power and authority, including the 'last enemy': death (1 Cor. 15.26). This particular formulation of a 'dying and rising' divine being is unique, with later accounts of the 'resurrection' of the gods like Adonis or Attis borrowing from the language of Christianity.

Similarly, Jesus' death by crucifixion appears to be unique among divine figures. Crucifixion was considered one of the most disgraceful and brutal forms of capital punishment, fitting only for the worst criminals, slaves, and dogs. Greek and Latin authors described the act in vivid and gruesome detail, or made reference to it as a cruel taunt. The Hebrew Bible called it a 'curse' (Deut. 21.23). Outside of Christianity, only the second-century CE author Lucian makes reference to the god Prometheus being nailed to a rock in a cruciform pose. But, it is unclear whether Lucian's imagery was inspired by the story of the crucified Christ.

About the author

Robyn Faith Walsh is assistant professor of New Testament and early Christianity at the University of Miami (Florida). Her research interests include the letters of Paul, the history of the interpretation of the synoptic problem, and Greco-Roman archaeology.

Suggestions for further reading

In this book

See also Chapters 21 (distinctions in religion), 29 (differences among religions), and 31 (Roman and Greek religion).

Elsewhere

Litwa, M. David. *Iesus Deus: The Early Christian Depiction of Jesus as a Mediterranean God*. Minneapolis: Fortress Press, 2014.

Smith, Jonathan Z. 'Dying and Rising God.' In *The Encyclopedia of Religion*, edited by Mircea Eliade (2nd edition), vol. 4, pp. 521–527. New York: Macmillan, 1987.

Philo, *Philo Volume II: On the Cherubim; The Sacrifices of Abel and Cain; The Worse Attacks the Better; On the Posterity and Exile of Cain; On the Giants* (translated by F. H. Colson and G. H. Whitaker). Loeb Classical Library 227. Cambridge, MA: Harvard University Press, 1929.

41

Why do some Christians not acknowledge evolution?

Arthur McCalla

Christians who do not acknowledge evolution are called creation-ists. Creationism is a modern movement that originated in the early twentieth century as part of the Fundamentalist reaction against biblical criticism and Liberal Protestantism. To understand creationism, then, we have to understand why these movements so troubled conservative American Protestants. Biblical criticism treats the Bible as an historical document whose various books reflect the intellectual, social, and political thought-worlds of their human authors. Liberal Protestantism theologically accom-modates recognition of the Bible as a historical document by reinterpreting various Christian doctrines: Genesis narratives, for example, become ancient Hebrew myths and Jesus a moral teacher. Conservative Protestants regarded any such accommodation as a betrayal of the faith that the Bible as God's eternal revelation to humanity transcends human history and therefore its every word must be considered absolutely true. This belief—the doctrine of biblical inerrancy—holds that to admit that the Bible contains errors or obsolete understandings of the world is to substitute some human standard for the Word of God and to undermine its testimony to the redemptive work of Christ. By the end of the nineteenth century conservative Protestants had identified biblical inerrancy along with certain beliefs about Christ as fundamental doctrines that all true Christians must affirm. Their defense of these fundamental doctrines became known as 'Fundamentalism.'

Fundamentalists' commitment to biblical inerrancy means that they reject all historical claims—including those made by the modern academic disciplines of civil history, archaeology, linguistics, and so on—that are incompatible with accounts contained in the Bible. For this same reason Fundamentalists reject biological evolution as incompatible with the biblical account of creation. Creationism—the name for Fundamentalists' opposition to biological evolution—defends the biblical doctrine of the special creation by God of every species in its current form against the origin of species through natural selection or any other evolutionary mechanism. The extensive scientific evidence for evolution is irrelevant because the critical issue for creationists is not the content of evolutionary science itself but the defense of biblical inerrancy.

There are three varieties of creationism:

- Old Earth creationism;
- Young Earth creationism; and
- intelligent design.

All three deny evolution but differ on the age of the earth. Old Earth creationists (OECs) are able to accept geological evidence for an ancient earth because they interpret the 'days' of the Genesis creation story figuratively so as to allow for a vast antiquity before the appearance of human beings while still upholding biblical inerrancy. The early Fundamentalists who campaigned to ban the teaching of evolution in public schools (the Scopes Monkey Trial of 1925 in Tennessee marked the high point of this phase of anti-evolutionary activity) were OECs. A new phase of creationism began in the 1960s with the shift to Young Earth creationism. Young Earth creationists (YECs) reject figurative interpretations of Genesis as placing human reasoning above the plain sense of the Word of God. They insist that Christians must accept that God created the world and everything within it in six 24-hour days approximately 6,000 years ago; that the three primary geological agents have been Creation, the Fall, and the Flood; and that physical death is a consequence of sin and so all fossils, as the remains of once-living creatures, must postdate the Fall (they deny the validity of radiometric dating techniques—remember, creationism is not about science but about defending biblical inerrancy). ID, finally, is a form of creationism that was introduced in the 1990s as an attempt to get around constitutional objections to teaching creationism in public schools by suppressing all references to the biblical basis of its program. It rejects evolution but does not (publicly, at least) insist on a young earth.

So, the problem of accounting for such things as, say, the discovery of dinosaur bones concerns the age of the earth and is a separate issue from evolution. All creationists both accept that dinosaurs existed and believe that, like every other species, they were created directly by God. The problem is how long ago did dinosaurs live? OECs and ID proponents need not reject the mainstream understanding of dinosaurs as having lived tens of millions of years ago because they accept an ancient earth. YECs, however, insist that God created the dinosaurs along with all other forms of life a few thousand years ago. They accordingly maintain that dinosaurs and humans coexisted within the last few centuries, that most dinosaur fossils are the remains of animals that perished in the Flood, that some (small!) dinosaurs may have been aboard Noah's Ark, and that dinosaurs became extinct (if they truly are extinct) only recently.

About the author

Arthur McCalla (PhD University of Toronto, 1992) is professor in the Department of History and Department of Philosophy/Religious Studies at Mount Saint Vincent University in Halifax, Nova Scotia. He is an intellectual historian working in the areas of nineteenth-century religious thought and the history of the study of religion.

Suggestions for further reading

In this book
See also Chapters 33 (who wrote the bible?), 16 (religion in politics), and 36 (Christian differences).

Elsewhere

Bowler, Peter J. *Monkey Trials and Gorilla Sermons: Evolution and Christianity from Darwin to Intelligent Design*. Cambridge, MA: Harvard University Press, 2007.

McCalla, Arthur. *The Creationist Debate: The Encounter between the Bible and the Historical Mind*, revised edition. London: Bloomsbury, 2013.

Numbers, Ronald L. *The Creationists: From Scientific Creationism to Intelligent Design* (expanded edition). Cambridge, MA: Harvard University Press, 2006.

42

Are Mormons Christian?

Linh Hoang

This is a complicated question that assumes an agreed upon definition of Christian. No formal definition of Christian ever appears in the Bible. But in the New Testament, the Greek word *Christianos* occurs three times (Acts 11.26; 26.28 and 1 Pet 4.16). It refers to outsiders seeking a label for the fledgling Jesus movement. But it does not provide the nuances of the term Christian used today. Nevertheless, if one defines a Christian as someone who believes Jesus Christ is the Son of God and the Savior of the world who suffered, was crucified, and resurrected from the dead and one day will return, then, anyone who claims this belief is a Christian.

From this perspective, Mormons are Christians since they do believe in Jesus Christ and that he established Christianity. When the Winter Olympic Games was held in Salt Lake City, Utah in 2002, the Church of Jesus Christ of Latter-day Saints sent out a media notice reemphasizing the centrality of Jesus Christ in its name. It stressed the Christian identity by altering the logo of its name by enlarging the type on 'Jesus Christ' and urged the media to use the long name, the Church of Jesus Christ of Latter-day Saints (LDS or LDS Church). This stressed their Christian identity and effectively denied the existence of an entity called the 'Mormon Church.' It is better, then, to refer to Mormons as the LDS.

The text of the LDS, *The Book of Mormon* (1830) claims to deepen the witness to Jesus Christ that was introduced in the New Testament. This is where it becomes complicated. The LDS believe that Christianity as originally established by Jesus Christ and his immediate followers, had gone through an apostasy in which the original authority—the priesthood—was lost. Thus, the LDS claims no part of traditional Christianity but accepts Christian heritage and faith. The LDS is a 'restoration of truth' or the restoration of Christianity from the historic churches of Roman Catholic, Eastern Orthodox, and Protestant. They are a 'new' Christianity since the LDS claims the historic Christian Churches to not be true followers of Jesus Christ of the New Testament.

The LDS have taught that Protestant reforms, the American Revolution, and the rise of democracy allowing freedom of religion, all prepared the world for the reintroduction of Christ's gospel. Their founder Joseph Smith's (1805–1844) First Vision told him that no current churches were true and claimed to have restored the original Christianity by divine authority. This is known as the restoration or the restoration of all things.

From an institutional side, the Roman Catholic and mainline Protestant churches do not recognize baptism of LDS as valid. For instance in 2001, the Roman Catholic Church required officially that any Latter-day Saints joining the Church needed to be re-baptized. Thus, LDS are not treated as separated brethren, a term that applies to some baptized Christians. This change came about because of the different doctrinal teachings of the LDS Church, especially on the Trinity and salvation that caused some concern. The LDS believe that the Trinity: Father, Son, and Holy Spirit are three gods which differs from the traditional Christian understanding of one God in three persons. Their understanding of salvation offers humankind exaltation into godhood in the highest Celestial kingdom. That is, human beings can become gods. This is clearly different from traditional Christian teaching. These are but a few of the theological differences between the LDS and other Christian Churches.

There is also a commonality between LDS and other Christian Churches. The concern for social justice and care of other are important aspects of the LDS that is shared by all Christians. There is a common moral value that all Christians share of working towards a stronger understanding of the Gospel of Jesus Christ in order to create a better human life.

Finally, the LDS Church is not part of mainstream Christianity but do want to be regarded as Christians. They claim to be a restoration of the whole grand sweep of Christianity, that is, the true church of Jesus Christ on earth today. It is difficult to have a definitive answer to the question because of the varied understanding of Christian and the ongoing disagreements between the Churches. But if believing and following the teaching of Jesus Christ is the sole criterion, then the answer is yes.

About the author

Linh Hoang OFM is an associate professor and chair of the Religious Studies Department at Siena College in New York. He has published articles and book chapters in the areas of Asian American Catholics, Vietnamese Catholicism, comparative religion, migration, globalization, historical theology, and inter-generational religious practices. His book *Rebuilding Religious Experience* was published in 2007.

Suggestions for further reading

In this book

See also Chapters 20 (how many are right?), 29 (differences among religions), and 36 (Christian differences).

Elsewhere

Davies, Douglas J. *An Introduction to Mormonism.* Cambridge: Cambridge University Press, 2003.

Webb, Stephen H. and Alonzo L. Gaskill. *Catholic and Mormon: A Theological Conversation.* Oxford: Oxford University Press, 2015.

43
What is biblical archeology?

Aaron W. Hughes

Biblical archaeology is a subgenre of archeology that involves the attempt to recover and investigate the material remains of the Ancient Near East (parts of which are not infrequently referred to as the 'Holy Land,' which roughly corresponds to the modern nation states of Israel and Palestine) with the aim of illuminating the descriptions found in the Bible, be it the Hebrew Bible ('Old Testament') or the New Testament. While it uses the same techniques as found in general archaeology, such as excavation and radiocarbon dating, whenever one appends the adjective 'biblical' in front of a science or social science, tensions naturally emerge.

Despite the sensationalism found in movies such as *Indiana Jones and the Raiders of the Lost Ark* and headline-grabbing discoveries (often later found to be forgeries) such as the James Ossuary or the Shroud of Turin, biblical archeology is—or ought to be—a very mundane activity premised on the general rules of archeological method. In this sense the goal of biblical archeology is, in theory, the same as non-biblical archeology: to understand and supplement our knowledge of the historical record through the excavation of material remains. Its goal ought not to be the confirmation of what religious Jews and Christian believe to have happened because it is mentioned in the Bible. Again, though, this is rarely the case. A quick perusal of titles on *Amazon*, for example, reveals books with titles such as *Biblical Archeology: An Introduction with Recent Discoveries that Support the Reliability of the Bible* or *The Popular Handbook of Archaeology and the Bible: Discoveries that Confirm the Reliability of Scripture.* Such titles show us that the field of biblical archeology is anything but straightforward or simply scholarly. Despite the sensationalist and implicit theological implications of such titles, and their contents, biblical archeology, in the hands of experts as opposed to religious dilettantes, is how we verify, discount, or add knowledge to our *historical* and *social* understanding of the biblical period, a period that spans from roughly 2000 BCE to late antiquity.

Since the adjective 'biblical' is put before the noun archeology, there are certain expectations or connotations that might not exist for other types of archeology. Roman or Greek archeology, for example, does not have the same mystique for religious believers because such archeology is seen as somehow more 'secular' or, at the very least, less invested in religious truth claims. Whereas many think that biblical archeology is a religious activity meant to support the biblical record, it rarely is or does. What, then, does one do if and when the archeological record contradicts the biblical account? Most biblical archeologists who are well trained, for example, are not interested in using archeology for apologetical purposes. There is no archeological evidence, for example, that shows that the Israelites were in Egypt, wandered in the desert, conquered the land in a military campaign and divided it among the twelve tribes of Israel. Nor, despite the Bible's claim to the contrary, is it difficult to maintain that the united monarchy of David and Solomon was anything more than a small tribal kingdom. If archeology cannot furnish any positive remains for these basic beliefs that emerge from the Bible, it can show, more positively, that the God of Israel had a female consort and that the early Israelite religion adopted monotheism only in the waning period of the monarchy and not at Mount Sinai. This is not to say, however, that there are some biblical archeologists who want to argue that, if archeology does not actually contradict the Bible, it at least confirms or illumines other aspects. So while archeology may confirm the existence of Jesus, it has no way of supporting that he was or is the 'Christ.'

Since the 'holy land' is also contested land between Israelis and Palestinians, we must also be aware that archeology in the region often has a political or ideological connotation as well. Many right-wing Israelis, which includes the current government, for example, use archeological remains as a way to prove ancient Jewish settlement in a particular region and, thus, as a justification for current settlement activity. Despite the fact that Palestinians see themselves as descendants of the ancient Philistines, they— perhaps for obvious reasons having to do with their occupation— engage in very little archeological activity.

In sum, then, biblical archeology can be, often in equal parts, mundane, apologetical, scientific, political, and territorial.

About the author
Aaron W. Hughes is the Philip S. Bernstein Chair in the Department of Religion and Classics at the University of Rochester.

Suggestions for further reading

In this book
See also Chapters 33 (bible's authors) and 37 (St. Paul).

Elsewhere
Cline, Eric H. *Biblical Archeology: A Very Short Introduction* New York: Oxford University Press, 2009.

Magness, Jodi. *The Archaeology of the Holy Land: From the Destruction of Solomon's Temple to the Muslim Conquest*. Cambridge: Cambridge University Press, 2012.

44

Is Europe less religious than North America?

Julie Ingersoll

To answer this question we need to have an operative definition of religion because we are trying to measure 'religiousness.' One way to answer our question is to look at attendance at religious events/ services. Alternatively, we might rely on survey data in which people are asked how often they do 'religious' things like praying, studying sacred texts, or participating in certain rituals.

These measures assume a certain set of characteristics as religious, and if we understand religion this way, then Europe is less religious than North America. But while this may be a default way to look at this question, it is only one way to do so.

Some people say that 'real religion' is deeply felt spirituality rather than something observable like attendance. This is a debate over authenticity where 'more religious' is equal to 'more authentically religious.' This is, of course, very subjective, making any kind of measurement impossible. For example, there are Christians who believe in the death penalty for homosexuality, others who believe the morality of homosexuality is between an individual and God, and Christian groups that embrace same sex unions and leadership by LGBTQ people. While people will have opinions about these issues and even opinions about what religion teaches (or should teach) about them, the question of who is more authentically Christian is a religious question and not an academic question.

To push this a bit further, other people suggest that religions are not really different from other social systems through which people organize themselves. In this view, religions are but one aspect of what is labelled social formation.

Indeed, there are good historical arguments to be made that what we perceive as 'secularism' (which we consider to be non-religious) that dominates Europe is a historical development directly from Protestantism. Protestantism decentered the authority of the Catholic Church, led to notions of individualism and the autonomy of human conscience from authority, and ultimately the privatization of religion and the limiting of its social significance. In that sense European secularism is as 'religious' as North American fundamentalism.

Bruce Lincoln offers helpful categories to understand this. According to Lincoln, there are really two kinds of religion: minimalist (as I just described developing out of Protestantism and the enlightenment) and maximalist (that rejects the modernist construction of religion as a private concern in favor of public religion that speaks to all of life.) With these categories we can start to see how examples that might look 'less' religious really are just differently religious. We can also see what used to be considered religious diversity might better be understood as different expressions of the same religion. For example, an interfaith group includes a Christian, a Jew, a Muslim (and maybe a Buddhist and a Hindu) and this is thought to be diverse. Yet these interfaith religious people are all minimalist and they have more in common with each other than they do some (maximalist) counterparts within their same traditions.

Some who approach religion this way say that religions are social formation strategies that root themselves in deities or transcendent authorities. Others in this camp argue that religions are no different from other social formation strategies at all.

So the answer to our question depends on how we are defining religion. But the exercise of discussing the question encourages us to be explicit about what we mean by the term (and by analogy other terms with apparently obvious meanings). It encourages us to question assumed definitions and assumed arrangements of categories (such as religious and secular as opposites). The next step in a religious studies course would be to explore how certain definitions and category arrangements might benefit some people and disadvantage others (i.e., explore how groups try to use them to their own advantage).

About the author

Julie Ingersoll is professor of religious studies and Religious Studies Program coordinator at the University of North Florida. Her PhD is from the University of California at Santa Barbara, and she teaches and writes about religion in American history and culture, religion and politics, and religion and violence.

Suggestions for further reading

In this book

See also Chapters 1 (ubiquity of religion), 12 (function of religion), and 15 (atheism or secularism as religion).

Elsewhere

Lincoln, Bruce. *Discourse and the Construction of Society: Comparative Studies of Myth, Ritual, and Classification*. New York: Oxford University Press, 1989.

Lincoln, Bruce. *Holy Terrors: Rethinking Religion after September 11*. Chicago, IL: University of Chicago, 2006.

Popkin, Richard H. *The History of Skepticism from Erasmus to Spinoza*. Berkeley, CA: University of California Press, 1979.

45

Were African slaves forced to become Christian when they got to plantations?

Sarah E. Dees

From the 1600s through the 1900s, the Transatlantic slave trade facilitated a system of race-based servitude in which Africans and African-descended people were violently removed from their homelands, traded as commodities, and forced to labor in the Americas. Slavery was legal when the United States was founded, and while Congress outlawed the importation of slaves in 1808, slavery remained legal in some areas of the country until the ratification of the Thirteenth Amendment to the United States Constitution in 1865. In addition to influencing slave-owners' treatment and management of slaves, Christianity shaped the Transatlantic slave trade itself; was a resource for both the pro-slavery and abolitionist movements; and played a role in the resistance, adaptation, and endurance of those who were enslaved.

Scholars have argued that the greater Christian tradition played a role in the ethical foundation of the practice of slavery. The Transatlantic slave trade was a massive network whose agents relied, in part, on negative assumptions about people from Africa to justify the system's inhumane practices. White European and American Christians' ideas about their own cultural and religious supremacy provided an intellectual and ethical foundation for the slave trade by perpetuating the idea of the cultural, psychological, and spiritual inferiority of Africans and African-descended people. Europeans and Euro-Americans misunderstood and discounted traditional African beliefs and ceremonies, assuming them to be misguided or unenlightened. Christian theological perspectives designated non-Christians as spiritual others and enemies.

Even so, these ideas about the inherent superiority of Christianity did not immediately lead to the forced conversion of African and African-descended slaves on plantations in the American South. In some regions, such as French Louisiana in the seventeenth century, all slaves were required to be baptized. However, not all slaveholders wanted their slaves to actively pursue Christian teachings. Christian worship often involved communal gatherings, and slaveholders regulated and restricted meetings of enslaved African Americans. In general, slave-owners forbade indigenous African practices, but spiritual alternatives could create their own challenges. Biblical teachings offered ambiguous statements on the nature of slavery and the status of slaves, and Christianity could be interpreted as challenging the racial hierarchies that legitimated slavery. Indeed, some slaves who were interested in Christian teachings argued that their conversion to Christianity meant that they should no longer remain in bondage. However, by the early eighteenth century, colonial governments passed laws indicating that slaves who converted to Christianity would not gain their freedom. Proponents of slavery argued that slaves could be free in spirit, but this did not equate to release from physical captivity.

By the Civil War, many slaves in the United States practiced Christianity. If they had not personally adopted Christian beliefs or practices, many were familiar with basic tenets of Christianity. Some slave-owners did allow slaves to gather for worship openly, at times even hiring preachers to minister to the slaves. Other religious leaders not sanctioned by slave-owners offered Christian teachings that were more meaningful for those enduring the conditions of slavery. In these cases, and in situations in which slave-owners did not allow their slaves to engage in religious gatherings, enslaved individuals gathered in secret to meet, pray, sing, and worship.

One of the main factors leading to the American Civil War was the practice of slavery. Members of many factions—Northerners and Southerners, white and black Americans, abolitionists and supporters of slavery—drew on Christian ideas to support their views. Some white Southern slave-owners argued that because Christianity was practiced in biblical times, the practice was religiously sanctioned. Some justified the institution of slavery by suggesting that it was ultimately a positive practice because it brought African descended people into contact with Christianity. At the same time, African-American and Euro-American abolitionists offered alternative interpretations of Biblical texts in support of efforts to end slavery.

The forms of Christianity that slaves adopted differed from the Christianities of white Southerners. Because white Southerners specifically discouraged literacy among African Americans, practices such as the singing and dancing, drawing on traditional African forms of music and percussion, were more prominent than the individual reading of scripture. Enslaved Christians shared biblical narratives through story and song. Preachers offered leadership and a religiously inspired vision of hope. In addition, some slaves drew of Christian motifs to conceal their continuing participation in traditions from their homelands in, resulting in new forms of blended traditions, such as Santeria. In addition, new African-American Christian denominations emerged, such as the African Methodist Episcopal (AME) church, in response to histories of racial subjugation that white Christians had in part perpetuated.

About the author

Sarah E. Dees (PhD, Indiana University) is a postdoctoral fellow at Northwestern University. Her research focuses on American and Indigenous religions.

Suggestions for further reading

In this book
See also Chapter 52 (African-American religion).

Elsewhere
Bailey, Julius H. *Down in the Valley: An Introduction to African American Religious History.* Minneapolis, MN: Fortress Press, 2016.

Johnson, Sylvester. *African American Religions, 1500–2000: Colonialism, Democracy, and Freedom.* New York: Cambridge University Press, 2014.

Raboteau, Albert. *Slave Religion: The 'Invisible Institution' in the Antebellum South* (2nd edition). New York: Oxford University Press, 2002 [1978].

46
Why are there so many radical Muslims in the world today?

Matt Sheedy

If we were to turn back the clock a few decades, we would not find the term 'radical Muslim' in common everyday use. Although recent historical events like the attacks of September 11, 2001, or the rise of groups like ISIS in an age of social media have called our attention to violent and authoritarian groups and individuals who identify as Muslim and justify their actions using religious language, conflicts described today in religious terms were often talked about in relation to ethnic identity (e.g., Arab Nationalism) or political affiliation (e.g., communist influenced) in the not too distant past. One important starting place, then, for addressing the question, 'Why are there so many radical Muslims in the world today?' is to historicize it by taking note of its past and present uses, and to ask what interests are being served in emphasizing religious identities and motivations over political, ethnic, and economic ones?

One important point to note is that 'radical Muslim' is a Western term used to describe outsiders that are perceived to represent a threat to things like national security and secular liberal values. Whether or not certain groups or individuals actually constitute such a threat should be considered on a case by case basis as the term is often thrown around with very little evidence, and is frequently assumed in advance based on common associations between Islam and extremism, where 'Muslim' sounding names (e.g., Muhammad), forms of dress (e.g., veiling), practices (e.g., daily prayer), and terms (e.g., *jihad*) are understood by some as inherently 'radical.' This tendency is due in part to common stereotypes about Islam that Edward Said famously termed 'Orientalism,' which refers to the long history of Western writers depicting the 'Orient' as the opposite or 'other' of Western civilization. Picking up on these ideas in his book *Reel Bad Arabs: How Hollywood Vilifies a People*, author Jack Shaheen details a number of common tropes about Arabs and Muslims found in Hollywood movies, such as the terrorist, the uncivilized desert-dweller, and the misogynist who is repressive or violent toward women. Whatever merits there may be to using the term 'radical Muslim' to represent the ideologies that some people hold, this history of racialized images and ideas about Muslims is important to bear in mind as it frequently prejudices the conversation on this topic and affects the ways that people respond, Muslim or otherwise.

The term 'radical Muslim' gained currency during the Cold War, where struggles for independence from colonial governments led to dramatic shifts in the national identities of a variety of states, as seen with the rise of 'Arab Nationalism' in the 1950s in countries like Egypt, Syria, and Iraq. Whereas these movements were commonly framed in terms of ethnic identification and as strategically aligned with the Soviet Union during the 1950s, 1960s, and 1970s, the Iranian Revolution in 1979 marked the rise to power of a theocratic government of considerable influence on the international stage and helped to spur the growth of what is sometimes referred to as 'political Islam' as a form of resistance against Western influence. It should also be noted that throughout the Cold War Western powers often backed and trained local 'Islamist' groups, who were fighting against secular nationalist and socialist movements, as a strategy to contain the 'communist threat' and to gain power on the world stage. Perhaps the best-known example of this strategy is what is sometimes referred to as the 'Afghan *jihad*' (1979–1989), where Western powers helped to arm and train foreign fighters from a variety of Muslim majority countries in a proxy war against the Soviet Union. It was during this conflict that Osama bin Laden rose to prominence and subsequently formed militant groups like Al-Qaeda. After the fall of the Soviet Union (1922–1991), many states re-aligned their identities along ethnic and religious lines, where 'Islamist' militant groups established during the Cold War were able to find a stronger foothold in national politics as an alternative to Western influence.

In sum, the term 'radical Muslim' is a recent invention that has a history in Cold War politics. While it attempts to describe the militant behavior of certain groups in the contemporary world, the current emphasis on religious identity minimizes the role of ethnic, economic, and geo-political causes and motivations, and creates the impression that such groups are acting for 'religious reasons' rather than a confluence of multiple variables working together, including a Western interest in obscuring its own role in such conflicts.

About the author

Matt Sheedy holds a PhD in religious studies and lectures at the University of Manitoba, Winnipeg. His research interests include critical social theory, theories of religion and secularism, as well as representations of Christianity, Islam, and Native traditions in popular and political culture.

Suggestions for further reading

In this book

See also Chapters 47 (types of Islam), 48 (*jihad*), 49 (Jewish, Christian, Muslim similarities), 50 (Sufism), and 51 (Sunni and Shia Islam).

Elsewhere

Alsultany, Evelyn. *Arabs and Muslims in the Media: Race and Representation After 9/11*. New York: New York University Press, 2012.

Buruma, Ian and Avishai Margalit. *Occidentalism: The West in the Eyes of Its Enemies*. New York: Penguin, 2005.

Mamdani, Mahmood. *Good Muslim, Bad Muslim: America, the Cold War, and the Roots of Terror.* New York: Doubleday, 2005.

Shaheen, Jack. *Reel Bad Arabs: How Hollywood Vilifies a People.* Northampton, MA: Olive Branch Press, 2009.

47

What is the difference between radical and non-radical Muslims in terms of the types of Islam?

Mushegh Asatryan

In the West, the term 'radical Muslims' denotes those Muslims who engage in violent acts in order to achieve political goals, and who justify their actions with recourse to the Islamic tradition. The 'non-radical Muslims,' then, are those who do not; they are regular people living regular lives. The 'radical Muslims' are not a homogeneous group, and comprise a great variety of individuals, living in various parts of the world, from different social, cultural, or ethnic backgrounds, and fighting for a variety of causes.

Although the term is sometimes indiscriminately used in political and popular discourse to denote any Muslim who is engaged in any military conflict—or who undertakes violent actions that go against Western (and in particular, American) interests, or which claim Western lives—it most commonly refers to militant groups resorting to violent acts in order to further their political interests. Radical Muslims tend to emphasize the militant elements found in the Islamic tradition, using them to justify their actions and to legitimate their goals. They frequently resort to the idea of *jihad* found in the Qur'an, Islam's holy scripture, and further elaborated in the Islamic tradition. This term primarily means 'war in the path of God,' aimed at expanding, or defending, the realm of Islam. For example, the violent actions undertaken by organizations like Al-Qaeda or ISIS, often involving heavy civilian casualties, have been framed by their authors as *jihad*.

Another feature that many of the radical Muslims share, also termed 'Islamic fundamentalism,' is a professed desire to return to a pristine, 'true' Islam of the time of the Prophet Muhammad. Because, due of the scarcity of historical sources, it is virtually impossible to know what this 'pristine' Islam actually looked like, such groups propose a vision of Islam that they see desirable. It usually involves the idea that society must be run according to the principles of the Islamic law, and that it is the duty of a believing Muslim to help achieve this goal by any means possible. Radical interpretations of Islam reject the practices of groups which they do not deem to be 'truly Muslim,' such as saint worship, found among many Sufi groups, or the practice of Shia Muslims to visit the graves of their Imams—presumably because these did not exist during Muhammad's time and are later, hence un-Islamic, additions to the religion. Frequently, this rejection is accompanied by acts of terror.

So, what is the difference between radical and non-radical Muslims in terms of the types of Islam? In other words, how does the 'Islam' of radical Muslims differ from the 'Islam' of everyone else? To answer this question, we must first examine what 'Islam' actually means. As any other religious tradition, Islam is not one thing, it does not have one, 'true' essence, or a correct and an incorrect way of practicing it. Islam is a collection of scriptures, legal treatises, theological works, communities, doctrines, and rituals. They have evolved throughout centuries, responding to the various political, cultural, and social circumstances at hand. Even the Qur'an alone is not homogeneous in its outlook, and it has passages ranging from openly militant to ones that preach love and peace. Throughout history, then, various groups of Muslims have interpreted their tradition in a way that best fit their situation. For example, in the middle ages, when Islam was the religion of a powerful empire, the legal and theological writings of the time presented Islam as a universal religion, and viewed the militant spread of this religion as a great virtue. During the period when large parts of the Muslim world had become subject to European colonial domination, the struggle against Western powers was often framed as a sacred war in the name of Islam. Likewise, radical Muslim groups nowadays resort to those verses of the Qur'an, and to those parts of the Islamic tradition, which promote warfare. Partly as a result of the actions of radical groups, in the West Islam is frequently viewed as an inherently violent religion, and all Muslims as potential terrorists. To counter these Islamophobic stereotypes, and to better integrate into the majority non-Muslim societies of North America and Western Europe, many Muslims in the west today solely emphasize the peaceful, pluralistic aspect of their tradition. Along the way, each group of Muslims tends to present their interpretation of the Islamic tradition (or, their Islam) as the only correct one.

About the author

Mushegh Asatryan (PhD, Yale 2012) is an assistant professor of Arabic and Muslim Cultures at the University of Calgary. His research interests include the interrelation between religion, society, and culture in the medieval Islamic Middle East, and his monograph, *Controversies in Formative Shi'i Islam: The Ghulat Muslims and their Beliefs*, was published in 2016.

Suggestions for further reading

In this book

See also Chapters 46 (radicalism in Islam), 48 (*jihad*), 49 (Jewish, Christian, Muslim similarities), 50 (Sufism), and 51 (Sunni and Shia Islam).

Elsewhere

Cook, David. *Understanding Jihad*. Berkeley, CA: University of California Press, 2005.

Lincoln, Bruce. *Holy Terrors: Thinking about Religion after September 11* (2nd edition). Chicago, IL: University of Chicago Press, 2006.

48
What does *jihad* really mean?

Mushegh Asatryan

The word *jihad* in Arabic means 'struggle' or 'exertion.' Just what exactly kind of struggle or exertion has depended on the contexts in which the term has been used throughout the history of Islam. At times when Muslims had to fight in self-defense, or when they fought to conquer, *jihad* denoted violent, military struggle aimed at defending, or spreading, Islam. During periods of relative peace and stability, *jihad* as fighting was relegated a secondary role, while the true, 'greater *jihad*' was said to be a spiritual struggle against one's vices. In modern times, different Muslims groups have variously emphasized either the peaceful (spiritual) or the militant aspects of the term, depending on their political goals and their orientation in regard to the non-Muslim world. Non-Muslims have also stressed the two different aspects of the term, either polemically, to argue for the supposedly violent nature of Islam (and hence, of all Muslims), or apologetically, to paint the 'true' religion of Islam as inherently peaceful.

The Qur'an, Islam's holy scripture, uses the term *jihad* in both of its meanings. In most cases, here it denotes obedience to God and an effort to be a better believer. However, the Qur'an contains several passages where *jihad* is used to refer to actual fighting, which reflects the turbulent history of the nascent community of Muslims in the seventh-century Arabian Peninsula. Initially a persecuted group of the Prophet Muhammad's followers, it gradually became a powerful military force, which was involved in (offensive and defensive) military encounters with the pagan and Jewish tribes of the Peninsula.

In the seventh and eighth centuries, the Muslims created a powerful empire stretching from Spain and North Africa in the west to Central Asia in the east. Unsurprisingly, in the Muslim writings of this period, the term *jihad* was used to denote an armed struggle in the path of God that was aimed at spreading Islam, and which was lavishly rewarded in the Hereafter. Later on, the threat from non-Muslim powers against Muslim territories, such as the Crusaders and the Mongols, provided a new impetus for the elaboration of the idea of *jihad* as military struggle to defend the realm of Islam.

The end of the wave of Muslim conquests enabled for peaceful interpretations of the term *jihad*. Muslim authors distinguished between two types, a 'greater' and a 'lesser' *jihad*. In this opposition, military struggle was only the 'lesser' one, whereas 'greater *jihad*' referred to a person's spiritual struggle against one's passions and vices.

The advent of modernity brought about two new developments that conditioned the further development of the doctrine of *jihad*. On the one hand, many of the historically Muslim territories came under European (i.e., non-Muslim) control. On the other, numerous Muslim communities emerged in non-Muslim majority countries in Western Europe and North America. These developments called for various responses on the part of Muslim thinkers and political actors. Thus, in many cases the struggle of Muslim populations against colonial rule was framed as *jihad*, a struggle to liberate Islam from foreign domination. The same idea and terminology has been frequently used to this very day by radical Muslim organizations such as Al-Qaeda and ISIS, who have described their violent attacks (often involving civilian casualties) as *jihad* in the name of true Islam.

In the West, *jihad* is often polemically used in anti-Muslim discourse as solely denoting struggle against the enemies of Islam (or the West), to indicate the supposedly violent nature of Islam and all Muslims. To counter this discourse, and in an attempt to enable Muslims to better integrate into the non-Muslim majority societies of Western Europe and North America, many Muslim authors and non-Muslim advocates of Islam apologetically argue that the 'true' *jihad* is the spiritual one (i.e., a person's struggle against one's passions), while the military *jihad* is only secondary.

To make sense of such a variety of meanings for the term *jihad*, we must bear in mind two points. First, this word does not indicate just *one thing*. It has been used by various people to indicate *various things* for various purposes—either peaceful or bellicose, either to achieve integration among communities or to separate them, or to mobilize popular support for whatever (peaceful or belligerent) cause. Second, Islam is also not *one thing*, and it does not have one, 'true' nature or essence. Like many other religions, it is a collection of authoritative texts, beliefs, communities, and rituals, some of which have a history of fourteen centuries, during which they and their meanings have endlessly mutated to adapt to their social, political, and cultural environments.

About the author
Mushegh Asatryan (PhD, Yale 2012) is an assistant professor of Arabic and Muslim Cultures at the University of Calgary. His research interests include the interrelation between religion, society, and culture in the medieval Islamic Middle East, and his monograph, *Controversies in Formative Shi'i Islam: The Ghulat Muslims and their Beliefs*, was published in 2016.

Suggestions for further reading

In this book
See also Chapters 46 (radicalism in Islam), 47 (radical and non-radical Muslims), 49 (Jewish, Christian, Muslim similarities), 50 (Sufism), and 51 (Sunni and Shia Islam).

Elsewhere

Bonner, Michael. *Jihad in Islamic History: Doctrines and Practice.* Princeton, NJ: Princeton University Press, 2006.

Cook, David. *Understanding Jihad.* Berkeley, CA: University of California Press, 2005.

Kepel, Gilles. *Jihad: the Trail of Political Islam* (4th edition; translated by Anthony Roberts). London: I. B. Tauris, 2006.

49

Are there similarities between Judaism, Christianity, and Islam?

Aaron W. Hughes

Judaism, Christianity, and Islam are frequently called 'Abrahamic' religions. This locution would seem to imply that these three religions are similar and, moreover, that they all derive from a common ancestor, Abraham. While they certainly share similar features, in large part the result of various Jewish, Christian, and Muslim social groups interacting with one another historically, they have many, many important differences. Within this context, such difference are often much more interesting than their similarities. So while Christians and Muslims might both revere Jesus, more interesting is the historical interactions between certain non-normative Arab Christian groups with Arab groups that would eventually emerge as Muslims in the Arabian Peninsula. This is not to say that the former simply influenced the latter, however; rather, it is to imply that distinct social groups shared a similar vocabulary that would eventually, using this example, eventually become orthodox Christianity and normative Sunni Islam. Similarities and differences, then, are the result of real *historical* interactions between social groups that make appeals to these three monotheistic religions. They are not based on some essential sameness or affinity.

Rather than see a set of superficial similarities between three generic and reified religions, it might be more useful to see smaller social groups interacting with one another and developing ideas either in common or in opposition to one another. Beliefs, practices, and ideas signified as 'religious,' in other words, are the result of social, historical, and cultural interactions between groups that make appeals to their respective religions. They do not, then, represent three manifestations of the same generic or timeless essence.

Within this context, it might be worth pointing out that the very term designated to name these three religions, 'Abrahamic religions,' is a modern construct that has only gained considerable popularity in our post-9/11 world. Like its predecessor 'Judeo-Christian,' it is an invented term that has little precedent in the premodern word and is meant to function as an inclusive and ecumenical category. Indeed, if anything, Jews, Christians, and Muslims have spent most of their histories degrading or, even worse, persecuting the other two on account of their perceived misunderstandings of Abraham.

Some might feel comfortable talking about an 'Abrahamic' notion of prayer, to wit, that all three religions have a similar notion of this activity based on a shared Abrahamic progeny. Such a position makes no historical sense, however, since each 'religion' is the result of distinct social processes that take place in distinct temporal and geographical contexts. It implies that there is a concept of prayer that *all* Jews, Muslims, and Christians share. Nothing could be further from the truth, however. Not only are there differences between the three religions, there also exist a great many differences within each tradition as well. Reform Jews do not pray in the same manner that Orthodox Jews do and the differences between them has nothing to do with an abstract sense of prayer, and more to do with real historical reasons for why the two concepts of prayer developed in the first place.

It should also be clear that attempts to show the similarities between the three religions tend to be based on ecumenical fantasy than anything historical. While this may be fine for interfaith groups, it does very little to help us understand the historical interactions between these groups.

Despite the artificiality of the rubric 'Abrahamic religions,' however, there are certain similarities between these three religions. Each later tradition, for example claims to have superseded the others. This is a classic example of each group trying to define itself by what it is not. Rabbis and religious scholars in Islam (the *ulama*) developed similar notions of law and legal interpretation based on their shared intellectual interactions in places like Baghdad.

About the author
Aaron W. Hughes is the Philip S. Bernstein Chair in the Department of Religion and Classics at the University of Rochester.

Suggestions for further reading

In this book
See also Chapters 46 (radicalism in Islam), 47 (types of Islam), 48 (*jihad*), 50 (Sufism), and 51 (Sunni and Shia Islam).

Elsewhere
Hughes, Aaron W. *Abrahamic Religions: On the Uses and Abuses of History*. New York: Oxford University Press, 2012.

50
Is Sufism part of Islam?

Aaron W. Hughes

Muslim identity is, like all identities, a potentially fluid concept. Attempts to define what is an 'authentic' part of Islam or any other religious tradition is thus a theological endeavor that the scholar of religion ought to resist. Instead, as should now be clear, it is the goal of the scholar of religion to show how identity—in this case Muslim—is contingent upon the *perceived* correct or normative interpretation of a message—in this case Muhammad's—that a community imagined to be divine. Within this larger context, Sufism, or Islamic mysticism, further reveals the dynamic use of Muhammad in the development of Muslim identity after his death. Historically, then, there can be no denial of the fact that Sufism is part of Islam. Indeed, later Sufis would go so far as to declare that Muhammad was the first Sufi and that they are simply following in his path. Sufism, for such individuals, represents the most authentic version of Islam. Alghazali (d. 1111), who perhaps did more than anyone bring together spiritual praxis associated with Sufism into the fold of the legal tradition associated with the more normative Sunni Islam, argues that Sufi teachings are what enable Muslims to perfect their commitment to the law. For some Sufi thinkers, then, Sufism is the most authentic version of Islam.

It is sometimes said that there are three 'denominations' in Islam: Sunnism, Shiism, and Sufism. This is in many ways incorrect because those Muslims who are Sufis or are attracted to certain teachings of Sufis also have commitments to either Sunnism or Shiism. One is a Sufi, in other words, *in addition to* being a Sunni or a Shiite.

Two groups in particular, however, want to deny Sufism's place in Islam. This is why this question is, in many ways, a political question based on the rhetoric of authenticity. The first group consists of those conservative or ultra-conservative thinkers who say Sufism is illegitimate on account of what they perceive to be its 'unorthodox' beliefs and practices. Such critics—in both the past and the present—argue that Sufism is heretical and contrary to the 'real' or 'authentic' teachings of Islam. They juxtapose Sufi teaching—especially its speculation about God and about attaining nearness to or absorption into Him—with the austere and radical monotheistic Islam that they have constructed in their own particular reading of the Qur'an and related sources. Such conservative critics—often called Wahhabis or Salafis—have labeled Sufism a *bida*, or 'innovation.' They have destroyed tombs commemorating Sufi *shayks* ('religious leaders'), which often functioned as sites of pilgrimage. Despite such conservative opposition, however, Sufism exists in all sorts of local variations and is integral to the way that millions of Muslims go about their daily lives from Morocco in the west to Indonesia in the east. Within this latter context, local versions of Islam often look nothing like the way Islam is presented in the classroom or in introductory textbooks to Islam.

Another group that wants to separate Sufism from Islam are those involved in the New Age movement. This movement seeks take the spiritual wisdom of the world's religions, abstract their teachings by overlooking their particularism and specific historical contexts, and then use these teachings for some kind of spiritual (but not religious!) fulfillment. Sufism, Kabbalah (Jewish mysticism), Vedanta, and so on become combined in a way that is based more on Western capitalism than anything resembling Sufism in its historical development in Islam.

About the author

Aaron W. Hughes is the Philip S. Bernstein Chair in the Department of Religion and Classics at the University of Rochester.

Suggestions for further reading

In this book

See also Chapters 46 (radicalism in Islam), 47 (types of Islam), 48 (*jihad*), 49 (Jewish, Christian, Muslim similarities), and 51 (Sunni and Shia Islam).

Elsewhere

Cornell, Vincent J. *The Realm of the Saint: Power and Authority in Moroccan Sufism*. Austin, TX: University of Texas Press, 1998.

Ernst, Carl. *The Shambhala Guide to Sufism*. Boston, MA: Shambhala, 1997.

Hughes, Aaron W. *Muslim Identities: An Introduction to Islam*. New York: Columbia University Press, 2013.

51
What are the main differences between Sunni and Shia Islam?

Aaron W. Hughes

Most sectarian divisions can usually be reduced to political squabbles and the desire to either subvert the existing status quo or to establish a new one. The religious legitimation or justification only comes later. The difference between Sunnism and Shiism are certainly no different. The main difference between them, the one from which all other differences emerge, concerns who has the right to be the legitimate ruler of the *umma* (i.e., the Muslim community) in the aftermath of the death of Muhammad—though it is important to be aware that, while the seeds were present at the beginning, what would emerge as normative Sunni Islam and normative Shia Islam would take centuries to work out. For those who would become Sunnis, authority resided in those that the elders of community agreed should lead the community based on political ability—this would culminate in the great caliphates of medieval Islam. For those who would become Shia, legitimate leadership resided solely in the *ahl al-bayt* (i.e., the family of the Prophet), particularly the descendants of Ali (599–661), the cousin and son-in-law of Muhammad. This distinction is the classic one articulated by Weber, namely, that between a prophet's charisma (in this case Shiism) or the ethical teaching that he inculcated in his followers (in this case Sunnism).

It is important not to assume, as many later sources want us to believe, that Sunni Islam emerged as normative from the chaotic period brought about by Muhammad's passing, and that Shiism emerged as a later heterodox movement. This is wishful thinking on the part of later Sunni commentators. What would emerge as Sunni Islam and Shia Islam represent the end products of several centuries of compromise and contestation between competing ideologies and interpretations of Muhammad's message. Rather than imagine separate tracks of development for these two movements, we need to regard them as intertwined at an early stage, and as deriving their potency from various ideological and sociological forces. Each group, in the process, used the other to articulate better is doctrinal contents and rituals.

Subsequent differences between the two groups are, as mentioned, derived from their different paradigms of leadership. Shiites—and there are several different subgroups—locate authority in the Imam, who is believed to be a direct descendent of Muhammad through his cousin and son-in-law Ali. The role of the Imam, who functions as a successor to the Prophet, is to provide his followers with the proper direction and to guide them toward a spiritual understanding of spiritual truths. There were—at least in Twelver Shiism, which is today the dominant form of Shiism—twelve Imams, with the final one going into occultation to return only as a messianic figure at the end of times. In the absence of this Imam, ayatollahs serve as the intermediary between the hidden Imam and his followers. In Sunni Islam, by contrast, leadership is much more mundane and political (as opposed to spiritual or prophetic).

Sunnis and Shiites also differ in their hadith collections. Hadiths are those sayings and deeds of Muhammad and other early Muslims that would go on to become an important legal source. Whereas Sunni Muslims are primarily interested in those hadiths that retell what Muhammad did and/or said, Shiites possess a large body of hadiths that they trace back to or through the various Imams. Sunnis, by contrast, would not see these hadiths as either authoritative or authentic. As developed in later Shiite legal theory in the fifteenth and sixteenth centuries, legal scholars (ayatollahs) would take over the legal duties of the occulted Imam. They interpret what they perceive to be the will of the Twelfth Imam through legal reasoning. There are, however, many parallels with Sunni legal thought. In addition, Sunnis and Shiites both regard the Qur'an as authoritative, believe that Muhammad was the prophet of God, pray five times a day, fast during Ramadan, go on the pilgrimage to Mecca (the *Hajj*)—though Shiites also go on pilgrimages to places associated with Ali and the other Imams.

Today, of the world's roughly two billion Muslims, around fifteen percent are Shiite (with the largest populations being in Iran, Iraq, Lebanon, and Yemen), the rest being Sunni.

About the author
Aaron W. Hughes is the Philip S. Bernstein Chair in the Department of Religion and Classics at the University of Rochester.

Suggestions for further reading

In this book
See also Chapters 46 (radicalism in Islam), 47 (types of Islam), 48 (*jihad*), 49 (Jewish, Christian, Muslim similarities), and 50 (Sufism).

Elsewhere
Hughes, Aaron W. *Muslim Identities: An Introduction to Islam*. New York: Columbia University Press, 2013.

Madelung, Wilfred. *The Succession to Muhammad: A Study of the Early Caliphate*. Cambridge: Cambridge University Press, 1997.

Mottahedeh, Roy P. *The Mantle of the Prophet: Religion and Politics in Iran*. Oxford: Oneworld, 2000.

52

Is there anything 'African' about African-American religions?

Emily D. Crews

In autumn 2016 I taught a course about global Christianities at a small liberal arts college in the American Midwest. Near the end of a discussion about Christianity among African and African-American slaves in the antebellum South a student asked, 'Is there really anything "African" about the Christianity the slaves believed in?'

Little did my student know that she was asking a question that had been debated, again and again, by scholars and lay people alike. Since their arrival in the late seventeenth century to what would become the United States, Africans and the cultures they brought with them have been the subject of great consideration and contention. The question of 'how African' slaves, freed people of color, and their descendants are is at the core of that discussion, and no part of their lives is subject to greater scrutiny or given greater possibility for meaning than their religious beliefs and practices.

Perhaps the most well-known and hard-fought version of this argument occurred in the early to mid-1900s between two well-known American academics—Melville J. Herskovits (an anthropologist) and E. Franklin Frazier (a sociologist). Herskovits believed that black people of the Americas retained a significant portion of their African heritage, and that African-American Protestantism in the United States and the Caribbean, in particular, served as evidence of a link to an African past. From its reliance on affect and performance, its inclusion of immersion baptism, and especially its profound links to music and dance, African-American Protestantism clearly showed traces of a deep and important African history.

Frazier took a directly opposing view. He argued that Herskovits exaggerated his findings and that, when the data was examined closely and critically, there was no evidence that the cultures Africans had brought to the Americas had survived the violence of slavery. He eventually—and definitively!—concluded, 'It is impossible to establish any continuity between African religious practices and the Negro church in the United States.'

Ironically, despite their opposing views, both Herskovits and Frazier sought to improve the situation of African Americans with their scholarship. For Herskovits, claiming an African past for African Americans—and linking Christianity to that past—meant dignifying and legitimizing an entire group of people. He believed that, should African-American culture prove itself to be rooted in civilizations that stretched back to ancient times, that culture would gain new respect from those people (namely, white Americans) who had sought for centuries to denigrate it. It would likewise prove that, even in the face of violent oppression and attempts at dehumanization, Africans had remained unbroken.

For Frazier, Herskovits's insistence on defining African Americans by their link to an African homeland and home culture prevented them from being understood—and understanding themselves—as truly American. Even aside from the methodological issues and lack of accuracy he perceived in Herskovits's work, Frazier felt that the search for an African past in the African-American present prevented blacks all over the world from being allowed and able to embrace a more positive future.

Many scholars of the late twentieth and early twenty-first centuries have entered into discussions similar to Herskovits and Frazier's, and support has been strong (and at times virulent) for both positions and many others besides. What does this continued debate mean for the study of African and African-American religions or the study of religion more generally? And how can new scholars or those who are interested in the study of religion make use of these questions for their own work and thinking?

Perhaps the most valuable lesson that can be learned is this: the statement that a person, a practice, an idea, or a religion is or is not African is an *ideological claim*. It is meant to advance or deny some kind of position; it is used to make an argument, even if that argument is only to oneself. Whether assigning the designation 'African' to someone's religion or dress or speech or thought is meant to be a compliment or an insult, a recognition or a denial, it is never without purpose. A scholar of religion must then be critical of all claims of the African-ness of a religious idea or action, regardless of its author or explanation, and we must treat them as we would any other claim within the field of religious studies. We must examine and interrogate them with close attention to evidence and be aware of their histories and contexts. We must ask, 'Who benefits from this claim? Who does this claim help and who does it hurt? How has it been used in the past? What other arguments does it make possible? What is at stake if it is true or false?'

About the author
Emily D. Crews is a PhD candidate at the University of Chicago Divinity School. Her dissertation investigates the role of religion (in its many forms) in Nigerian immigrant communities in the United States.

Suggestions for further reading

In this book
See also Chapters 3 (classifying religion) and 45 (religion on plantations).

Elsewhere
Raboteau, Albert J. *Slave Religion: 'The Invisible Institution' in the Antebellum South*. Oxford: Oxford University Press, 1978.

53

Are Eastern religions as connected to violence as Western religions seem to be?

Jason W. M. Ellsworth

When approaching the subject of violence in religions, there has been a view that Eastern religions are inherently peaceful compared to Western religions. The 'Western' gaze (read North American and European) at times views all Buddhists as non-violent pacifists or Hindus as comparatively more compassionate because of their vegetarian ideals. In this way the East has been mystified and exoticized to be a place of peace and tranquil bliss. It is thus surprising for some when news breaks challenging the peaceful view of the East that has persisted, instead describing Buddhists in Thailand taking up armed conflict against Muslims, monks burning themselves alive, or the violence attributed to Hindu nationalist groups in India such as the Bharatiya Janata Party (BJP). Often one finds easy answers to these challenges. Some will state that the Buddhists taking up arms are not true Buddhists or that the Buddhist in this case is justified in using self-defense. The very question pushes one to further examine the components of the question itself.

The first question we should ask is what is violence? Who decides what it means to say that a person or group is violent?

Where is the line drawn when deciding who is violent and who is defending themselves? Answers to these questions may seem obvious to some at times, however often when examining cases it is difficult to distinguish who are the antagonists of violence. When the United States of America bombed Iraq in 2003, was the USA exhibiting violent behavior or was it, as stated by the government, a form of pre-emptive defense and protection of the vulnerable in Iraq? Are those that eat meat involved in a form of violence towards non-human animals? The Hindu Bharatiya Janata Party has categorized Muslims who eat beef as violent and in response those Hindus themselves take up arms against Muslims to defend vegetarian ideals. The choice of terms to classify violence is highly contentious and can tell us much about who is describing the act. Is water-boarding torture or enhanced interrogation? Who decides what is an act of terrorism, war, or a preemptive defensive strike? By examining who is making the claim of violence and the type of violence, we can begin to understand who benefits from the rhetoric that is deployed.

Second, where are we drawing the line between the East and the West? At one point in religious studies classrooms, Islam was considered an Eastern religion and today it is now usually situated as a Western tradition. The line that divides the East and West is highly subjective and contested. It is a line that moves and is often an arbitrary classification system. Now that we find Buddhist practices all over the planet, do we define it as an Eastern or Western tradition? When something of this nature is subjective the question returns to who is classifying religions into this dual scheme and for what advantage? Who gains from this very split?

Edward Said's *Orientalism* critiqued the European (Western) representation of the 'East' as an imagined, manufactured and stereotyped image of the people of the Middle East. In deconstructing the West's stereotyped image, Said was able to show how the very divide of East and West was constructed and used to promote the West as superior. Said broke down the power relations involved to show how a people (mainly Muslims and Arabs) had been stereotyped, discriminated against, and oppressed. One mechanism that helped the colonial powers was the very classification system of East and West that had been deployed by scholars, politicians and writers.

Third, attributing violent acts to 'religions' ignores the vast interrelated societal influences. Blanket statements that view an imagined East or West as more violent than the other due to religion looks to bypass the depth of factors inherent in the process such as politics and economics. By ignoring these other factors and trying to blame violence on religions of an entire region also displaces the diversity of traditions.

Some media and politicians portray Islam as a religion of violence to excite hysteria over immigrants, often culminating in the use of the term terrorist for anyone that may be from the Middle East. While others champion Islam as a religion of justice and peace, this displays the very dichotomy of the question we see above. We are left wondering who is East and who is West, who has the right to decide what is violence or peace, and which practices of a society should be reduced to *religion*. When hearing that an entire region (East or West) can be labeled as violent or peaceful due to a subjective denominator such as *religion* it is best to ask who benefits from these statements.

About the author
Jason W. M. Ellsworth is a doctoral student in social anthropology at Dalhousie University and a sessional lecturer at the University of Prince Edward Island. Jason received his MA in religion and culture from Wilfrid Laurier University (2010), an honors BA in religious studies from Saint Mary's University (2009), and a BComm in marketing from Saint Mary's University (2003).

Suggestions for further reading

In this book
See also Chapters 3 (classifying religion), 48 (*jihad*), and 58 (Buddhism as philosophy).

Elsewhere

Said, Edward. *Orientalism*. New York: Pantheon Books, 1978.

Jerryson, Michael K. and Mark Jurgensmeyer. *Buddhist Warfare*. Oxford: Oxford University Press, 2010.

54
Do Native Americans worship nature?

Sarah E. Dees

Native American spiritualty and religious traditions are frequently associated with land, nature, and the environment. At times these associations can verge on the stereotypical. The image of the 'ecological Indian,' an archetypal Native American figure who is spiritually in tune with elements of the natural world, has long been present in European and Euro-American imaginaries. In many ways, this stereotype is problematic: it can be unwittingly conflated with racialized ideas about the development of 'civilized' religion; it flattens and simplifies diverse forms of American Indian religiosity; and it downplays the ways that Native American religions have always developed and changed in response to new situations. Even so, land, the environment, and nature are crucial components in most Native American religious traditions.

As the academic study of religion developed in the nineteenth century, European and American scholars correctly noticed that nature was a key component in many aspects of Native American ceremonial life. Scholars used the term 'animism' to describe the religions of Indigenous communities. This term was meant to convey how Indigenous communities believed that features of the natural world—from trees and animals to the wind and geological formations—were imbued or animated with spirits. While this theory of Native American and Indigenous religions accurately depicted the ways that many Native Americans have long recognized many spiritual entities in nature, early scholars of religion viewed these beliefs about the natural world as superstitious or childish, and saw animistic forms of religion as inherently inferior to monotheistic religions. When studying the role of nature in the spirituality of Native American communities, it is important to be aware of this history.

Native American cultures are numerous and diverse, and this diversity is due in part to the many different environmental regions that communities have inhabited. Scholars estimate that, upon the arrival of Europeans, there were a thousand languages spoken by inhabitants of the Americas, with approximately 250 spoken in the present-day United States. The US federal government currently recognizes more than 550 Native American tribal nations, each maintaining a separate system of tribal government. More distinct Native American cultural communities exist without federal or state recognition. Each of these nations has a unique history and cultural identity.

Historically, many different features Native American cultures—from characteristics of their material culture and forms of subsistence to societal structure and complexity—were directly related to the type of environment in which the community lived. Scholars have thus categorized different Native American cultural areas based on geographical areas. Origin stories from numerous nations describe the ways that their communities came to settle on their homelands. In many cases, the people were guided to a specific place with the help of animals or forces of nature. These entities also helped to teach people how to live and thrive. Generations ago, members of these communities developed intimate knowledge of the landscapes, flora, and fauna in their regions. They determined optimal ways to hunt, farm, gather food and medicinal plants, and produce objects for use or for trade. Significant ceremonies often reflected yearly cycles or significant events, such as planting crops or hunting. Even Native American forms of Christianity regard the natural world as sacred.

As important as these elements are for Native American communities, political struggles have affected their abilities to maintain place-based traditions. Through centuries of colonial contact, Europeans and Americans have sought control over Native American lands and resources and forced communities to leave their homelands. These processes of incursion, violence, and removal have resulted in the disconnect of Native American people from their homelands. In military and legal battles over these lands, members of Native American communities have long described the sacred qualities of their lands. A shared discourse about the protection of Mother Earth has emerged among members of disparate communities. While some non-Native scholars have suggested that this type of discourse is a relatively recent historical development, Native Americans maintain that it represents deeply held and longstanding concerns about the well-being of the environment.

Contests over Native American sacred lands continue to the present day. At times, non-Native environmental or animal rights organizations have disagreed with some Native communities' hunting practices or decisions to allow mining on tribal lands. These disagreements reveal an important aspect of Native American environmental ethics: ultimately, communities are concerned with the environment as well as the future of their own communities and the relationships between humans and their environments.

About the author

Sarah E. Dees (PhD, Indiana University) is a postdoctoral fellow at Northwestern University. Her research focuses on American and Indigenous religions.

Suggestions for further reading

In this book
See also Chapters 3 (classifying religion) and 56 (Shamanism).

Elsewhere

Kidwell, Clara Sue, Homer Noley, and George E. 'Tink' Tinker. *A Native American Theology*. Maryknoll, NY: Orbis Books, 2001.

Nabokov, Peter. *Where the Lightning Strikes: The Lives of American Indian Sacred Places*. New York: Penguin, 2007.

Vecsey, Christopher and Robert Venables (editors). *American Indian Environments: Ecological Issues in Native American History*. Syracuse, NY: Syracuse University Press, 1980.

55
Is yoga religious?

Steven Ramey

To answer if yoga is religious depends on what the terms 'yoga' and 'religious' reference. Yoga is typically understood in the context of the US as involving physical exercises that incorporate poses, controlled breathing, and sometimes meditation. Forms, of course, vary between instructors and even more so between different traditions of physical yoga. Yoga, however, can refer to a broader range of practices or approaches. The Bhagavad Gita, for example, describes three different yogas to connect to the divine: karma yoga (often translated as the way of action), jnana yoga (the way of knowledge), and bhakti yoga (the way of devotion). Yoga is also the standard name for one of the six traditional schools of philosophy commonly associated with classical Hinduism. The Yoga school incorporates a variety of methods, including but not limited to physical exercises, to experience and realize fully the philosophical ideas concerning human existence.

Like yoga, people employ the term 'religious' variously, even when associated with yoga (as in the question). For example, a popular understanding connects something religious with interacting with something supernatural, while in another sense, something religious involves a system of ritual, beliefs, and morality around which people organize their lives. With either of these general definitions, yoga can be identified as religious, depending on which meaning of yoga is used. The notion of bhakti yoga fits both definitions, as devotees often organize their lives, in part, around their relation to the divine. Forms of physical yoga could fit both definitions, as some variations incorporate a notion of the divine that participants address as part of the ritualized exercises, and the meditative reflections can inform their way of living.

The point that physical yoga can be practiced in a manner that some identify as being religious raises a more precise question, 'Is physical yoga inherently religious?' If people perform the exercises simply as physical conditioning without addressing a divine being or reflecting on their place in the universe, do the practices maintain that religious character automatically? Such questions have been significant in court cases involving teaching yoga in US public schools. The Encinitas (California) public school district, for example, developed a program to teach one form of physical yoga in a way that excluded references that could be deemed religious. When some parents filed suit, a judge had to decide if the school district's program was an unconstitutional government promotion of religion. The opponents of the program argued that the exercises in the school promoted particular views of the world that drew on the religious nature of yoga and that the religious character of the exercises was inherent and thus could not be removed simply by altering the language and divine references. In 2015, the judge, however, ruled that this particular yoga program was not religious.

From a different perspective, the Hindu America Foundation (HAF) has promoted a 'Take Back Yoga' campaign to assert that yoga is originally and inherently a Hindu practice. That designation, however, does not automatically make yoga religious; some who identify as Hindu assert that Hinduism is a way of life, not a religion. While the HAF description of yoga as focusing on the individual gaining moksha (release from the cycle of death and rebirth) through understanding their position in this world could be identified as religious, the campaign emphasizes the cultural ownership of yoga as Hindu, rather than emphasizing a religious character. HAF's campaign argues that current forms of yoga in the US have diverged from yoga's original form and that many teachers and businesses have appropriated a diminished form of yoga for their personal gain. Others, however, contest the equation of yoga with Hindu origins, asserting that the physical exercises commonly labeled as yoga developed in the interaction between Indian and European exercise practices since the nineteenth century.

In the responses from the California judge, the Hindu America Foundation, and others, the complexity of finding an answer becomes apparent. While the judge focused on one yoga program, HAF incorporates many different approaches into their general sense of physical yoga. In their differing assertions, the judge ruled on a legal question about one specific program within a tradition of US jurisprudence, while the HAF emphasized the origins of yoga in their interest to promote Hindu cultural ownership of yoga, and thereby promote positive images of Hinduism in the United States. Thus, the answers to the question depend on the definitions that a person holds and what he/she wants to accomplish, whether legal definitions, cultural ownership, or historical origins.

About the author
Steven Ramey is professor in the department of religious studies at the University of Alabama, where his research and teaching has focused on contested identifications and practices in contemporary India and the United States. He is the author of *Hindu, Sufi, or Sikh* (Palgrave, 2008) and editor of *Writing Religion* (University of Alabama Press, 2015), and he has an edited volume, *Fabricating Difference* (Equinox, 2017).

Suggestions for further reading

In this book
See also Chapters 3 (classifying religion), 12 (function of religion), 13 (rituals v. habits), and 14 (spiritual but not religious).

Elsewhere
Jain, Andrea. *Selling Yoga: From Counter-Culture to Pop Culture*. Oxford: Oxford University Press, 2014.

Singleton, Andrea. *Yoga Body: The History of Modern Posture Practice*. Oxford: Oxford University Press, 2010.

56
What is shamanism?

Suzanne Owen

Shamanism is often described as humankind's earliest religion, evidenced by prehistoric cave paintings and ancient artifacts, such as the Pashupati Seal found in the Indus Valley depicting a seated horned deity or a man in a headdress surrounded by animals. There are several problems with this view. It assumes an evolutionary theory that regards shamanism as the universal origin of religion, eventually superseded by more 'advanced' religions. It then regards contemporary indigenous religions as 'remnants' of this prehistoric religion, an interpretive leap supported by little evidence.

'Shamans' first came to the attention of Russian explorers and later ethnographers in Siberia after Russia had conquered the region in the late sixteenth century. Šamán, in the Tungus language of the Evenki, has a complex etymology as it is thought not to be a Tungus word. It referred to a person with the knowledge and skill to work with spirits. S. M. Shirokogoroff speculated on a Manchu link, while later scholars, including Romanian-born historian of religion, Mircea Eliade, thought it could have entered the Tungus language from Sanskrit owing to similarities with the term *śramana*, denoting a wandering ascetic. However, he viewed Evenki shamanism as the 'classic' form to measure all other shamanisms.

In his highly influential book *Shamanism: Archaic Techniques of Ecstasy* (first published in French in 1951), Eliade was fascinated with ethnographic accounts of Evenki shamans' characteristics and reduced them to a set of practices (techniques) that could be found in many cultures around the world, universalizing the term beyond its semantic origins. By regarding these practices as 'archaic,' Eliade is also importing evolutionary theory into his 'history of religions' project. In particular, he highlighted the 'soul journey' a shaman makes while in an 'ecstatic' trance, or heightened state of consciousness, which fueled psychological interest in the subject. It led other scholars, such as Piers Vitebsky at the Scott Polar Research Institute in Cambridge, UK, to note the similarities between various cosmological descriptions of contemporary shamanic groups from different parts of the world. In his book *Shamanism* (originally published in 1995 as *The Shaman: Voyages of the Soul from the Arctic to the Amazon*), he compares, among others, Siberian and Western Ojibway 'shamans' based on his own ethnographic fieldwork as well as historical accounts.

Another issue with the Eliadian approach to shamanism is that it privileges certain types of activity (e.g., the active, conscious 'soul journey'), while ignoring or dismissing unconscious or passive experiences of shamans, such as 'possession' states. The idea of the shaman as a 'master' of spirits continues in more recent scholarship, such as Merete Demant Jakobsen's *Shamanism: Traditional and Contemporary Approaches to the Mastery of Spirits*. Another issue is the gendering of shamans. Among the Evenki, a shaman is not restricted to one gender. However, the paradigmatic 'shaman' is depicted as male and active (conscious mastery of spirits) while a medium is often depicted as female and passive (unconscious possession by spirits). In fact, both types and much in between are described in ethnographic accounts of Siberian shamans.

If shamanism could be regarded as a set of universal techniques, it would be possible for urban Europeans and North Americans to enter into altered states of consciousness by adopting these practices. This became an attractive idea in the 1960s and 1970s. As a visionary on the edge of society—sometimes described as a 'madman'—the shaman became an emblem or motif of artists and poets, such as American environmental poet Gary Snyder. The idea of the shaman was also popularized through the novelistic works by Carlos Castaneda, who gained a PhD in anthropology from UCLA, told as the author's apprenticeship to a Yaqui Indian named Don Juan. Another anthropologist, Michael Harner, went on to develop training programs in what he called Core Shamanism, based on insights from his experimentation with *ayahuasca* (an etheogenic vine) during fieldwork in the Amazon and combined with Native American drumming practices, which did not require hallucinogens for achieving trance states.

Some scholars dispute whether such 'neo-shamans,' as they are often labelled, are legitimately practicing 'shamanism,' but what is of interest to us as scholars of religion is how the term is employed, by whose criteria, and for what purpose. Shamanism may then be best understood as a discursive category for placing sets of selected characteristics together and imbuing them with romantic primitivist longings of the civilized discontent. The 'shaman' is as much a representation of an untamed life that is at home in nature, free of the expectations of a modern, rational society, as it is a type of figure in Siberian societies.

About the author

Suzanne Owen is a senior lecturer in religious studies at Leeds Trinity University, UK. She obtained her PhD from the University of Edinburgh and researches contemporary indigenous and pagan religions.

Suggestions for further reading

In this book

See also Chapters 14 (spiritual but not religious) and 54 (nature worship).

Elsewhere

Eliade, Mircea. *Shamanism: Archaic Techniques of Ecstasy*. Princeton, NJ: Princeton University Press, 2004 [1951].

Hutton, Ronald. *Shamans: Siberian Spirituality and the Western Imagination*. London: Hambledon & London, 2001.

Jakobsen, Merete Demant. *Shamanism: Traditional and Contemporary Approaches to the Mastery of Spirits.* New York: Berghahn Books, 1999.

Sidky, Homayun. 'On the Antiquity of Shamanism and its Role in Human Religiosity.' *Method and Theory in the Study of Religion* 22 (2010): 68–92.7

Vitebsky, Piers. *Shamanism.* Norman, OK: University of Oklahoma Press, 2001.

57

Is being a vegetarian a religious thing for some people?

Jason W. M. Ellsworth

In the city of Palitana, located in the Indian state of Gujarat, one might find Jains heading to the market or visiting the city on pilgrimage. For many who claim to be Jain, Palitana is considered sacred and thus the city should represent their values as Jains. For many Jains eschewing meat is connected to their values to protect all animal life—thus why Jains often claim to be vegetarian. In 2014 a group of Jain monks went on a hunger strike to petition the government to make Palitana a vegetarian city. Successfully winning their bid Palitana is now a vegetarian zone banning the slaughter of animals and the sale of both meat and eggs in the city. It is often depicted in the media as the world's only vegetarian city.

For Jains, however, their definition of vegetarianism varies from how others use the term. In addition to not eating meat, Jains often do not eat eggs, so one could categorize them as Lacto-vegetarian (one who does not eat meat, fish, fowl, or eggs). Vegetarianism is best examined as a spectrum with multiple subcategories such as vegan, ovo-vegetarian, lacto-ovo-vegetarian, plant-based diet, pescatarian, pollotarian, newly arising categories such as ostro-vegan, and many others. The continued addition of qualifiers leaves one to wonder who or what is vegetarian. Those that require their food to not be cooked beyond a specific temperature add the qualifier raw food to their definition as well. Jains add another aspect by often eschewing garlic and onion, items that are often considered okay for vegetarians. Do we need another term beyond vegetarian or lacto-vegetarian to describe Jain eating habits?

The identities that are constructed from claiming a specific form of vegetarianism help create an image of who is part of the in-group for a community such as the Jains. At the same time, the claim also separates out those that do not participate in the same practices. In the city of Palitana the government-imposed vegetarian zone appeased Jains, however it was not met with the same acceptance from the Muslims who make up 20 to 25 percent of the population. The Muslim inhabitants claimed that their own religious rights that allows for animal sacrifice have been impinged upon, not to mention the fisherman and butchers in the area.

Hare Krishnas, some Hindus, various Taiwanese Buddhist organizations, Shaolin monks, Jains, or Adventists are just some of the commonly referred to vegetarian religious groups practicing some form of vegetarianism. While vegetarians exist within varying traditions the question may also be raised if vegetarianism in itself is a *religion*? Veganism (often defined by one who does not eat or use animal products in any form) is often labeled with a pseudo-religious connotation. The argument often lies not in whether veganism is associated with a sacred, transcendent being or other wordily entities, but rather that veganism is overly strict with its 'doctrines' in a similar manner to some communities that are categorized as religious. The comparative nature of the analysis leaves open the question of what exactly is a religion? By claiming that veganism is a religion one might be trying to discard the practice as being too hard lined and too similar to structured organized religious communities.

On the other hand, claims that vegetarianism or veganism are in some fashion similar to those things we consider to be religious—such as 'creeds'—are taken up to legitimize the practice. In 2016 in Ontario, Canada it was argued that vegetarians have the right to be protected under the human rights commission due to the creedal nature of the practice. In doing so, those that use this argument not only look to legitimize the practice but also allow them to file for accommodation similar to those that look to protect their religious rights.

By categorizing the spectrum of vegetarianisms as religious, one risks disregarding the vast diversity of reasons that defines each of the practices into an assumed set of similarities under the banner of religion. Rather than state that being some form of vegetarianism is in some way related to a set of practices that we define as religious, one might better ask who is claiming a particular vegetarianism as a religious thing? In this question one can break down what is at stake and for whom in making these claims? What type of identity is one trying to construct in opposition to others?

About the author

Jason W. M. Ellsworth is a doctoral student in social anthropology at Dalhousie University and a sessional lecturer at the University of Prince Edward Island. Jason received his MA in religion and culture from Wilfrid Laurier University (2010), an honors BA in religious studies from Saint Mary's University (2009), and a BComm in marketing from Saint Mary's University (2003).

Suggestions for further reading

In this book
See also Chapters 3 (classifying religion), 13 (rituals v. habits), and 14 (spiritual but not religious).

Elsewhere
Crowther, Gillian. *Eating Culture: An Anthropological Guide to Food.* Toronto: University of Toronto Press, 2013.

Hamilton, Malcolm. 'Eating Ethically: "Spiritual" and "Quasi-religious" Aspects of Vegetarianism.' *Journal of Contemporary Religion* 15 (2000): 65–83.

Zeller, Benjamin E., Marie W. Dallam, Reid L. Neilson, and Nora L. Rubel (editors). *Religion, Food, and Eating in North America.* New York: Columbia University Press, 2014.

58

Isn't Buddhism more of a philosophy than a religion?

Nathaniel J. Morehouse

Elsewhere in this book others have dealt with the question of defining what makes something a religion or not. Such a definition (if it exists) will easily allow us to separate things into different camps such as 'philosophy' or 'religion,' safely placing them where they belong and allowing us to move on with life. Sadly, things are never quite that simple.

Many things happen when you label something a 'religion,' especially in modern American culture. Briefly, religions in the Unites States are granted special rights and privileges. Legally religions and the 'churches' associated with them are tax exempt, pay no property or income taxes as well as receiving other beneficial treatment under American tax law. Those associated with specific religions are allowed to perform ceremonies which affect the public sphere (e.g., weddings, which while often seen as 'religious' in nature are a civil contract with specific rights and privileges under civil law). Religions also are granted a degree of respect regarding the beliefs and practices of those who identify with that tradition. Finally, freedom of religion limits what civil authorities can require of groups which are identified as 'religious.'

When a tradition is labeled a religion it also perceived (given the normative notion for what we think of as 'religions' is largely based of a Judeo-Christian-Islamic notion) that one can only subscribe to one religion and once one does this they must not dabble in other religions. Consequently, once someone labels something like Buddhism a religion it then enters into some degree of competition with other religions, whereas when it is a philosophy it is possible to then both embrace Buddhism as a philosophy while still maintaining a Christian (for example) identity. Likewise, many American college students (again for example) are turned off by 'organized religion' and may well want to label Buddhism as a philosophy rather than a religion so that they may maintain their disdain for 'religions' while embracing Buddhist 'philosophy' and thus happily avoid any cognitive dissonance.

Perhaps most importantly we also have to question what we mean when we say 'Buddhism,' as if this is something that is monolithic and unchanging. Part of the problem here comes from the way in which Buddhism is typically taught in introductory college courses. We tend to focus on things like the four noble truths, the eight-fold path, and the doctrine of anatman. With limited time in survey courses there may well be time to deal with some differences between various groups of Buddhists, but not much else. We may well read some sutras and look at the importance of the monastic way of life, wherein we examine the emphasis on meditation and renunciation. This, of course, privileges the monastic viewpoint above all others and even more it places a tremendous emphasis on textual considerations. This leaves out a great section of the lives of those who consider themselves to be Buddhists.

When Tibetan Buddhism was initially studied by Europeans they were primarily interested in examining texts to understand 'true' Buddhism, and did not consider the practices or even oral traditions of the people who practiced and identified as Buddhist, often believing that they had degraded the 'truth' of Buddhism. These Europeans own logocentric focus on texts determined what the data was, and from that data they determined what 'real' Tibetan Buddhism was. Had different data been chosen, they would have developed a different first impression of Buddhism.

The Buddhism that we frequently see in textbooks is in essence a Buddhism that is the creation of European and

American scholarship (along with—perhaps—the category of 'religion' as a whole), and may well not be all that familiar to individual Buddhists living in mountain villages in Tibet, or Pure Land Buddhists in Japan. What then does it mean when we speak of 'Buddhism'? Is Buddhism truly the texts, the monks, and the meditation; or is it the rituals of the individual Buddhists who do not live in monasteries, those who look to the monks to help them battle cosmic forces, who perform rituals, who never meditate, but make pilgrimages to holy sites? Finally, why do we privilege one of these over the others, and why do we privilege the claims that one is true Buddhism while the other isn't? And of course, who is it that gets to make those claims?

About the author

Nathaniel J. Morehouse earned his MA in religious studies from New York University and his PhD in religious studies from the University of Manitoba. He currently lives in Northeast Ohio where he teaches courses in religious studies and philosophy. His first book *Death's Dominion Power, Identity, and Memory at the Fourth-Century Martyr Shrine*, was published in 2016 by Equinox.

Suggestions for further reading

In this book

See also Chapters 3 (classifying religion), 6 (religion v. philosophy), and 59 (the Buddha).

Elsewhere

Childs, Geoff. *Tibetan Diary: From Birth to Death and Beyond in a Himalayan Valley of Nepal*. Berkeley, CA: University of California Press, 2004.

Lopez, Donald S. *From Stone to Flesh: A Short History of the Buddha*. Chicago, IL: University of Chicago Press, 2013.

59

Why do the statues of Buddha sometimes depict him as being overweight?

Kendall Marchman

If you're lucky enough to visit Chinese restaurants or Buddhist temples, you will inevitably encounter a statue of a jolly, over-weight man comfortably lounging and laughing while children play around him. This indeed is Buddha, but let's get a bit more specific: this is *a* Buddha—or one day will be—and his name is Maitreya. The migration of Buddhism around the world has produced many names for Maitreya, which is why this depiction of him is simply identified as the 'laughing Buddha' or even 'fat Buddha.' Therefore, the quick answer to this common question is that the overweight Buddha is actually a different Buddha than the historical one, called Siddhartha Gautama or Sakyamuni, who lived and taught in ancient India. Let's unpack this answer, though, to see how it came about.

First off, the statement that there are multiple Buddhas might come as a surprise to many. The term 'Buddha' is a title—not a name—that means 'the awakened one.' Although only Sakyamuni has achieved Buddhahood in recorded history, Buddhists believe that there have been many in the distant, irretrievable past, and that there will be more in the future. Maitreya was first mentioned in a sermon attributed to Sakyamuni, in which he names Maitreya as his successor who will appear after a period of global chaos. The birth of Maitreya will restore virtue to humanity, because once he becomes a Buddha, he will reinvigorate the dharma (the teachings of the Buddha) that was lost during the age of chaos. Until that time, Maitreya observes the world from his heavenly abode known as Tusita, planning how he will teach the world once he becomes a Buddha. Therefore, because he has not actually become a Buddha yet, Maitreya is recognized as a bodhisattva, or a 'Buddha in waiting.' As the death of Sakyamuni grew more distant, Buddhists anticipated the birth of Maitreya, and some resolved to be reborn in Tusita or here on earth once Maitreya finally started teaching as a Buddha. These goals remain attractive to some Buddhists still today, because a Buddha is recognized as an unmatched teacher who can help the community gain enlightenment quickly.

Buddhist teachings and practices continued to mature and adapt as they migrated out of India through Central Asia and into China. A division emerged during this time between the Mahayana (the Great Vehicle) and the pejoratively labeled Hinayana (the Lesser Vehicle). Mahayana teachings introduced the idea that Buddhahood is possible to all living beings. Like Maitreya, those who vowed to one day become a Buddha technically became bodhisattvas, though it would take a lot of effort and time before they reached his level. A key part of this 'bodhisattva vow' included delaying the transition into Buddhahood out of compassion to help all other sentient beings reach that status as well. Hinayana schools did not accept these new teachings, which led to Mahayana schools derisively labeling Hinayana as 'lesser' Buddhist teachings. Today, Theravada is the only remaining Hinayana school, and they certainly reject the idea that their teachings are a lesser version of Buddhism. Despite these and many other differences between the two sides, Maitreya acts as a bridge. Although Mahayana introduced many new buddhas and bodhisattvas into their expanded cosmology, both sides still recognize Maitreya as the next Buddha on this world.

Not only were the teachings and practices evolving during this transition period, but so were the graphic representations of Maitreya. Early representations of Maitreya depicted him as a slender, regal prince with a crown, often seated in a pensive posture. Over time, through a blend of Buddhism and Chinese folklore, his appearance transformed. Tradition points to a tenth-century Buddhist monk named Budai as the model for the popular 'laughing Buddha' statue. Local villagers and children loved Budai because of his jovial disposition, generosity, and uncanny abilities. Budai eventually disappeared, and instead of assuming that he died, villagers spread the belief that he was Maitreya visiting from Tusita, to which he had returned. Kindled by the popularity of the myth, depictions of Budai became synonymous with Maitreya, leading to the current global popularity of the 'laughing Buddha' statue. Scholars have suggested that this depiction has endured due to its links to popular folklore and Buddhism, and that the image represents cultural ideals, such as prosperity, satisfaction, joy, friendship, and family. Many cultures share these values, not just Buddhists, which explains why the image of the laughing Buddha has become so ubiquitous in homes, restaurants, taxi cabs, and much more.

About the author

Kendall Marchman received his PhD in religious studies at the University of Florida, and is currently an assistant professor in the Department of Religion and Philosophy at Young Harris College. His research focuses on Pure Land Buddhism in medieval China.

Suggestions for further reading

In this book

See also Chapters 58 (Buddhism as philosophy) and 60 (Origins of Buddhism).

Elsewhere

Ch'en, Kenneth. *Buddhism in China: A Historical Survey*. Princeton, NJ: Princeton University Press , 1973.

Leighton, Taigen Dan. *Faces of Compassion: Classic Bodhisattva Archetypes and Their Modern Expression*. Boston, MA: Wisdom Publications, 2012.

60

I've heard the founder of Buddhism was Hindu—so how did the one develop from the other?

Travis D. Webster

While no Hindus can be found in the centuries preceding the work of Siddhartha Gautama (fifth century BCE, known by the title of the Buddha, or the enlightened, or awoken, one), we can distinguish a class of people described in the text known as the Ṛig Veda (10.90) as *brahmanas* (an ancient Sanskrit term), a priestly group said, in one of its texts, to have emerged from the mouth of the 'cosmic person' (known there as *purusha*). Along with performing hymns to various deities, these Vedic priests (*brahmins*) also preserved sacrificial rituals upholding the law and order of *dharma* (a term used to name the cosmic system of duties and obligations). Well before the time of the Buddha, as demonstrated with the elaborate horse sacrifice and solemn rites of the Kuru kingdom (*c.*1000 BCE), royal patronage of such Vedic rites led to complex relations between kings and priests. By the eighth century BCE, however, the royal court had become the epicenter of philosophical tournaments hosted by local chieftains as far east as the river basin between the Ganges and the Yamuna rivers (in what is today known as northeastern India), where debates about *dharma* were held between *brahmins* and wandering ascetics.

This shift away from Vedic ritualism, along with the rise of urbanization in the Ganges valley during the sixth century BCE and the gradual eastward movement of Vedic-Brahmanical religion provide the socio-political context in which to consider the foundations of Buddhism. For scholars of Buddhism, moreover, the term 'shramana' signifies the 'ascetic tradition' in which Buddha is said to have sought enlightenment. Nevertheless, it should be emphasized that until about the time of King Ashoka (c.268–232 BCE) Brahmanical religion included a role for such renouncers, that is, 'those who strive' (shramanas). Although nineteenth-century scholarship tended to frame Buddha as a reformist of Brahmanical religion, the polemical aspects of Buddhist hagiography are very probably a product of the time in which they were written (that is, several hundred years after the Buddha's death). For the Buddha, as a product of his time, would have likely been rather keen to use the Brahmanical apparatus to his advantage, for as we know it was the Vedic god Brahma who urged Buddha to teach *dharma* for the sake of humanity.

The Buddha is referred to in the earliest inscriptions as Shakya-muni, the 'sage of the Shakyas.' The tribal appellation, 'Shakya,' can be derived from 'Shaka,' an ethnic name of Iranian steppe nomads whose Central Asian descendants may have been among the earliest Indo-Aryan speaking immigrants in eastern India. Textual evidence also suggests archaic forms of Vedic ritual were preserved in the Buddha's vicinity of Magadha (a region in northeastern India) but clearly the acculturation of early Vedic and Brahmanical religions was ongoing prior to the time of the Buddha. In fact, the enduring influence of Buddhism is most closely related to indigenous practices generically described as 'yoga' and in this regard we may note that recent research has sought to authenticate insider claims that Buddha was taught some Brahmanical forms of meditation by two different yogis.

Although there is no evidence that the Buddha received any specialized training or education in the Vedas, his first sermon is believed to have 'set rolling the wheel of *dharma*,' a Sanskrit term that initially appears in early Vedic literature and is then shared with a variety of non-Brahmanical traditions. *Dharma*, in its prior usage, refers to the correct performance of Vedic rituals and represents the main subject matter of the 'ritual portion' of the Vedic texts. For Buddhists, however, *dharma* means the teachings of the Buddha, which concerned doctrines on the cycle of rebirth (*samsara*), the results of actions (*karma*), and the condition of liberation (*moksa*)—all of which seem to have stimulated much interaction between Brahmanical and non-Brahmanical schools of thought at that time. All of this suggests that, in its historical context, the Buddha and his teachings might not best be understood by us as something entirely apart from the Vedic practices and debates of his time (what we might today just call Hinduism).

It seems quite obvious, then, that the Buddha formulated his teachings in opposition to central claims of the Upanishads (another well-known Hindu text), albeit revalorizing some concepts (e.g., *karma*, *dharma*, etc.) and skillfully refuting others, but doing so as a *shramana*; striving for enlightenment, he primarily may have tried to avoid two 'extreme doctrines' by repudiating the belief that there is either anything permanent or that nothing endures. For the Buddha, discovering a middle-way meant rejecting the most axiomatic category in Vedic discourse: the self (*atman*). At the same time, accepting the notion of rebirth and karmic continuity between lives (i.e., past deeds determine future rebirths), he seems to have refused to settle for any nihilistic perspective that prohibits the acquisition of liberating knowledge. What's more, the Buddha's combination of *shramanic* and yogic practices was readily amenable to newly emerging political alliances of the time, that were being forged beyond the hereditary class of kings and priests; but the more important synthesis of Indian religion would have to wait for some Brahmanical response to missionary campaigns sponsored by emperor Ashoka, whose own conversion to Buddhism (said to have occurred after his army's conquest of the kingdom of Kalinga, in central east India, around 260 BCE) initiated a long period of zealous proselytizing throughout Asia.

About the author

Travis D. Webster received his PhD in Indian Subcontinental Studies from the School of Languages and Cultures at the University of Sydney, Australia. His area of specialization is the Upanisads with a cognitive anthropological approach to Advaita Vedanta.

Suggestions for further reading

In this book

See also Chapters 58 (Buddhism as philosophy) and 59 (the Buddha).

Elsewhere

DeCaroli, Robert. *Haunting the Buddha: Indian Popular Religions and the Formation of Buddhism*. New York: Oxford University Press, 2004.

Gombrich, Richard F. *How Buddhism Began: The Conditioned Genesis of the Early Teachings* (2nd edition). Abingdon: Routledge, 2006.

Parpola, Asko. *The Roots of Hinduism: The Early Aryans and the Indus Civilization*. New York: Oxford University Press, 2015.

Wynne, Alexander. *The Origin of Buddhist Meditation*. London: Routledge, 2007.

61

Are religions in Asia all connected in some way?

Kendall Marchman

Before answering this question, we must break down the two troublesome categories—religion and Asia. Plenty of entries in this volume handle the former, so let's take a moment to consider the latter. Asia is easily the largest continent on the planet, and six out every ten people on earth live there. Yet, despite its superiority in size and population, the concept of 'Asia' was not constructed by any of its indigenous peoples or cultures. Instead, Europeans constructed the concept in order to explain what was *not* European, and in doing so, created the way we have come to understand the world. In categorizing the world, and then proliferating those Western views across the globe through colonialism and imperialism, the West became (and remains) a hegemon.

The reality of shared European culture (e.g., the Latin root of Romance languages) due to the Roman Empire led Europeans to assume the same about Asian culture. As a result, vastly disparate Asian cultures and peoples were lumped together in a single category, originally termed the 'Orient.' Therefore, the early study of Asian cultures was often flawed and blatantly interested in perpetuating Western hegemony. The ramifications of this early scholarship are still felt today when college students enroll in 'world religions' courses, and expect to learn about religions in tidy, unique categories. Unfortunately, the reality of the world is much messier.

This brings us back to the question of 'Asian religions,' but what does that even mean? After all, if we look at the prescribed borders of Asia as generally defined, it is clear that all of the classically understood 'world religions' actually began in Asia! The Abrahamic traditions all began (and remain) in Asia, yet they are not considered as 'Asian religions.' This reality shifts us to the 'Middle East,' which takes an alternate meaning: it is neither completely foreign (it is the home of the Abrahamic traditions, specifically Christianity, which the West has always treated as superior to Judaism and Islam), and yet it is not European. The meaning of 'Asia' in the question of Asian religions is then isolated to only part of the continent, mainly the southern, southeastern, and eastern sections.

Historically, South Asian culture has been dominated by India, which was so large that premodern India (which encompasses much more territory than the national boundaries of India today) was recognized as a subcontinent. Indian history offers perhaps the greatest assortment of religions in the world—Hinduism, Buddhism, Jainism, and Sikhism are the most recognized indigenous Indian religions. All these 'isms' are the results of European constructs, much like Asia as whole. Yet, these identities have been accepted, and represent a reality for billions of practitioners globally. Are the religions connected? Of course! They evolved out of the same culture. In the cases of Buddhism and Jainism, they began as counter movements to the beliefs and practices we identify as Hinduism today. Moreover, they often share the same vocabulary and a similar cosmological view. Sikhism too demonstrates Indian culture, while notably drawing from Muslim influence in North India.

Eastern Asia substitutes Indian culture for the equally influential Chinese culture, which dominated throughout the eastern portion of the continent. Still, some Indian influence remains due to the presence of Buddhism, though it was heavily adapted to Chinese culture before reaching its zenith in China. The Chinese produced their own indigenous systems of philosophy, practice, and belief in Taoism and Confucianism. Again, like India, these two traditions arose out of the same context, and certainly connect through the idea of *tao* (or dao, the now preferred term among scholars and Chinese alike, written in pinyin [the official romanized version of Chinese]), though they understand in contrasting ways. These Chinese traditions are even apparent in Shinto, despite the uniquely Japanese focus of Shinto mythology. Southeastern Asia shares the influence of Indian religions (largely Hinduism and Buddhism) and Chinese culture, along with the major import of Islam. These larger traditions are integrated into local popular religious practices to make them unique and acceptable to each independent culture.

Yes, there are some connections between Asian religions. However, if these connections are highlighted simply to suggest that all Asian religions are the same, it neglects the multiplicity inherent to each religion throughout Asia. For instance, the Buddhism of Bhutan looks very different than the Buddhism of Japan. Moreover, this diversity is not restricted to crossing national borders. The Hinduism of Pondicherry in South India is not the same as the Hinduism in Jaipur farther north. Asian religions are complex and multifaceted because they include such a vast collection of cultures and populations. Furthermore, the term 'Asian religions' inherits the messiness of meanings and categorizations that are a legacy of the hegemonic campaign of the West.

About the author

Kendall Marchman received his PhD in religious studies at the University of Florida, and is currently an assistant professor in the Department of Religion and Philosophy at Young Harris College. His research focuses on Pure Land Buddhism in medieval China.

Suggestions for further reading

In this book

See also Chapters 28 (conflicts over beliefs) and 60 (origins of Buddhism).

Elsewhere

Masuzawa, Tomoko. *The Invention of World Religions, Or, How European Universalism Was Preserved in the Language of Pluralism*. Chicago, IL: University of Chicago Press, 2005.

Said, Edward W. *Orientalism*. New York: Penguin, 2007.

The study of religion

62
Where did the study of religion come from?

Michael Stausberg

There is no one point of origin of the study of religion. It did not just materialize out of nowhere, to remain with us ever since. Let's rephrase the question as 'where, when and why did the study of religion first appear?' These three subquestions are interrelated. The underlying question is: what is the study of religion? There is no simple answer to this question as the aims and methodological and theoretical frameworks of this academic enterprise have changed during the course of its history—and disagreement about its nature and function remain part of the business of scholarship.

The discipline has had different names. There are five main varieties, each reflecting somewhat different agendas and emphases:

- 'Religious studies' is the broadest but also most unspecific denominator—it can include virtually all ways of approaching religion including studying religion for religious purposes.
- 'Comparative religion' emphasizes the desire to go beyond the supremacy of one religion in interpreting religion.
- 'History of religions' highlights an approach that puts religion in historical perspective, for example by embedding the history of Israelite and early Christian religion in the context of Iranian, Mesopotamian and Eastern Mediterranean religions.

- 'Science of religion' is a term that has been used early on and continues to be used mainly by German, Scandinavian, French and Brazilian scholars, but given that the word 'science' in English excludes the humanities it did not have much of a success in Anglophone countries—in the United States the related term 'scientific study of religion' commonly refers to social scientific research on religion, mainly sociological and psychological.
- 'The study of religion' has emerged as a common denominator for non-religious and non-confessional scholarship during the past two to three decades. (I prefer the term 'study of religion(s)' to indicate that since its origins the discipline always aimed at going beyond studying religion in the singular: never just one religion, but at the same time concerned to relate the variety of religions to each other with the singular 'religion' as the theoretical point of reference.)

The canon of academic disciplines, as we know it at most universities today, emerged over time since the first modern research university were established in the nineteenth century. Sociology and social anthropology, for example, only emerged around the turn from the nineteenth to the twentieth century. While the study of history and languages such as Hebrew, Arabic, Greek and Latin has had university chairs for centuries, the first chairs of Sanskrit and archaeology were established in the early nineteenth century; comparative philology, or linguistics, emerged at about the same time as the study of religion/s, namely since the later 1870s.

The establishment of two of the first chairs in the study of religion/s that had a sustainable institutional impact was a side-effect of redefining state/church relationships in the Netherlands and France respectively. In the Netherlands, the constitution of 1848 had separated church and state, and the Higher Education Act of 1876 decreed the de-confessionalization of Dutch faculties (divisions) of theology. As part of this transformation, history of religions and philosophy of religion were introduced as new additional subjects. Chairs in history of religions were established in Leiden and Amsterdam in 1877. In France in 1885, the faculties of theology were disbanded altogether and a new institution for studying religions was erected in their place. Carried forward by an internationally connected group of scholars, the new academic enterprise soon found institutional recognition across the globe. In the United States, the first department of 'comparative religion' was established in 1892. In Japan, the first department was established in 1905.

The study of religion/s remained a highly international but minor affair until after World War II. In line with the worldwide expansion of tertiary education, the discipline has experienced an unprecedented expansion since the 1960s and 1970s. Departments were founded and grew at an increasing number of universities. The discipline spread to new parts of the globe, for example in some Africa countries and in South Korea. In the United States (soon followed by Canada), cultural, religious, political, and legal developments such as a new interpretation of the First Amendment by the Supreme Court boosted a lasting yet partial process of separation of the discipline from religious frameworks and Christian theology.

About the author

Michael Stausberg is professor of religion at the University of Bergen, Norway. He has published on a broad variety of topics, including early modern intellectual history, the intersections of religion and tourism, the category of magic, theories of ritual and theories of religion, and Zoroastrianism (a pre-Islamic Central Asian and Iranian religion allegedly founded by Zoroaster).

Suggestions for further reading

In this book
See also Chapters 2 (origins of the word religion), 63 (first scholar of religion), and 65 (religious studies v. theology).

Elsewhere

Stausberg, Michael. 'History.' In *The Oxford Handbook for the Study of Religion*, edited by Michael Stausberg and Steven Engler, 777–803. Oxford: Oxford University Press, 2016.

63

Who was the first scholar of religion?

Michael Stausberg

This question implies another one: what is 'scholarship of religion'? Or even what is 'scholarship'? Any take on these issues results in different answers. Is it sufficient to say that scholarship of religion is any kind of learned study of one's own religion, or would the range of erudition also need to include religions other than one's own? In the former case, would it be required that this study is historical or critical? In the latter case, would it be required that one studies that other religion in a non-polemical manner, not subjecting it to truth-claims put forward by one's own religion? Does 'scholarship of religion' allow for religious perspectives or does it have to be strictly 'secular' and maybe even critical of religion? Does scholarship require specific media? Is a travelogue scholarship? Or maybe not any travelogue but only such travel reports that give precise dates and times and provide sufficient details and are written in a non-sensational, non-deprecatory manner? Or is scholarship limited to books or journal articles? If so, what kind of books and journals? Does any literature count as scholarship or only texts that have references to sources and other texts, or even footnotes? This is not just hair-splitting. Each question addresses different modes of dealing intellectually or academically with religion. And for each variety one could seek to trace a 'first' protagonist.

This is not limited to the West. For example, certain Muslim scholars are sometimes acknowledged as early scholars of religion, most famously al-Biruni (973–1048 CE), a scholar who contributed to several natural sciences and also published works on linguistics and history. He lived in what today is Afghanistan and travelled to India. Based on his travels, he published works on India in which he sought to give an impartial, unbiased account of the customs, beliefs, and practices of the Hindus, even though he acknowledged them as the religious antagonists of the Muslims. Around a century later, al-Shahrastani (1086–1153 CE), who lived in Iran, wrote *The Book of Sects and Creeds* in which he provides a survey of different creeds, philosophies and religious communities.

The scholarship of these Islamic scholars, however, did not result in any institutional establishment of religious studies. At the al-Azhar university in Cairo—founded in the late tenth century CE—students would study logic, philosophy, Arabic grammar, astronomy, and Islamic law. In medieval Europe, theology, that is the study of Christian teachings and scriptures, was considered the supreme subject taught at universities. In both cases, knowledge about religions apart from Islam and Christianity respectively was not part of the curricula.

Since the sixteenth century, in tune with the European expansion across the globe scholars studied an increasingly broad variety of cultures, languages and religions––from South and North America, through Africa, the Middle East, Central Asia, to South and East Asia. However, the idea of establishing a 'science' of religion was first expressed programmatically in the late 1790s— after the Enlightenment, the French revolution and the Kantian revolution of thinking—by a handful of German philosophers and theologians. Their ideas, however, did not find much resonance.

While scholarship on religions expanded throughout the nineteenth century, it was only in 1874 that the idea of establishing a science of religion was once more proclaimed—this time more forcefully and again by a German, Friedrich Max Müller (1823–1900). Müller came to England in 1846 and remained there for the rest of his life. In 1867 Müller published 'Essays on the Science of Religion' and in 1873 *Lectures on the Science of Religion*. For Müller, this was only one of the sciences he hoped to establish; he was as much concerned with comparative linguistics and mythology. Müller's main interest was in ancient Indian scriptures. He was something like an academic celebrity at Oxford with a wide international network of contacts. Though he never held a chair in religious studies and his ideas on religion were soon deemed uninspiring and dated, he came to be regarded as something like a founding figure of the nascent field of the comparative and historical study of religion when the first histories of this enterprise were published in the early twentieth century. One reason for this reputation may also have been that none of the scholars who were appointed to the first chairs of comparative religions that were established since the late 1870s would outshine Müller in in terms of intellectual and entrepreneurial achievements.

About the author

Michael Stausberg is professor of religion at the University of Bergen, Norway. He has published on a broad variety of topics, including early modern intellectual history, the intersections of religion and tourism, the category of magic, theories of ritual and theories of religion, and Zoroastrianism (a pre-Islamic Central Asian and Iranian religion allegedly founded by Zoroaster).

Suggestions for further reading

In this book

See also Chapters 2 (origins of the word religion), 62 (origins of the study of religion), and 65 (religious studies v. theology).

Elsewhere

Girardot, N. J. 'Max Müller's *Sacred Books* and the Nineteenth-Century Production of the Comparative Science of Religion.' *History of Religions* 41(3) (2002): 213–250.

Stausberg, Michael. 'History.' In *The Oxford Handbook for the Study of Religion*, edited by Michael Stausberg and Steven Engler, 777–803. Oxford: Oxford University Press, 2016.

64
Why is it important that we study religion?

K. Merinda Simmons

This question is an interesting one because, so often, there is some assumed substance to the term 'religion' that might be studied. Typically, there are also some go-to examples that stand in for a definition: What's religion? Well, Hinduism is a religion, some might say. This common approach makes sense of why students entering my 'Introduction to religious studies' course often expect, they have told me, a survey of 'world religions' that includes descriptive units about Buddhism, Christianity, Islam, Judaism, Rastafarianism, and other traditions or systems of belief that are deemed to fit beneath the 'religion' umbrella. These students are surprised when I make plain on the first day of class that the course offers no such survey but is, instead, a chance to think in a bit more depth about how we come to identify certain things as 'religion' at all and about the consequences of doing so. On one hand, the term is so frequently used that such an approach might initially seem like an unnecessary exploration of what is already common sense. But if we think seriously about the fact that 'religion' is a word like any other whose meanings have changed a great deal over time and over a great many number of geographical, political, and social contexts, the seemingly common sense nature of the term suddenly seems not so common after all. That familiarity (or lack thereof) with the term is, therefore, what appears worth exploring.

With that in mind, it is not especially important that we study *religion*. Or at least, not if that means analyzing something existing naturally in the world that we scholars passively recognize and describe upon locating it. What *is* important is learning to ask questions about the labels we tend to use more or less unconsciously and the qualities we give them. One of those labels—one to which many people attach a great deal of significance—is, of course, 'religion.' If a system of beliefs or practices is called a religion—as opposed to a 'cult' or 'radical fringe group,' for example—that designation will bring with it a higher level of social, political, and economic legitimacy. The importance of looking at language becomes quickly apparent when considering, for example, how politicians (this is certainly the case in the US currently) simultaneously embrace 'religion' and condemn 'extremism.' What traditions or practices come to be included in either category? Who makes those decisions and how? Studying religion with these kinds of questions in mind allows us to think about how boundaries get established and subsequently defended, policed, or challenged.

What's more, seeing such boundaries and classifications not as natural or stable but as tools people use differently in different settings is crucial if we are to become aware of our own investments in various terms and ideas. We tend not to have to think much about what is familiar (and, thus, 'normal') to us, even as we use it as an important starting point. Religion is one of those familiar points that help chart a course on the map of ideas and concepts that we use to navigate our social worlds. So, there is much to be gained in defamiliarizing ourselves with the term by thinking about it in ways we typically don't have to and by asking what kinds of assumptions and expectations appear in conversations about religion.

If we can start becoming curious about ourselves—how we come to call certain things familiar and how we come to identify other things as strange—then we can start engaging the local and larger worlds around us with more sophistication and complexity. Everything (or nothing) is 'important,' depending on who's talking about it. So it seems that the substance of our study is not the thing called religion—is 'it' even a thing? A set of practices? Beliefs held deep inside ourselves? One sees how quickly one might start sliding down particular rabbit holes. Instead, more productive is looking at what's at work when this or that person or group calls something 'religion' at all.

About the author

K. Merinda Simmons is associate professor of religious studies at the University of Alabama. Her areas of teaching and research focus on identifications of race, gender, and religion in the Caribbean and the American South.

Suggestions for further reading

In this book

See also Chapters 72 (studying religion in public schools) and 75 (interdisciplinarity).

Elsewhere

Martin, Craig. *A Critical Introduction to the Study of Religion*. New York: Routledge, 2014.

McCutcheon, Russell T. *Studying Religion: An Introduction*. New York: Routledge, 2014.

Nye, Malory. *Religion: The Basics*. New York: Routledge, 2008.

65

Is there a difference between religious studies and theology?

Jason N. Blum

Unequivocally, yes. To summarize somewhat simplistically (but not inaccurately): theologians study the supernatural; religious studies scholars study what people say about the supernatural.

One place to begin understanding the difference is the academic institutions associated with each field. In the United States, a degree in religious studies—either a Master of Arts (MA) or a Doctorate in Philosophy (PhD)—is earned through an academic department that typically has 'religion' or 'religious studies' in its name (i.e., a 'Department of Religious Studies' or 'Department of Religion'). Such departments are found within both public and private universities and colleges. By contrast, degrees in theology are known as Master of Divinity (MDiv) and Doctorate in Theology (ThD), and are typically bestowed by seminaries and schools or departments of theology—that is, by academic institutions that are explicitly religious in nature (this distinction is not always as clear in other countries, where programs in religious studies and theology may operate out of a single department, or the terms may be used interchangeably). The MDiv degree is the standard prerequisite for individuals seeking to become priests or ministers, whereas a degree in religious studies typically does *not* indicate a career in the professional ministry.

These institutional distinctions reflect a very important difference in the purposes and the kinds of training that characterize academic programs in religious studies and theology. Religious studies is an *etic* endeavor, or the study of religion 'from the outside.' In other words, the professor of religious studies is not necessarily religious herself. A religious studies scholar does not necessarily practice or believe in the religion that she studies; just as a chemist's or a mathematician's profession indicates nothing about her personal religious beliefs (or lack thereof), a religious studies professor's personal religious beliefs or practices (or lack thereof) are irrelevant to her teaching and research. Someone who researches and teaches about Hinduism, for example, might be Christian, Muslim, Hindu, or atheist.

Conversely, theology may be described as an *emic*—or 'insider'—practice. A theologian is by definition a member of a particular religion, who is engaged in the intellectual exploration and study of his or her own religion. What crucially distinguishes the work of a theologian from that of the religious studies scholar is that the former operates 'from within' the tradition: the theologian identifies with the religion he studies (i.e., a Christian theologian studies Christianity *and* identifies as Christian). Historically, the term 'theology' arose first with regard to Christianity, but the kind of work that a theologian does can and has been performed with respect to many different religions. Any individual who both identifies with a given religion and who is professionally engaged in the study of it may, therefore, be described as 'doing theology.'

By contrast, religious studies is, in short, the secular study of religions. It does not engage the question of whether or not a religion is true, or whether or not the supernatural (e.g., God) exists. These questions are 'bracketed,' or put to the side as outside the purview of religious studies. Rather, her primary interests are in things whose existence is far less debatable: texts, practices, doctrines, institutions, etc. While it is controversial whether or not a given religion is true or whether or not God exists, it cannot be denied that people engage in certain publicly observable activities (such as praying or making pilgrimage), hold certain beliefs (such as in the existence of God or the reality of karma), create institutions (such as churches, mosques, and temples), and hold certain texts (such as the Bible) or individuals (such as the Buddha or the prophet Muhammad) to be authoritative in terms of how to live a good life. In other words, when a religious studies scholar studies religion, she studies things that *people* do, say, and make; she does not study the supernatural itself. Therefore, the kinds of things that the scholar of religion studies are undeniably real (although we scholars of religion love to debate how to label, understand, and explain those things). Theology, by contrast, is not limited in the same way. Although theologians may (and often do) use the same methods and tools as religious studies scholars, they also may make claims that cannot be supported through those methods (i.e., claims concerning supernatural entities or forces that cannot be proven or disproven through empirical research). Whereas the religious studies scholar relies on reason and historical evidence (broadly construed) in her analyses, the theologian may use these *in addition to* scripture or other specifically religious sources of authority as evidence; the latter are considered inadmissible within the field of religious studies as evidence.

About the author
Jason N. Blum teaches at Davidson College. His research focuses on theory and method in religious studies, and topics at the intersection of philosophy and religion, particularly the relationship between science and religion, religious experience, and religion, society and ethics.

Suggestions for further reading

In this book
See also Chapters 6 (religion v. philosophy), 12 (function of religion), and 62 (origins of the study of religion).

Elsewhere

Pals, Daniel. *Nine Theories of Religion*. New York: Oxford University Press, 2014.

Schilbrack, Kevin. *Philosophy and the Study of Religions: A Manifesto*. New York: Wiley Blackwell, 2013.

Wiebe, Donald. *The Politics of Religious Studies: The Continuing Conflict with Theology in the Academy*. New York: St. Martin's Press, 1999.

66
What is exegesis?

Aaron W. Hughes

Exegesis is another word for interpretation. In religious studies it tends to refer to the interpretation of texts that adherents
deem canonical or as somehow sacred. Because these texts possess
such qualities they are often imagined to contain the seeds of all
wisdom, and it is up to the exegete (or interpreter) to tease out
the requisite legal, mystical, or philosophical meaning, often with
the help of agreed upon criteria. Exegesis is thus the activity that
enables exegetes to get scripture to conform to their own ideological positions—though, of course, they would never admit to this
and would instead claim that they are simply doing God's will. A
gay-friendly Muslim exegete, for example, will read the quranic
text in such a manner that it conforms to his or her agenda. That
which does not conform to said agenda can either be ignored
or, more profitably, interpreted away by using the principle that
even though the Qur'an (or any other scripture) literally says
something, it was not meant to be understood literally, but only
symbolically or metaphorically.

   The biblical phrase 'an eye for an eye' offers a startling example
of the way exegesis can subvert the literal level of the text. In its
discussion of punishment, the book of Exodus says 'an eye for
eye, tooth for tooth, hand for hand, foot for foot' (21.24), which is
usually seen as the biblical version of *lex talionis* (i.e., a person who
has injured another person is to be penalized to a similar degree).
Despite this verse, however, the rabbis of the Talmud argued that
one could not take an 'eye for an eye' because if someone was

blind in one eye, taking the other eye would not be fair as it would completely blind them. Using this as their guiding principle, the rabbis argued that, despite what the Bible *literally* says, it does not really mean it and that what that verse is advocating for is a form of monetary compensation.

The role of allegory, as can be seen from these examples, plays an important role in exegesis. The biblical book known as 'The Song of Songs' or 'The Song of Solomon,' to use another example, does not mention God at all in it, and instead appears to be a 'secular' erotic poem between a lover and a beloved. In the hands of Jewish exegetes, however, the book became an allegory of the love between God (the beloved) and Israel (the lover). In Christian exegetical hands, the exact same book is read as an allegory of the love between Jesus (the beloved) and the Church (the lover). Despite the fact that the book mentions neither God nor Israel, neither Jesus nor the Church, allegory allows the interpreters to read such ideas into the text.

Exegesis is also the way that later scholars derive legal rulings from scripture. So while the Qur'an, for example, forbids the drinking of date-palm wine, it does not mention bourbon or marijuana. Does this, then, mean that a Muslim can drink bourbon or smoke marijuana, and must only avoid palm wine? The answer, of course, is no, because later exegetes forbade both of these intoxicants that were not available to the earliest Muslims on account of the same reason that the Qur'an forbade palm wine, namely, that it impairs cognitive ability.

Often we hear people ask questions like 'what does the Qur'an say about *x*?' Such a question is very difficult to answer because it assumes that what a book literally says is how people interpret it. As should now be clear from the above, however, a clever interpreter or interpretation can take even the most bellicose verse and turn into a spiritual one (e.g., when the Qur'an mentions *jihad*, it does not mean a literal 'holy war,' but an internal or spiritual 'struggle'). In like manner, the most peaceful verse can be turned into the most venomous.

Exegesis, in sum, is the activity that enables people either to read what they want into scripture and/or to take out that which they believe to conform to their own ideological position.

About the author
Aaron W. Hughes is the Philip S. Bernstein Chair in the Department of Religion and Classics at the University of Rochester.

Suggestions for further reading

In this book
See also Chapters 33 (bible's authors), 37 (St. Paul), and 65 (religious studies v. theology).

Elsewhere
Hughes, Aaron W. 'Making the Past Present: the Genre of Commentary in Comparative Perspective.' *Method and Theory in the Study of Religion* 15(2) (2003): 148–168.

Smith, Jonathan Z. 'Sacred Persistence: Toward a Redescription of Canon.' In his *Imagining Religion: From Babylon to Jonestown*, 36–52. Chicago, IL: University of Chicago Press, 1982.

67

What do you do when you do fieldwork in religion?

Russell T. McCutcheon

There are those who, traditionally, thought religion was all about texts—reading them and interpreting them the proper way, in order to understand their meaning. Whether so-called scriptures or theological treatises, the study of religion for many meant going to a library, checking out a book, and reading it in the light of what was called the secondary literature around the book—a body of literature that could stretch back years, all depending on the importance of the book in question. The common assumption was that religion mainly concerned orthodox (i.e., proper, correct) expressions of an otherwise inaccessible experience or feeling. Thus there was what some might now term a rationalist bias in the newly emerged field—the effort was to systematize and thereby make sense of this otherwise seemingly irrational (or, better put, non-rational) affectation that some people claimed to have. And if we add to this the tendency in history writing at the time to (understandably) rely on written sources as ones primary datum, then to study a religion meant to read texts, sometimes ancient texts and sometimes contemporary texts (yet still written by authoritative interpreters of the tradition—or maybe even penned by the colonialists, soldiers, and missionaries who actually travelled to various distant places). And so, early on, for example, one of the field's founders, the German scholar Friedrich Max Müller (d. 1900) established and edited a massive effort to translate what were then—from the European point of view, to be sure—newly discovered texts now classed as scriptures, the so-called Sacred Books of the East series (fifty volumes were published by Oxford University Press from 1879 to 1910). This was the day of so-called armchair anthropologists who did their work in British libraries and archives in France or museums in Germany.

This model took some time to give way—it's not hard to find to this day, in fact—for it wasn't immediately clear that, for instance, reading texts meant seeing the world only through the eyes of its various authors and editors. Instead, authors were often assumed not to have viewpoints and simply to be innocently narrating events or conveying timeless meanings. But over time the existence of a text prompted some to ask why anyone would even write something in the first place, that is, raising questions about interests and alternative positions that must have once existed and which prompted one side to write, or maybe both sides, with historical happenstance determining that this, and only this, particular ancient text lasted until we could read it today (ancient libraries were razed, after all, and who knows what all could happen to destroy a scroll or parchment). In other words, the historical situation of the text itself—either its origins and thus composition or even its continued existence as a material artifact—started to attract scholars' attention. And if we add to this the mid-twentieth century turn toward fieldwork in anthropology, associated with the work of the influential Polish anthropologist, Bronislaw Malinowski (d. 1942)—in which scholars began to leave the library and, instead, immerse themselves in the everyday cultures of human beings, learning their languages and their customs over years of careful immersion and engaging in what came to be known as thick description and participant observation (where the sometimes fine line between participant and observer was often straddled)—it was just a matter of time before the almost exclusive reliance on reading texts would give way to talking to people.

We therefore arrive at a moment, today, when the onetime credentials of the field (e.g., learning ancient languages and studying religion in antiquity) have, at least in part, given way to scholars studying what they call religion on the ground, lived religion, or material religion—all terms that prioritize so-called lived experience over books and second-hand descriptions. Presuming that alternative voices need to be recovered, rather than just studying elites who have access to reading and authoritative writing, the field has been affected by feminist and Marxist studies from a generation or two ago, inasmuch as many scholars of religion now seek out understudied groups which represent either marginal or perhaps even oppositional viewpoints (when compared to so-called mainline religions). Immersion with these groups' members (which, in many cases, requires the acquisition of language skills, of course) has therefore become a qualifier in this field, not unlike how modern anthropology uses it as evidence of scholarly competency.

But with the day-to-day intimacy and access necessary for useful ethnographic works to be produced come some difficulties that can't be overlooked. Case in point: there's a long history in the study of religion in which scholars have debated the role of scholarship on religion: whether it is here to *explain* the beliefs and behaviors of the people studied or, instead, merely to *interpret* and thereby *understand* the meaning of their claims and actions. Whereas the latter has been critiqued as aiming to appreciate, even authenticate and assist, the people under study, inasmuch as it studies them empathetically, the former has sought to maintain a critical distance from the interests of those being studied—which has earned for it criticisms of its own, at least from those who see the study of religion as being a humanistic rather than a social scientific endeavor. Yet to the latter—from social theorists to cognitive scientists—the familiarity needed to produce ethnographies risks that their authors compromise on important scholarly principles. Thus the turn toward nuanced fieldwork has, at least for some, precluded a style of scholarship very much associated with the founding of the field in the late-nineteenth century: theorizing religion's origins and modern functions. So the gains of detailed fieldwork has meant that, at least for some scholars, the field ends up acting more as a guest in other people's cultural houses, careful not to tread too heavily on other people's presumptions and interests. The price paid is a lack of interest in *explaining* why anyone would ever believe or do the things that we can now so closely witness people doing; it leads to a lack that could be argued to naturalize and thereby legitimize those very beliefs and actions, inasmuch as they now are simply *described* and never questioned or examined critically.

So, to answer the question posed at the outset, we might conclude that what we do when we do fieldwork in the study of religion is to risk authorizing the religious insider as expert on their own behaviors, thereby lessening our own relevance as scholars. For the premise of the academic study of religion, as with all of the human sciences, is that participants are not necessarily experts on their own worlds. For just because one might be a native English speaker does not mean that one necessarily knows why, for example, English speakers place adjectives in a very particular order when describing their worlds (i.e., that we say 'large, blue pond' and not 'blue, large pond' might therefore strike the linguistics specialist as curious when it's not even noticed by speakers themselves).

About the author

Russell T. McCutcheon is professor and chair of the Department of Religious Studies at the University of Alabama; his work is on the theories of religion, approaches to the study of myth, as well as focusing on the history of the study of religion and the practical effects of classification systems.

Suggestions for further reading

In this book

See also Chapters 69 (texts v. fieldwork) and 76 (contributions of the study of religion).

Elsewhere

Clifford, James and Georger Marcus (editors). *Writing Culture: The Poetics and Politics of Ethnography*. Berkeley, CA: University of California Press, 1986.

Gregg, Stephen E. and Lynne Scholefield (editors). *Engaging with Living Religion: A Guide to Fieldwork in the Study of Religion*. Abingdon: Routledge, 2015.

68

In what ways can religion be legally discussed in US public schools?

Michael Graziano

The First Amendment to the United States Constitution reads in part: 'Congress shall make no law respecting an establishment of religion, or prohibiting the free exercise thereof.' While these words have long been central to how Americans interact with religion, they also offer little practical guidance for how to settle day-to-day disputes about the place of religion in public life. The Amendment says nothing about school principals, for example, or whether a biology teacher can instruct her students in intelligent design. Few areas of public life in the United States have been as consistently divisive as the role of religion in public schools.

Religious freedom in the US is not absolute. In general, while Americans may *believe* whatever they wish, they may not necessarily *act* on those beliefs simply because such beliefs are 'religious.' Furthermore, the Supreme Court sees public schools as areas of special concern, since schoolchildren are captive audiences—they are legally required to attend school until a certain age—and subjected to the influence of authority figures (teachers, principals, other school officials, etc.). As a result, a patchwork of rules has developed to regulate when, and how, religion may be discussed in public schools.

Students and school officials may discuss religion in different ways. For example, teachers can instruct students about religious texts, such as the Hebrew Bible or Muslim Qur'an, so long as these texts are part of a larger program of secular education. These texts could be approached as works of literature, for example, or as windows onto the historical contexts of their invention and revision. However, since school staff are also state officials, they may not use religious content to make theological claims about the value of individual religious traditions or ideas. Schools also cannot mandate or initiate prayer. According to the Court, this is still the case even if the prayer is both voluntary and non-denominational, since this would put the schools in the position of endorsing prayer, and religion, in general. Instead, schools must stay neutral in such debates. The goal of religious discussions must be education and awareness, rather than approval or disapproval.

Students have more flexibility. Unlike teachers and administrators, they do not represent the state's authority. Students may pray by themselves or in groups throughout the school day, subject to the same rules as other speech activities. Furthermore, students may discuss their feelings or ideas with reference to their own religious beliefs. These comments cannot be silenced or marked down by school authorities so long as the student's comments are related to course materials.

Given the variety of people and perspectives involved, it is difficult to draw a clear line between discussing religion academically and discussing religion devotionally. A good example is the controversy over discussing creationism in schools. Some groups object to the teaching of biological evolution and cosmological theories of the universe's origin (such as the 'Big Bang') and have requested equal time for students to learn about alternative explanations more appealing to some religious groups (such as 'intelligent design'). These alternative explanations were ruled unconstitutional on account of being religious rather than scientific. Yet this controversy raises an interesting question: if legal, *which* creation story would be taught? While many who objected to teaching biological evolution likely favored Christian origin stories, this is not the only alternative. For example, students in this hypothetical 'equal time' situation might learn that the universe was created by Brahma and preserved by Vishnu. It was just such a debate over creationism and intelligent design that gave birth to Pastafarianism, a new religious movement that pushes for the teaching of its own creation story—in which the Universe is created by the all-powerful Flying Spaghetti Monster—as part of public school curricula.

Challenges in adjudicating these disagreements are exacerbated by the diversity of religious ideas within the United States. Is it possible to teach about a religious tradition's history or literary output—even in an 'academic' and 'secular' setting—without also advocating for the tradition's worth on some level? In a curriculum of finite time and resources, teaching about one tradition might come at the expense of teaching about another. Which traditions should be prioritized? And who gets to decide? These controversies suggest the many different—and often contradictory—ways in which Americans continue to understand religion, belief, and religious freedom.

About the author
Michael Graziano specializes in American religious history. He teaches religious studies at the University of Northern Iowa.

Suggestions for further reading

In this book
See also Chapters 65 (religious studies v. theology) and 72 (studying religion in public schools).

Elsewhere
American Civil Liberties Union. 'Joint Statement of Current Law on Religion in the Public Schools.' Retrieved from www.aclu.org/joint-statement-current-law-religion-public-schools.

Chicago-Kent College of Law at Illinois Tech. 'School District of Abington Township, Pennsylvania v. Schempp.' *Oyez*. Retrieved from www.oyez. org/cases/1962/142.

Haynes, Charles C. *A Teacher's Guide to Religion in the Public Schools*. Nashville, TN: First Amendment Center, 2004. Retrieved from www. firstamendmentcenter.org/madison/wp-content/uploads/2011/03/ teachersguide.pdf.

69

Do scholars of religion study texts or do they study the religion firsthand, as an anthropologist might?

Richard Newton

The short answer is that they study both.

Scholars of religion understand that their object of study, first and foremost, is a human activity. That human activity encompasses all manner of effective expressions. Through much of the nineteenth century, scholars chronicled 'religion' by referencing particular beliefs, rituals, leadership structures, social organizations, communal laws, reported sensations, and yes, texts. Twentieth century scholarship did not depart from this so much as it focused those efforts toward the question of how to define religion. So if you're thinking that religion can refer to anything, you're not alone. It largely has. This sort of observation has led early twenty-first century scholars to turn their attention to why.

Like anthropology, religious studies is curious about the things people do. People place meaning not simply in their conspicuous sacrosanct behaviors, but also—and even more so—in the behaviors they assume routine. Anthropologists and religion scholars approach a community with questions about the stuff that communities would otherwise take for granted.

Let's say I've sat for dinner with a number of Christian families who say table grace before meals. Faith statements might peak your interest, but there are all sorts of things to consider. Do breakfast and lunch meals demand a blessing or just dinner? Are we blessing food, the hands that prepared it, or some divine source for indirectly providing it? Who gets credit for the food before us? And who gets to deliver the prayer—a matriarch, a patriarch, a child maturing into the tradition, or everyone gathered? Are prayers to be read, sung, a memorized speech, or an extemporaneous riff? If extemporaneous, why is it still pretty formulaic, like a 'Dear God' letter to the editor? How come the words sound old-fashioned or sappy? What is the appropriate length to keep people's undivided attention? And what are people really thinking during the grace? These are just some of the questions a scholar of religion might investigate in an attempt to better understand human beings and what they deem significant.

Anthropologists and religion scholars alike recognize that humans inhabit a potentially meaningful world. We watch how humans invest their time and energy into filling it with significance. In cataloguing their ingenuity we note patterns—so much so that humans appear to follow a sort of script. What an anthropologist may call a 'cultural text,' a religion scholar might label as 'scripture.' The former emphasizes the pervasive development of a specific form of communication (i.e., literacy). The latter takes a specific example from Christendom (i.e., the Bible) and relates it to instances identified as comparable. Both are a testament to the influence of the written word and other social technologies in human history.

Though each discipline takes a different route to this observation, anthropology and religious studies understand texts to be noteworthy tools for building civilizations. As media, they may be complex. Their messages may even mystify. You're likely aware of sophisticated investigations into the authors, readers, contexts, and consequences of a text. But our inquiry also probes the forms and behaviors enveloped in textual engagement. The critical question subtending all of this is what is the story behind the people who engage them.

For instance, many Evangelical churches provide Bibles in the pew or display verses on a screen. So why do members insist on bringing their personal Bibles to worship services? When is a tattered Bible a sign of devotion or blasphemy? Are community members encouraged to write notes in their Bibles or is that disrespectful? What do people do with Bibles when they are not being used? Were we solely to focus on reading, we would miss out on the other unquestioned customs that happen around texts.

Texts are a site to watch humans relate to one another. Yes, the texts may index myths and histories and theologies and customs. But they are also at the center of interpersonal and intra-personal drama. The scholar of religion takes an interest in this drama, and if texts are involved, so be it. When we designate human activity as our focal point, texts become an accidental part of the equation. This frees us to appreciate the nuances behind their appearance in society.

About the author

Richard Newton is assistant professor of religious studies at Elizabethtown College. His research focuses on the anthropology of scriptures. He is also the founder of the student-scholar blog, *Sowing the Seed: Fruitful Conversations in Religion, Culture, and Teaching*, and host of the companion podcast, *Broadcast Seeding* (sowingtheseed.org).

Suggestions for further reading

In this book
See also Chapters 67 (fieldwork), 75 (interdisciplinarity), and 76 (contributions of the study of religion).

Elsewhere
McCutcheon, Russell T. 'What is the Academic Study of Religion?' Retrieved from http://rel.as.ua.edu/pdf/rel100introhandout.pdf.

Smith, Jonathan Z. 'Religion and the Bible.' *Journal of Biblical Literature* 128(1) (2009): 5–27. Retrieved from www.sbl-site.org/assets/pdfs/presidentialaddresses/JBL128_1_1Smith2008.pdf.

Wimbush, Vincent L. 'Scriptures.' *Oxford Bibliographies* (September 13, 2010). Retrieved from http://oxfordbibliographiesonline.com/view/document/obo-9780195393361/obo-9780195393361-0055.xml.

70

Is it possible to study religion academically and still be religious?

Richard Newton

The brand of religious studies modeled in this volume represents a disciplined commitment to the history of religion as an opportunity for academic scrutiny. It stops itself from pronouncing judgments and instead examines the complexities that inform human striving.

This approach entails description, explanation, interpretation and comparison. Those performing these investigations consider the enterprise a critical—that is, insightful, analytical, and worthwhile—pursuit of human understanding.

The question asked in this chapter surfaces one aspect of that debate: the scholar's relationship to the object of study—religion—and its affects—the religious. It plumbs the depths of the more fundamental question, 'What does it mean to call something, someone, or even oneself religious?' A given answer is not about solidifying truth but observing just some of the dynamic relationships people have around the idea's legacy.

If by 'religious' you mean one who has intimate knowledge of a specific tradition or set of traditions, a scholar may be perceived as especially religious by those who confess to know very little in comparison. I'm reminded here of the countless plane rides I've taken where small talk turns toward the question of occupation.

No matter how I qualify my work, most people end up considering me religious. They assume that the years I have spent devoted to understanding the subject of 'religion' must constitute some superior level of religiousness to their own. So to those who understand religion as a matter of intellectual investment, an academic may be primed to be religious.

At the same time, many religious studies students can attest to the social reality that there are 'right' and 'wrong' types of knowledge. There were so many times in my undergraduate career where professors introduced ideas that I could hardly raise in the church of my upbringing. And regardless of background, my religious studies students agree that many of the arguments pressed in our conversations would put them at odds with the religious communities from which they hail. Discussions of social construction, cognitive science, and discursive functionalism are too blasphemous to be entertained. The discipline's humanistic tenor has earned a reputation of making students 'lose their religion.' I know of campus ministers who've discouraged students from taking religious studies classes for this very reason. For those who understand religion as a matter of questions to be tabled, then an academic may be precluded from being religious.

In both of these scenarios, there is a presumed element of volition. I made a choice to become a religious studies scholar, just as I choose to follow the rites and customs of a certain community of religious people. But when we take a long hard look at the history of religion, being religious is often less an issue of choice than of circumstance. In my estimation, the label 'world religions' points to discourses with aspirations, if not, a legacy of this. You might think of the persons born into Jewish or Catholic families who, despite their best efforts at distancing themselves from these religions, will ne'er always be Jews and Catholics. From the atheist philosopher of religion who says 'God Bless You' when someone sneezes to the agnostic Saudi-American historian of Islam who drinks at department get-togethers just as earnestly as he fasts during Ramadan, an academic may not help but be religious. The most pervasive, far-reaching examples of religion are the systems that persist regardless of our compliance.

Whether one can be religious and study religion academically is a question of identity. The intellectual enterprise in which we trade can be a credit or a liability depending on one's interests. And from a certain point of view, the knowledge professed by the scholar of religion is a testament to the influence and currency of our subject matter, making religiosity not a zero-sum game but a matter of degree. But the hallmark of a scholar of religion is their commitment to identify religion as a human activity. As long as other commitments—religious or otherwise—do not inhibit this work, religious studies can continue.

About the author

Richard Newton is assistant professor of religious studies at Elizabethtown College. His research focuses on the anthropology of scriptures. He is also the founder of the student-scholar blog, *Sowing the Seed: Fruitful Conversations in Religion, Culture, and Teaching,* and host of the companion podcast, *Broadcast Seeding* (sowingtheseed.org).

Suggestions for further reading

In this book

See also Chapters 65 (religious studies v. theology) and 71 (existence of God).

Elsewhere

Martin, Craig. 'How to Read an Interpretation: Interpretive Strategies and the Maintenance of Authority.' *The Bible and Critical Theory* 5(1) (2009): 06.1–06.26. Retrieved from http://genealogyreligion.net/wp-content/uploads/2011/01/How-To-Read-An-Interpretation2.pdf.

Miller, Monica R. 'Black Death and the Godz of the New Pop Art.' *JSTOR Daily* (May 28, 2015). Retrieved from http://daily.jstor.org/black-death-godz-new-pop-art.

Smith, Leslie Dorrough. 'Debating the System.' *Culture on the Edge: Studies in Identity Formation* (May 19, 2016). Retrieved from http://edge. ua.edu/leslie-dorrough-smith/debating-the-system.

71

Does the academic study of religion deny the existence of God?

Blair Alan Gadsby

The academic study of religion—religious studies (RS)—is in no position to either affirm or deny god's existence. As a matter of academic constraint, it may *not* appeal to a god when constructing its theories and forming its descriptions as it has a research role closer to that of the social sciences and less oriented towards the philosophy of religion or theology where such appeals may be made. In a way, this very question suggests some of the complexities of studying religion when there are religions whose very doctrines deny the existence of god—Buddhism, Jainism, certain forms of Judaism, among others.

Nevertheless, monks in a Christian monastery, for example, performing Latin traditional Plainchant, or Gregorian chant, to their monotheistic God share certain other characteristics with monks in a Tibetan Buddhist monastery chanting OM to an empty universe. Though in fact, the Christian monks share more characteristics in their *manner* of chanting to Theravada Buddhist monks whose atheism, in turn, is not entirely similar to the Tibetan monks' and could be considered a stricter or purer form of Buddhist atheism. The challenge for RS is to study, define, and categorize all the various elements of religious beliefs and behavior in a manner consistent with objective research.

In doing so RS must remain grounded in the social sciences as those disciplines are conventionally practiced. If not, it risks losing its status as a science—which it has fought so hard to establish over the past century and a half. RS as an independent academic discipline typically demonstrates this scientific orientation by conforming to the rules of methods and theories developed in cognate disciplines and by adding its own unique contributions. As a result, references to the untestable or unverifiable are precluded in RS as *all* researchers from *all* disciplines must be able to share in the observations made and confirm the sources from which RS theories and conclusions are developed and drawn.

One historical example of the formal and institutional separation of RS from theology took place with the liberalization of late nineteenth-century European thought. This liberalization (sometimes associated with secularization and a relaxing of religious restrictions) was primarily the result of the explosion of scientific knowledge that had been developing since the Enlightenment of the 1700s—a time in which the general growth of knowledge led to a rapid development in areas of specialization such as linguistics, geography, and historiography. The Dutch theologian and historian Cornelius P. Tiele (1830–1902) was, after some controversy, appointed to the chair of history of religions at the University of Leiden in 1877 marking one of the first such 'historical schools of religious research.'

Sometimes RS scholars *do* make their views known. Sigmund Freud did so. He explicitly declared that religion would one day be recognized for the 'obsessional neurosis' that he thought it was, and that religion would disappear in the face of a general increase of science. He stated this in 1927, and nearly 100 years on nothing could be further from the truth. Conversely, Carl Jung also studied religion from a psychological viewpoint without coming to Freud's conclusions.

A better example of how current RS scholars treat their subject matter is reflected with the following comparison of two very different approaches: when humans accept and act upon what one recent RS theory describes as the 'belief in supernatural compensators' (the promise of rewards), then we are dealing with an element in human life which rests on rational bases, according to this *rational choice/exchange theory* (see Stark and Bainbridge's *A Theory of Religion*, listed at end of this chapter). But is it so clear that it is a *rational* act to accept supernatural compensators, or rewards? Or is something more non-rational involved? As in Rudolph Otto's *numinous*—a non-rational 'category of value' that 'cannot be strictly defined.' Otto's view is referred to as the *phenomenology of religion* and is about as descriptively close as any objective academic discipline can get without crossing the line into more speculative theorizing, or affirming the existence of god.

Whether the religious behavior in question is rational or non-rational, or whether the researcher is employing rational choice/exchange theory or the numinous of the phenomenology of religion, according to Max Weber, another RS founding scholar, it is to *this world* which religious activity is directed, not the spirit world, and it is to this world that our academic gaze must be cast. In this way, no reference to god is required to interpret, theorize, or otherwise analyze religious behaviors.

About the author

Blair Alan Gadsby is a graduate of the University of Toronto's Centre for Religious Studies (MA, 1992) and is currently adjunct faculty of religious studies at Mesa Community College in Arizona teaching world religions, among other courses. He is also researching the pluralistic forms of Islam on the east African coast in the city of Mombasa in Kenya, where he lived in the 1980s and witnessed firsthand the multi-religious civic harmony that can be achieved in a dominantly Islamic region.

Suggestions for further reading

In this book

See also Chapters 8 (belief in a higher power), 9 (sacred books), 10 (miracles), and 70 (studying religion v. being religious).

Elsewhere

Berger, Peter. *The Sacred Canopy: Elements of a Sociological Theory of Religion*. New York: Anchor Books, 1967.

Freud, Sigmund. *The Future of An Illusion* (translated by James Strachey). New York: W. W. Norton, 1989 [1927].

Jung, Carl G. (editor). *Man and His Symbols*. New York: Dell, 1964.

Otto, Rudolph. *The Idea of the Holy: An Inquiry into the Non-Rational Factor in the Idea of the Divine and its Relation to the Rational* (translated by John W. Harvey). London: Oxford University Press, 1972 [1923].

Stark, Rodney and William Sims Bainbridge. *A Theory of Religion* (Toronto Studies in Religion, vol. 2; edited by Donald Wiebe). New Brunswick, NJ: Rutgers University Press, 1996.

Weber, Max. *The Sociology of Religion*. Boston, MA: Beacon Press, 1993 [1922].

72
Should the study of religions be mandatory in US schools?

Julie Ingersoll

More than half a century after the US Supreme Court removed school-sponsored prayer and devotional Bible reading from public schools, conflict over what place religion may or may not have in public education persists. Some religiously minded citizens fight to teach creationism, 'Christian' American history, the Bible, and more. Many secularists, seeking to preserve the secular character of public institutions, reject the idea that these topics are appropriate to a public school curriculum. The result of this secularist position, though, is that people in the US suffer from a dangerous religious illiteracy.

Americans often do not know that the version of 'creationism' taken for granted as the only possible reading of Genesis dates only to the middle of the twentieth century. They have no critical skills to see how popular understandings of what the Bible says (on issues like race, slavery, gender and more) have changed over time. They can easily be manipulated into thinking that the version of Islam espoused by Al-Qaeda or the so-called Islamic State is representative of Islam as a whole, or even that it is a more pure version of Islam than that held by their Muslim neighbors, when they know nothing of Islam.

There is a third alternative to the dichotomy between promoting religion in public schools and ignoring it altogether. That alternative is the academic study of religion, the goal being to teach about religion as an important aspect of culture drawing on the methods of history, literature, sociology, anthropology and various other academic disciplines.

Many people think that the separation of church and state in the US precludes education about religion in public schools but this is not the case. Indeed, scholars of religion claim that the academic study of religion may be the one discipline that the US Supreme Court has recognized as essential to a proper education. In the 1963 decision, *Abington School District v. Shempp*, in which the court ruled that devotional Bible reading in public schools was a violation of the Establishment Clause of the First Amendment, the court also asserted that one cannot be an educated person without a proper understand of the world's religions and the ways in which they have functioned throughout history. The court recognized the teaching of the bible as literature and an important historical/cultural artifact as not only appropriate but necessary.

This approach, however, does have its challenges. For the most part, primary and secondary level public school teachers often do not have the necessary background to teach about religion well. They may know one version of one religious tradition from their background, upbringing and even their personal commitments but they are unlikely to have wide-ranging knowledge of a variety of traditions and sophisticated comparative skills. The temptation to extrapolate from what we know, to assume that 'all religions' are really the same, is powerful. Moreover, it's too easy for us to think we are being religiously neutral when in fact we are not. Even among scholars of religion who understand our work as being 'about religion' rather than being 'religious' we often critique each other for subtle biases, but that's the nature of striving for objectivity.

Yet the advantages of tackling the difficulties are strong. Basic global literacy requires that students understand the religious traditions that shape how people organize their social worlds and how they construct a functional sense of reality. But, more than acquiring facility with content about religions (as valuable as that is), the study of religions also helps students learn to set aside their own ways of seeing the world, to understand the assumptions, frameworks, and structures, that organize someone else's world.

So yes, the study of religions should be a part of a sound public school curriculum.

About the author

Julie Ingersoll is professor of religious studies and Religious Studies Program Director at the University of North Florida. Her PhD is from the University of California, Santa Barbara and teaches and writes about religion in American history and culture, religion and politics and religion and violence.

Suggestions for further reading

In this book

See also Chapters 68 (legality of religion in public schools) and 70 (studying religion v. being religious).

Elsewhere

Braun, Willi and Russell T. McCutcheon. *Guide to the Study of Religion.* London: Cassell, 2000.

Prothero, Stephen. *Religious Literacy: What Every American Needs to Know—And Doesn't.* New York: HarperOne, 2008.

Smith, Jonathan Z. *Imagining Religion: From Babylon to Jonestown.* Chicago, IL: University of Chicago Press, 1982.

73
How do you study the religions of cultures that no longer exist?

Vaia Touna

By now it should be evident that to use the category 'religion' to talk about the ancient world, or of cultures that no longer exist comes with certain difficulties, especially because this term cannot be found in the vocabulary of many of these cultures (see the works by Barton and Boyarin and by Jonathan Z. Smith in the suggested reading list at end of this chapter). So, let's leave religion aside for a moment and let's see how we study cultures that no longer exist. My own field of expertise is ancient Greece so I will use that as an example, although, scholars studying other ancient cultures use pretty much the same methods.

The difficulty of studying cultures that no longer exist is that scholars cannot do fieldwork in the sense of visiting those cultures, that is, they can't time travel and talk to the people of that time period, and have a firsthand understanding of their cultures. Instead, scholars have to rely on and study what is often referred to as primary sources, that is, material artifacts found in archaeological sites (such as statues, buildings, burial sites, epigraphs, inscriptions found on stelae, etc.) and of course, when possible, study ancient texts which requires learning and becoming proficient in the language of the culture under study. Furthermore, such scholars also study what is often referred to as secondary literature, that is, commentaries and interpretations written about that ancient culture and its various aspects by subsequent archaeologists, historians, anthropologists, religious studies scholars, etc.—all of which is necessary in order to begin to understand that remote world.

Although, we have an abundance of material artifacts, for example, from ancient Greece, scholars understand that our knowledge of the ancient Greek past is still very fragmented because a lot has being lost and therefore we should always be self-aware and mindful of the historical gaps we are encountering, and how we, as interpreters of that past, fill those gaps *with our own narratives*. To give an example: when we talk about ancient Greece it is more than likely that we are actually referring just to ancient Athens because most of the material artifacts we have come from that one city—this is something that modern tourists who annually visit the city know only too well—and also many of the texts we possess come from them as well; residents of the other still well-known ancient city, Sparta, on the other hand, didn't leave any textual material, so what we know of them comes, most of the time, from Athenian authors, who had their own political interests to depict Spartans the way they did (the cities, along with each of their supporters, famously went to war with one another from 431–404 BCE, after all), something of which scholars should be aware when making claims about what life in Sparta was like.

Now, when it comes to study the 'religion' of a culture that no longer exists, as we have seen in previous entries of this volume, 'religion' as a category people use to name aspects, or items, in their worlds, is not universal; therefore, people in other parts of the world (removed from us both in space *and* time) organized and named their worlds differently. So now our question gets a little more complicated; how can we study the religion of a culture whose members don't even have the idea of religion itself? There can be different approaches to this puzzle. For example, there are plenty of scholars who see religion as something that is manifested in the ancient Greek gods, heroes, the various cults, and rituals (such as bloody and bloodless sacrifices and offerings to the gods and demi-gods) and statues, inscriptions, or texts concerning these topics therefore become their primary sources. Yet, there are other scholars who are more suspicious of so easily project-ing backwards in time this very modern category 'religion,' and, instead, they turn their attention to comparing ancient Greek texts (primary sources) and the way those texts have been trans-lated and interpreted (secondary literature) by modern scholars. Engaging in this kind of comparison one can easily find that what determines what counts as religion in the ancient world is not that this category can self-evidently be found in those ancient texts, or that it is part of a natural classificatory system by which ancient people organized their worlds. To give you another brief example, gods and the practices that were related to them seem not to have consisted of a distinct sphere that was separate from, say politics, at least as we understand it today; instead, this distinction is often-times the result of modern interpretation and translations of the artifacts that remain, that insert into the ancient world our under-standing of religion as if it corresponds to ancient Greek words like, for example, *eusebia* or *threskeia*. Yet, taking a closer look, one sees that these words had little to do with our modern understand-ing of religion (that is, of private faith and inner feelings), but, instead, some scholars now suggest that those words had more do with naming proper social behaviors and relationships. So, again: one should be very careful and self-aware when projecting anachronistically modern words and modern assumptions onto cultures that no longer exist.

To conclude, the theories and methods that we use to study distant cultures, both in time (i.e., those cultures that no longer exist) and in space (i.e., those today that are different from our own), and the various categories that we use to understand those ancient groups (such as religion, ritual, sacred, even polytheism and monotheism) are relatively modern and thus specific to the scholar who is doing the study. This means that the scholar must always be self-reflexive, and self-aware that the criteria and the categories used to name, identify, classify and organize items in the past do not necessarily correspond to the culture that she or he happens to study—an unresolved gap may in fact persist. If so, then, we may now see that we don't necessarily study things 'religious' (thereby assuming that there is some essential element in the things that we can then naturally identify in that remote world, and then study); instead, our object of study now may not even be located in the past but, rather, we may find ourselves studying modern scholarly discourses that assume (and for what purpose?—now that's the question to ask!) that religion is a natural identifier in those cultures that are so far removed from our own.

About the author

Vaia Touna is assistant professor at the Department of Religious Studies at the University of Alabama, USA. Her scholarly interests range widely, from looking at specific concepts of religion in the Greco-Roman world to methodological issues concerning the study of religion in general.

Suggestions for further reading

In this book

See also Chapters 75 (interdisciplinarity) and 76 (contributions of the study of religion).

Elsewhere

Barton, Carlin A. and Daniel Boyarin. *Imagine No Religion: How Modern Abstractions Hide Ancient Realities*. New York: Fordham University Press, 2016.

Johnston, Sarah Iles, ed. *Religions of the Ancient World: A Guide*. Cambridge, MA: Belknap Press, 2004.

Konaris, Michaeil D. *The Greek Gods in Modern Scholarship: Interpretation and Belief in Nineteenth and Early Twentieth Century Germany and Britain*. Oxford: Oxford University Press, 2016.

Smith, Jonathan Z. *Relating Religion: Essays in the Study of Religion*. Chicago, IL: University of Chicago Press, 2004.

Touna, Vaia. *Fabrications of the Greek Past: Religion, Tradition, and Modern Identities*, Leiden: Brill, 2017.

74
What is the cognitive science of religion?

Robyn Faith Walsh

The cognitive science of religion (CSR) is a subfield that considers the role the physical sciences can play in the academic study of religion. Utilizing data from the cognitive and neurosciences, computer science, psychology, philosophy and linguistics, scholars who engage in this research study the mind/brain as a product of the physical world and evolution. Such research takes the position that human thought and behaviors are fully embodied, natural states, and they should be studied as such.

The CSR stands in contrast to more traditional ways scholars sometimes describe religion, using terms like spirit/the spiritual, belief, experience, or transcendence. The scholarly objection to these concepts is that they reduce human consciousness and behaviors to subjective descriptions of reality that are not testable or observable. Such perspectives privilege human beings and human minds as somehow able to process reality outside of the laws of nature. This perspective is also sometimes called 'mind/body dualism,' which refers to the idea that human beings are a mind/soul that inhabits a physical and mortal body. Proponents of CSR advocate for an 'embodied' approach that brings cutting edge research in the sciences—on questions like the nature of consciousness and the meaning of personhood—to the scholarly study of religion. In so doing, their goal is to better understand and describe religious phenomena, like why people are willing to accept that supernatural agents like gods exist without direct, physical evidence.

Critics of the CSR approach note that much of this science is still in its infancy (e.g., neuroscientific studies on the nature of consciousness) and to integrate this complicated and, at times, inconclusive research into a field like religion is irresponsible. Critics also site that religious studies scholars lack expertise in the sciences, which might incline them to cherry-pick studies that simply support their pre-determined hypotheses. Others critics maintain that, regardless of what the cognitive sciences tell us, all human behavior and understandings are ultimately social, so we should focus on how discourses and practices (like the development and use of language) shape our understandings, not on the inner-workings of the brain itself.

About the author

Robyn Faith Walsh is assistant professor of New Testament and early Christianity at the University of Miami (Florida). Her research interests include the letters of Paul, the history of the interpretation of the synoptic problem, and Greco-Roman archaeology.

Suggestions for further reading

In this book

See also Chapters 62 (origins of the study of religion) and 76 (contributions of the study of religion).

Elsewhere

Pyysiäinen, Ilkka, *How Religion Works: Towards a New Cognitive Science of Religion*. Leiden: Brill, 2003.

Slingerland, Edward, *What Science Offers the Humanities: Integrating Body and Culture*. New York: Cambridge University Press, 2008.

Tremlin, Todd, *Minds and Gods: The Cognitive Foundations of Religion*. New York: Oxford University Press, 2006.

75

Is the study of religion related to other academic disciplines?

Jennifer Eyl

One word suffices to answer this question: Yes. That is to say, the academic study of religion pertains to almost all fields of academic inquiry, because the practices and beliefs that many people today call 'religion' pertain to every aspect of human behavior. This is not to suggest that all human behaviors are religious all the time, of course (such a claim would bankrupt the very word of meaning), but rather, the things we call 'religion' and 'religious' are not separate from all other things that people do, say, or think. The study of religion tends to be associated with the disciplines of history, anthropology, and sociology, but these disciplines themselves are quite broad. Because the study of religion asks questions about power, social structure, and the constitution of subjectivity (as well as the constitution of social groups), there are few, if any, arenas of human practices beyond the scope of the topic.

The study of religion comes out of a nineteenth-century German school of thinking called *Religionsgeschichtliche Schule* ('history of religions school'). Early scholars of religion imagined that human intellectual and psychological development began in primitive stages prone to animism and polytheism, but grew and developed toward the ideal (or, fully developed) form of religion, namely, monotheism. This teleological notion of 'development' has been abandoned by scholars due to the self-congratulatory privileging of Christianity and European culture inherent in such a position. Likewise, many scholars have questioned the usefulness of the category 'religion' in the first place, as the category is imposed upon the practices of people who do not classify their own activities in the same way. Thus, the study of religion is simultaneously a study of how (mostly) Western scholars classify the practices of people around the world and in history, as well as the examination of the practices and beliefs themselves (usually pertaining to gods or other invisible beings). And such practices touch upon all aspects of life.

For example, religion and economics often overlap. When people donate money to churches or temples, when religious organizations manage money, or when the IRS gives religious organizations tax breaks, we see clearly how intertwined religion and economics can be. Discourses about morality and gods often overlap with ideas about money—especially with regard to who is entitled to money (or not), who has been shown divine favor (or disfavor) via wealth, etc. Religious ideology can even contribute to the justification for broad economic systems: at the present historical moment, for example, many Americans believe capitalism to somehow be divinely ordained.

Religion and technology are also intimately connected, such that technological innovations find their way into religious practices, as much as religious concerns motivate technological innovation. For example, some of the most important advancements in technology and communications of the early twentieth century were motivated by concerns about the afterlife. Alexander Graham Bell, the inventor of the telephone, was attempting a device so sensitive that the living could talk to the dead. Thomas Edison, inventor of the phonograph, believed it possible to develop an apparatus that could record voices of the dead, just as the phonograph captures voices of the living. A nineteenth-century religious movement called 'Spiritualism,' which included the dead tapping on walls to communicate to the living, gained ground right after the invention of the telegraph. Thus, the study of telecommunications and the study of religion are sometimes co-implicated.

I point to the above examples to demonstrate that even when one imagines the domain of 'religion' to be obvious and separate from other things, one discovers that what we call religion reflects the material conditions of living. Thus, it is common to find university courses and academic books about the anthropology of religion, or the history of Christianity, or sociological studies on various religious groups. The connection between the study of religion and other fields such as history, anthropology, and sociology, is explicitly imbedded in the university curriculum. Yet, the academic study of religion extends even further to fields such as political science, economics, philosophy, psychology, gender studies, critical race theory, art, dance, creative writing, and every field in which discourses and practices about gods, ethics, morality, or invisible powers take place.

This, of course, leads one to ask: if we can speak of religion and politics, religion and sports, religion and science, religion and economics, religion and gender, etc., then what, exactly, is religion? It is not the task of this chapter to answer such a question, but the question should provoke thought about how we construct categories and classify human practices and beliefs.

About the author
Jennifer Eyl is an assistant professor of religion at Tufts University. She works primarily on ancient Christianity.

Suggestions for further reading

In this book
See also Chapters 69 (texts v. fieldwork) and 76 (contributions of the study of religion).

Elsewhere
Martin, Craig. *A Critical Introduction to the Study of Religion.* New York: Routledge, 2012.

Masuzawa, Tomoko. *The Invention of World Religions, or, How European Universalism was Preserved in the Language of Pluralism*. Chicago, IL: University of Chicago Press, 2005.

McGarry, Molly. *Ghosts of Futures Past: Spiritualism and the Cultural Politics of Nineteenth-Century America*. Berkeley, CA: University of California Press, 2008.

Nongbri, Brent. *Before Religion: A History of a Modern Concept*. New Haven, CT: Yale University Press, 2015.

76

Why do we need the study of religion if we already have historians, anthropologists, sociologists, psychologists, and folklorists?

Paul-François Tremlett

I am going to suggest that we need the study of religion because it challenges the traditional organization of knowledge and expertise in the academy. Specifically, the study of religion promotes inter-disciplinarity, which despite being a bit of a mouthful is an accelerator for disruptive knowledge, or knowledge that transforms the way we experience and understand the world around us.

When not in their offices or teaching, historians are known for their predilection for archives. Their chosen site of research is typically an airless, artificially illuminated, basement. Until time travel is invented, these solitary creatures are destined to spend long hours amidst faded documents and photographs. Anthropologists by contrast, like to put their feet up and watch television. Abroad. Apparently, there is no better way to understand a culture than to listen in on the ways people discuss their favorite television programs. Sociologists and psychologists sit in the middle of the continuum somewhere between misanthropic historiographers and gregarious anthropologists: they like people but only just enough to make them fill out questionnaires and set them tests. While folklorists … well, who knows what *they* do?

When they return to their departmental offices, colleagues and students, these scholars return to environments where everybody broadly shares the same vocabulary in terms of the methods they use to do their research. The only difference is their topic. And that's pretty much the key to understanding how the academy has traditionally been organized. Historians work in history departments, anthropologists in anthropology departments, sociologists and psychologists in sociology and psychology departments. This means that there might be only one historian specializing in religion in a history department among colleagues specializing in a range of other subject areas that could include anything from public health, to policing or sport. And the same goes for all the other departments. As a sarcastic British wit once put it, 'the winter nights must fly by.' That's why we have the study of religion. A study of religion department groups scholars together on the basis of their research interests rather than their research methods. Which doesn't necessarily guarantee good conversation but it does engender something called 'inter-disciplinarity.' And it is also a clue as to why the study of religion idea is such a good one.

Sometimes when we talk about history, anthropology, sociology and psychology we talk about 'disciplines.' We refer to them in this way because each of these subjects—or disciplines—coalesced in distinct ways around specific scholars, texts, theories and most importantly, methods. It's the methods that are 'disciplinary.' For example in Britain, anthropology developed from the works of E. B. Tylor and Bronislaw Malinowski, initially favoring a library-based, taxonomic approach to religions and cultures before embracing ethnography as its distinctive method. Importantly, this did not merely change how anthropologists conducted research. It also meant a conceptual shift in the way religions and cultures were understood. The key point about methods, then, is that they are akin to spectacles. Once you put them on you start to see things in a certain way. The other disciplines—including history, sociology and psychology—also have their spectacles, ways of seeing or perspectives. And so, when we speak of inter-disciplinarity we mean mixing different lenses in our spectacles. Which could mean double vision but what it should mean is developing new, complex perspectives rather than blurring them. The study of religion model encourages methodological syncretism and is arguably a laboratory for original thinking and problem-solving. In a study of religion department historians, anthropologists, sociologists and psychologists develop curricula and research plans that reflect this inter-disciplinary environment, encouraging their students and wider publics to see religion from multiple perspectives. Which brings me to folklore: the fact is that the folklorists have always been outliers. Their analyses of folk tales and folk beliefs and practices combine methods culled from literary analysis and anthropology. When the anthropologist Claude Lévi-Strauss put these together with linguistics back in the 1940s, the chemical reaction was so strong it created a completely new school of thought that became known as 'Structuralism.' Structuralism influenced not only anthropology, folklore and linguistics but also literature, painting and music. That's inter-disciplinarity. And it lies at the heart of the study of religion.

About the author

Paul-François Tremlett is a senior lecturer in religious studies at the Open University in the UK. He got his PhD from the School of Oriental and African Studies in London. He is currently interested in processes of rapid social change and intersections of politics and religion.

Suggestions for further reading

In this book

See also Chapters 62 (origins of the study of religion) and 75 (inter-disciplinarity)

Elsewhere

Bielo, James, S. *Anthropology of Religion: The Basics*. Abingdon: Routledge, 2015.

Nongbri, Brent. *Before Religion: A History of a Modern Concept*. New Haven, CT: Yale University Press, 2013.

Tylor, Edward B. *Primitive Culture*. London: John Murray, 4th ed. 1903 [1871].

77

Can't I just learn about religion in my church, mosque, or temple?

Brent A. Smith

The short answer is yes, but a longer answer is needed. As a practitioner you are 'inside' of a particular understanding of what
religion is and involves. Along with fellow 'insiders' you are studying religions you are 'outside of' and looking at the activities and
meanings of others through the 'lens' of your own tradition. This is
a theological way to study religion but it is only one way. Another
way is through the field of religious studies, the academic study of
religion that looks at human being, being religious using 'glasses'
not worn by insiders residing in a particular religious tradition.

An analogy can illustrate the difference. Let's say you want
to learn to play a game other than 'your' game, basketball, and
someone suggests soccer, a game you've never heard of. You visit
my university's soccer coach and she says the game, like basketball,
is played with a ball, involves dribbling and passing, and players
score by putting the ball in a goal. She shows you a strange-looking
ball, says dribbling and passing must be only with the feet, and
the goal is on the ground with little scoring! You realize you are
being taught a game completely different from 'your game,' and
suspect you cannot understand soccer through your knowledge
of basketball and what you first thought were comparable similarities. Later on you learn the game the US calls soccer is called

football (or futbol) in other countries, and if you ask directions to the university's football field you will end up in a much different location! You are learning about a new and particular game, and that other pursuits might also be games though they involve different activities, equipment, terminologies, aims, etc. If you maintain your insider status as a basketball player learning soccer/football, not only will you not learn soccer but you can become even more confused when another friend asks you to learn 'the game of golf' and you're given a small, hard ball, can find no netted goals and no game clock, and are handed long sticks! Something similar could be said about studying the religions of others from inside of your own.

In religious studies we create concepts to evaluate how various activities function religiously through an understanding formed by our concepts. It's like creating concepts to study the human activity of 'game playing' to understand better how playing soccer, basketball, and golf function for insiders playing each game. Part of the discipline of the academic study of religion is to realize we create and critique these concepts, that they are related to our personal experience and history, and that we will bring them to human activity in various traditions, cultures, and locales that are different from one another and our own experience. For example, a foundational concept is the sacred/profane distinction. Activities that function religiously mark off sacred space and time from profane or ordinary space and time. Eating a Jewish Passover Seder meal at a synagogue and grabbing lunch today at a fast food place both involve consuming food but carry different understandings of time and place, and the significance of actions taking place there and then. The sacred/profane distinction helps us understand that difference, and what experiencing the Seder meal means to a Jew, a very different meaning than communion to the Christian insider though both involve eating. We apply concepts created in our field to describe and analyze insider activity as functioning religiously to the insider; like, asking what coordination means to the basketball player on the hardcourt and the swimmer in the pool will use the same concept involved in different activities and experiences.

We use other academic disciplines—most specifically philosophy, anthropology, psychology, sociology, and today even neurology and film studies!—and integrate their thoughts and findings into our methods of study. Our approach is not 'objective.' Anyone studying someone else's religion does so from inside of some place of meaning and method, be it a church, mosque, synagogue or a religious studies department down the hall from the other university departments. So, while you can study other religions from inside your own building, community, and tradition, you can also study from inside of religious studies and use the concepts of the academic study of religion to describe and analyze how activities function religiously for insiders residing within various traditions (and actually, other cultural phenomena and activities as well).

About the author
Dr. Brent A. Smith is assistant professor in the Religious Studies Program at Grand Valley State University, a 25,000 student public university in Grand Rapids, Michigan, USA. He received his Masters from the Divinity School of the University of Chicago in 1983, his Doctorate from Meadville Theological School in 1984, and served Unitarian Universalist Churches for 26 years before coming to GVSU in 2010.

Suggestions for further reading

In this book
See also Chapters 71 (existence of God), 73 (ancient religion), and 75 (interdisciplinarity).

Elsewhere
Aden, Ross. *Religion Today: A Critical Thinking Approach to Religious Studies*. Lanham, MD: Rowman & Littlefield, 2013.

Kessler, Gary E. *Studying Religion: An Introduction through Cases*. New York: McGraw-Hill, 2003.

McCutcheon, Russell T. *Studying Religion: An Introduction*. Sheffield: Equinox, 2007.

Rodrigues, Hillary and John S. Harding. *Introduction to the Study of Religion*. Abingdon: Routledge, 2009.

78

Can one study one's own religion objectively?

Rebekka King

Once I went to the doctor complaining about severe headaches. Having performed a perfunctory internet search, I was convinced I had a brain tumor. The doctor began a routine examination and asked me questions about my health and lifestyle. It was soon revealed that the actual cause of my headaches was caffeine withdrawal and the diagnosis was take Advil, drink some coffee, and start to cut back gradually. Despite the fact that I was the one experiencing the pain, she was the one who was capable of identifying its root cause. Clearly, my doctor had specialized training, experience, and knowledge which I lacked. The same is true for the academic study of religion. Like medicine, there are specific norms and values that are associated with the methods of investigation we make use of and the way that we think about our own relationship to our subject of study.

As with most of the entries in this book the answer to the question, 'Can one objectively study their own religion,' is 'yes,' 'no,' 'maybe,' and 'it's complicated.' In the academic study of religion, this question is sometimes known as the insider/outsider debate. Some people think that only an adherent of a particular religion is capable of truly understanding what it is like to be part of that tradition. For example, if you haven't spent hours in Hebrew school preparing for your bar or bat mitzvah can you really understand what it is like to grow up Jewish? In contrast, others argue that someone who grew up in a tradition might have a difficult time looking past their own experiences and be too narrow in their analysis. A Southern Baptist might misunderstand the significance of the Eucharist to a Roman Catholic.

When done poorly, the insider's approach to the study of religion amounts to either polemical attacks against a belief or practice or it becomes a defense or celebration of a religion. Both approaches move us into the realm of theology or apologetics. The task of the academic study of religion is not to prove whether not a given doctrine or practice is right or wrong, but rather to understand how it works within a specific social context. In other words, there is a difference being a scholar of religion and being a practitioner of religion. But the distinction is not as clear cut as you might imagine. At issue is not so much whether or not someone is a religious believer or adherent, but rather the approach they take to studying religion. One can engage in 'insider discourse' without believing in the tenets or practicing the rituals of a particular faith. For example, someone like Richard Dawkins could be considered an 'insider' to Christianity, despite the fact that he is an avowed atheist. This is because his books engage with Christianity at the level of theological discourse. He takes the actions and beliefs of Christianity at face value and critiques them in such a way that advocates his own, anti-religious stance and works to uncover why he believes religion is wrong.

In both cases—polemics and apologetics—involve taking a stance on the teachings or the truth claims within a religious tradition. Our understanding of who counts as an insider is broad: current affiliates, former members, and everyone who engages in the conversation at the level of truth claims. You may have heard the question of insiders versus outsiders compared to other fields or objects of study: Must one be a woman to study women's studies, Latin American to study Latin American studies, or more bizarrely, must one be a bird to study ornithology, or a tree to study forestry? Perhaps we should ask the trees before we answer too confidently.

The question of objectivity goes both ways and is as much a question of *should* as it is of *can*. The insider *can* aim to adopt an objective or outsider's viewpoint—one that does not assume any kind of religious commitment and instead attends to the norms of the discipline and empirical analysis, but *should* she? In my opening analogy the doctor's objective analysis of my lifestyle led to an appropriate diagnosis. It would have been more difficult were she diagnosing herself or a close family member. This practice is discouraged by medical ethicists. Not all doctors are great doctors, in fact, misdiagnoses happen all the time. And some people probably aren't cut out for medicine. So it goes for the study of religion.

About the author

Rebekka King is an assistant professor of religion in the Department of Philosophy and Religious Studies at Middle Tennessee State University. Her specialties include North American religions, cultural anthropology, sociology of religion, and religion and diversity in the public sphere.

Suggestions for further reading

In this book

See also Chapters 64 (importance of religious studies), 65 (religious studies v. theology), and 70 (studying religion v. being religious).

Elsewhere

Fitzgerald, Timothy. *The Ideology of Religious Studies*. New York: Oxford University Press, 2000.

McCutcheon, Russell. *Critics Not Caretakers: Redescribing the Public Study of Religion*. Albany, NY: State University of New York Press, 2001.

Spickard, James, J. Shawn Landres, and Meredith B. McGuire. *Personal Knowledge and Beyond: Reshaping the Ethnography of Religion*. New York: New York University Press, 2002.

79

What is this CE and BCE dating system that I've seen used throughout this book?

Aaron W. Hughes

Any of the above entries that mention a date tend to employ the BCE and CE designation. The former term means 'before the Common Era' and the latter means 'Common Era'. The terms perfectly correspond to, for some, the more traditional dating of BC ('before Christ') and AD (*anno domini*, literally 'in the year of our Lord', sometimes also thought to be 'after death'). 40 BCE, for example, corresponds to 40 BC, and 592 CE corresponds to 592 AD. It is worth noting that according to the BCE/CE dating, like the BC/AD one, there is no year zero. The year 1 CE immediately follows 1 BCE. It is not at all clear, however, that Jesus was born in 1 CE. It might be worth noting that BC/AD, which BCE/CE essentially replicates, was not introduced until 525 AD/CE, when Dionysius Exiguus began to count the date from the death of Jesus.

There are, of course, problems with this schema. Most immediately, none living in the BCE period would have considered themselves to have been living in a period before the 'common era' because they would have had no idea what the common era was. In like manner, no one who lived in the BC period would have known that they were living 'before Christ', just as no Buddhist or Hindu individual would imagine themselves as living 'in the year of our Lord.' This is the main reason that most scholars no longer employ BC and AD, but instead prefer to use BCE and CE.

Some readers might think that replacing the BC and AD designations with the BCE and CE ones is based on political correctness since both, after all, correspond to the same date. This brings up a more interesting question about religion and dating, however. All religions have their own calendars because they all date their social worlds in ways that are considered meaningful to them. These dates are often grounded in often mythic events in the distant past that are deemed significant. The year 2017, for example, corresponds to the year 5777 in the Hebrew calendar. The assumption here is that, according to traditional Judaism, the world is 5777 years old (though there are rabbinic stories that suggest this dating ought not to be taken as literal). 2017 and 5777, in turn, correspond the year in 1438 the Muslim calendar. According to the Muslim tradition, Muhammad led his followers out of Mecca and into Medina 1438 years ago. In like manner we can say that the Second Temple of the ancient Israelites was destroyed in 70 CE, but to a traditional Jew that means very little since he or she would know that they temple was destroyed on the 9th of Av (i.e., the ninth day of the month of Av), which is a holy day in Judaism, a day on which traditional Jews fast.

Despite this, and perhaps for obvious reasons, secular scholars of religion insist on measuring the calendars of other religions using the BCE/CE designation, one that is intimately tied to western and largely Christian history. Rarely do we take a course or read a book, for example, in which the professor or scholar uses non-Western dates. This would only introduce confusions, and it also means that we measure other peoples' histories using our own calendar. Despite the claim, then, on the part of the academic study of religion to be neutral or objective, the very dating that it uses to measure other cultures and their religions is based on a western model, one that—despite the switch from BC to BCE and AD to CE—is unique to the religious history of the West.

About the author

Aaron W. Hughes is the Philip S. Bernstein Chair in the Department of Religion and Classics at the University of Rochester.

Suggestions for further reading

In this book

See also Chapter 3 (classifying religion).

Elsewhere

Dubuisson, Daniel. *The Western Construction of Religion: Myths, Knowledge, and Ideology* (translated by William Sayers). Baltimore, MD: Johns Hopkins University Press, 2008.

The future

80
What is the future of 'religion'?

Russell T. McCutcheon

Although we know that readers will not necessarily work through this book's chapters in sequential order, we nonetheless thought that it ought to end in some way, such as by addressing a 'where to from here' question. So, invoking our editorial right, we opted to each tackle one last question, with an eye not simply on religion (as addressed in the next and final answer), but, as made evident in some of the previous answers, also our tendency to think that certain things in the world ought to be called religious.

So, just what *is* the future of this term that so many of us use so easily when we talk about our world? (Warning: answering this might take just a little more than five minutes to read.)

At the time of writing this, there's a bit of political turmoil in the air here in the US, where I live and work—something on which, despite their many differences, so-called liberals and conservatives would likely agree (if those old distinctions still matter). But their agreement may end there, since the source of this turmoil for the former is the view that the recently inaugurated president may be illegitimate, yet for the latter, there's the opinion that protestors across the country are 'sore losers' who fail to respect the office. Among the things that are fascinating about this moment of unrest, at least for a scholar of religion, was President Trump's address to the National Prayer Breakfast on February 2, 2017, at which he said the following:

It was the great Thomas Jefferson who said, the God who gave us life, gave us liberty. Jefferson asked, can the liberties of a nation be secure when we have removed a conviction that these liberties are the gift of God. Among those freedoms is the right to worship according to our own beliefs. That is why I will get rid of and totally destroy the Johnson Amendment and allow our representatives of faith to speak freely and without fear of retribution. I will do that, remember.

Freedom of religion is a sacred right, but it is also a right under threat all around us, and the world is under serious, serious threat in so many different ways. And I've never seen it so much and so openly as since I took the position of president.

The world is in trouble, but we're going to straighten it out. OK? That's what I do. I fix things. We're going to straighten it out.[1]

At least two things are worth looking at in this quote, if we keep in mind this notion of social unrest (apart from the strategic use of an authoritative figure to ground and thereby authorize the claims). First, the Johnson Amendment that he wishes to repeal (i.e., 'totally destroy') was proposed and then adopted as part of the US tax code in 1954, and was named after its original sponsor (who later became president of the United States); it specified that non-profits—what are commonly called a 501(c)(3), in reference to the part of the tax code that applies to them—cannot engage in political campaigning. Inasmuch as members of churches, temples, mosques, etc., have status as a non-profit organization in the US (with certain tax benefits then coming their way, such as exemptions from paying federal income tax or an exemption for religious leaders from paying federal and often state tax on whatever they pay toward the cost of their home [or homes]), the amendment, which is still in effect today, mandates that they must not engage in campaigning (such as from the pulpit, as part of a sermon)—one of the bricks in the US's so-called 'wall of separation

---

1 Retrieved on February 4, 2017 from http://time.com/4658012/donald-trump-national-prayer-breakfast-transcript.

between Church and State' (quoting Jefferson, once again, this time from a letter of his, from January 1, 1802—a phrase that has been repeated so many times since then that many think it is written into the Constitution).

Although it might seem to be a minor example (though the president's focus on it so early in his term suggests otherwise), it's indicative of the practical effect, in a liberal democracy such as our own, of something being classified *as* religion; in fact, it's an example that (once again, with the notion of social unrest in mind) presses us in the direction of entertaining that, contrary to how we often see it, the term might better be understood as a management device, as a way of classifying just some actions, claims, institutions, etc., the consequence of which is to sort and rank those actions, claims, and institutions: this is allowable, but just here and not there, and when done by you but not them. If seen in this way, who should obtain the benefits associated with the designation then becomes a point of debate—think of the (at times heated) discussions, also taking place as this piece is written, over whether, for instance, Islam is a religion or instead what some term a political ideology (and thus not deserving of the benefits received by being ranked among the religions of the world). Or what about those seemingly nationalist, Sinhalese Buddhist monks in Sri Lanka who have been reported in the news, for the past few years, stirring up trouble, engaging in violence—that can't be religion, can it? What about those within Judaism who claim that the name identifies an ethnic or kin group and not a religion? In fact, it's not difficult to find Christians who retreat from the designation, inasmuch as—or so they would argue—it's not nearly a big enough or deep enough term to name what they claim to have.

But to return to the Johnson Amendment: does it actually bring benefits to religions—if it did then why destroy it? After all, freedom of speech is a much-heralded right in this country, and the amendment (which applies far more broadly than just churches, of course) certainly seems to curtail that—but in exchange for certain perks. But is the trade-off worthwhile? Does it place what would be called in law 'an undue burden' on religious people (as the current administration, and its supporters, likely would argue), inasmuch as it curtails their political speech when in a religious setting? What's more, just what is the difference between these two modes of speech that the amendment, and many of us, seems to take for granted? Simply put, why do we even seek to categorize Sri Lanka Buddhists as either religious or political?

Might calling something religious be itself a political act—as already suggested, a tactical way of managing people?

Trying to answer such questions leads to the second item in President Trump's prayer breakfast comments that stands out to us: this notion of religious freedom. What happens if the federal government, let's just say for the sake of argument, sanctions same-sex marriage (as recently happened in the US, in fact) and you (again, just for argument's sake), claim that such unions are sinful, inasmuch as a your community understands some passages in what you hold to be your divinely inspired scripture to forbid homosexual relationships. Has the government just legislated morality? As we see happening in the US, might the longstanding notion of religious freedom (guaranteed in the constitutional documents of many liberal democracies, and not just in the US in its Bill of Rights's First Amendment) be a way to counter what, on such occasions, some see as the federal government's overreach, thereby creating a safe space not unlike that which was made by means of the above-described tax exemptions? For claiming such protections, by seeing religious people as being persecuted by so-called secular powers, and thereby prevented from freely exercising their religion (the other famous part of the First Amendment) could have the effect of carving out a space in which expressing such beliefs, and thereby acting contrary to what has become settled law, is actually protected from being judged unlawful, discriminatory behavior (as some others will undoubtedly claim it to be).

So refusing service to someone, for instance, might come to be understood as tolerable, even protected by law, if it can be claimed to have been done for this as opposed to that reason. If your organization can be described *as* religious, or your motivations and goals designated *as* religious, then you may have freedoms others do not—for then refusing service might be classed as discrimination and prosecuted.

There are all sorts of other examples we could use. To select one from the other end of the spectrum, does one's 'sincerely held religious beliefs' (for this is the way it is often phrased on law and political discourse) enable one to, say, withhold that portion of ones taxes that might go toward funding the nation's military? Yet the point remains the same: in starting to offer an answer to this chapter's question we should perhaps pay attention to the practical effects of that term, religion, as it is used in the consequential modern discourse we call law.

So, keeping our eye on the word itself, and how legal and political frameworks handle something so designated, our question concerns the future utility of using this term, applied in one of the many ways in which it may or may not be defined, to name and thereby manage people and their doings (for naming, and thereby grouping like and unlike things, is a form of management, no?). For, looking back, it has been a crucial device that nation-states across the globe have used to identify groups motivated by what are presumed to be internal states and private dispositions (variously known as belief, faith, experience, deep feeling, etc.)—non-empirical dispositions that are commonly distinguished from observable actions and modes of organization (thus our common opposition of religion and politics, premised on the distinction between private faith and public action). Such distinctions—which amount to a conceptual fence that, once in place, allows us, as noted above, to separate and sort people and their goals—have proved extremely useful to help manage the many (sometimes conflicting) subgroups within the nation (recall the possibly inevitable amount of unrest that we find within any group); for we are not homogeneous populations (as that recent US election has made painfully evident to some), with completely overlapping interests and shared aspirations. But if some of those competing interests and possibly contradictory aspirations can be removed from public sphere—and cordoned off somehow—then perhaps a certain sort of town square, and thus public discourse, can be created …

All of this, to be sure, is premised on the durability of the conceptual and social fences that we use. But it's not difficult to imagine that fencing falling apart—all fences, whether on the unruly frontier or in a quite suburb, need maintenance and mending from time to time, so their future is really in our hands. So, depending on their state of repair claims and actions that were once allowed only in certain venues on specific occasions could become part of routine, day-to-day life (perhaps like what some once thought of limited to 'locker room talk' making its way into public discourse in a political campaign?). Case in point: might the 1963 US Supreme Court case known as *Abington v. Schempp* be overturned, thereby paving the way toward once again finding bible readings and prayers starting each day in public schools? If so, then these routines might no longer strike us as religious inasmuch as they're just what we routinely do on a Monday morning at 8:30. For over fifty years these once regular actions have been unconstitutional, and thus illegal in the US (inasmuch as they were seen to contravene the First Amendment's Establishment Clause), but only as a result of the Court's decision and, since then, government's will to prosecute infractions brought to its attention. Sure, students were still free to assemble, privately, around the school's flag pole, for instance, to say prayers prior to the start of the school day, or, inasmuch as they were members of a sanctioned student club, they've always been able to use the school's rooms after hours for such things as bible study groups; the state, which includes its various policing apparatuses, was able to understand those actions as allowable inasmuch as they were seen as distinct from the school's leadership (i.e., a public school's principals and teachers, all of whom are paid by a diverse collection of citizens, aka: taxpayers) acting in ways that seemed to 'respect the establishment of religion' (as the First Amendment phrases it), such as by leading prayers indicative of specific religions or reading from a certain edition of the bible (yes, different groups use different bibles). But what happens if the bible reading is complemented, from time to time (how often would this be required?) by a reading from a Hindu or a Sikh text? And what if 'respecting the establishment of religion' is interpreted by the courts to mean the need to be nondenominational and thus inclusive (as opposed to utterly neutral on the matter of religion in general)? What happens to this longstanding brick in that wall of separation?

While I'm not suggesting that some dystopic future is in the offing if these demarcation devices are revised—readers interested in that scenario are recommended to try Margaret Atwood's 1985 novel, *The Handmaid's Tale*—I am arguing that the future of using religion, and all that comes with it, to name parts of our social worlds is intimately linked to the sorts of social worlds that we wish to inhabit. Simple as that. There was a day, just a few generations ago, when many scholars agreed that human beings would inevitably overcome the need to be religious; it was called the secularization thesis. Perhaps they'd find a better way to vent anxiety (we here think of Sigmund Freud's theory of religion) or maybe they'd finally establish a classless and thereby just society, with no alienation and conflict (Karl Marx's thoughts on religion's function comes to mind)—but, one way or the other, religion would surely decline. But that, of course, didn't happen (the role of Islam in the Iranian Revolution of 1979 is often cited as the first of many counterexamples to the once popular secularization thesis). But I'm not so bold as to predict that religion—or, better put, our interest to call things religious and thereby separate them from other things we say and do, naming them as political or secular—is on the way out or, instead, on the brink of thriving all the more. Rather, I simply wish to bring to a reader's attention that this question is for *them* to answer, knowing that *they* are inhabits of worlds that, for some time now, use this term, religion, to do practical work in the most mundane of situations. It is therefore *their* term, to be defined as *they* see fit, in contrast to how others might define and use it—all of whom are trying to affect the world in who knows what ways.

About the author

Russell T. McCutcheon is professor and chair of the Department of Religious Studies at the University of Alabama; his work is on the theories of religion, approaches to the study of myth, as well as focusing on the history of the study of religion and the practical effects of classification systems.

Suggestions for further reading

In this book

See also Chapter 81 (future of religion).

Elsewhere

Arnal, William E. and Russell T. McCutcheon. *The Sacred is the Profane: The Political Nature of 'Religion.'* New York: Oxford University Press, 2013.

Atwood, Margaret. *The Handmaid's Tale*. Toronto: McClelland & Stewart, 1985.

81
What is the future of religion?

Aaron W. Hughes

Scholars are not always the greatest prognosticators. With that caveat in mind, however, it is important to distinguish at least three different subquestions lurking in the shadows of the present question. The first, perhaps the most obvious, is what will religion look like in the future and what will happen to it? This subquestion is probably the most difficult to answer. The second is how will religion be classified and by whom? And the third is what does the future hold for those of us who have devoted our lives to the academic study of religion? Will we still be relevant? Before I undertake to answer these questions, it should go without saying, given the previous questions and answers that this volume has put forth, that religion offers one of the primary means for creating group identity. Such identity works on the assumption, to paraphrase Jonathan Z. Smith, that people are LIKE US and that people are NOT LIKE US, and that we must try to articulate how, why, when, and where such perceived similarities and dissimilarities reside. Such distinctions lead to a host of, for lack of a better term, coping strategies as various groups seek to make sense of their often highly chaotic social and political worlds. Religion, of course, contributes to this social cartography because it, more than any other discourse, is that which accounts for sameness and difference through its creation of narratives (e.g., myths), categories and rhetoric that elevate sameness and difference to the level of ontology or metaphysics.

To return to those subquestions mentioned above: What might religion look like in the future? Religion, framed in this light, would seem to offer simplicity in the face of chaos and certainty in times of uncertainty. This is religion's virtue, for many, just as it is simultaneously one of the greatest threats to global stability. As the world become more chaotic and more uncertain, one possible future for·religion—with its discourse of absolutes sublimated to the level of divine agency—is that it will become more entrenched in drawing stark lines between 'us' and 'them' on the one hand, and between 'good' and 'evil' on the other. We have to realize, of course, that the terms in the previous sentence with quotation marks around them ought to be seen as relative or unstable. Too often, however, they are not perceived in this manner. They are instead seen as categories or markers that are as natural as can be. We see this almost daily as battle lines are drawn between a Euro-American Christian West on the one hand and Islam on the other. Islam, increasingly defined as hostile to Western values, is constructed as the villain, that which threatens to undermine world order. In like manner, we cannot deny the fact that certain Muslim jihadists use the exact same rhetoric to portray the West, now seen as anathema to Muslim values, in a highly negative light. Religion, or whatever name we decide to give it, has always carved the world up in this manner. There is no reason to believe that any of this will change in the future, whether near or otherwise.

We have all witnessed the repercussions of this over the last few years. There is a fear, for example, to take in refuges or displaced migrants from Muslim countries lest they be furtive or future 'terrorists' or that their numbers will pose a risk to a fragile and fearful white, Christian majority. The current president of the United States has recently signed an executive order that prevents travel to the United States from seven predominantly Muslim countries (and in which he does not have business interests). Though the order has recently been challenged in the courts, it seems to be relatively popular among those rank-and-file

Americans who supported the president, many of whom would consider themselves to be 'good' Christians. Here we see, then, just how the rhetoric of religion—'good' versus 'bad' ones, 'real' versus 'fake' ones, 'spiritual' versus 'ideological' ones—plots social groups on an imagined map that threatens global stability. Such a cartography unfortunately risks becoming even more acute in the future.

Scholars of religion have to resist the urge to follow suit. Many scholars are guilty of echoing back such rhetoric that seeks to differentiate between so-called good and bad religions. I have written a great deal about how scholars of Islam now tend to be in the business to carving out 'good' Islam and, in the process, denigrating as inauthentic those versions of the religion with which they disagree. Such moves are not helpful, however, as they forget that religions are but social constructs that sublimate human ideology to the level of that which they perceive to be transcendent. If we say that some religions do this better than others or that some forms of a particular religion do it better than other forms, then we exacerbate the problem.

This brings us to the second subquestion: How will religion be classified in the future and by whom? It seems quite clear that this is now, at least in the United States and other liberal democracies, largely a question for the courts. As scholars like Jonathan Z. Smith and Russell McCutcheon have well argued, it is the courts, and not scholars of religion, where matters of religion and secularism—what gets to count as 'religious' and what does not—are not only decided but increasingly enforced. Perhaps, then, we ought to be as interested in study legal rulings—in the United States, in Europe, in India, in Israel, to name but a few examples—both in the past and the present as much as we tend to study so-called religious texts. It is such legal decisions that are responsible for how others understand both their own religions, but perhaps just as importantly those of other peoples.

Here the future of the courts in the United States, and how they decide to adjudicate such matters, will be telling. Perhaps now more than ever, the Establishment Clause in the First Amendment, which prohibits Congress from preferring or elevating one religion over another, is under threat. Once again, the future of religion—both in the United States and other places—will intimately be connected to legal and governmental (if they are in fact different) fiat. The question becomes, do we account for diversity (do we celebrate it or do we fear it?) and legalize it (say, as Canada does with is legal policy of Multiculturalism as enshrined in the Charter of Rights and Freedoms) or do we legalize against it?

This brings us to our third subquestion: What role will scholars of religion play in this future? I think this depends on how we define the task of the academic study of religion. If we define its task as bringing to light the 'sacred' in the world's religious traditions, as facilitating interfaith or interreligious dialogue, or as differentiating 'good' from 'bad' religion, then I would imagine that the future for the field is rather bleak. The study of religion will increasingly be out of sync with the world in which we inhabit. It will become, if it has not already, a form of liberal ecumenism.

If, however, we define the academic study of religion as that which attunes us to the ways in which social groups imagine and construct their inherited and perceived realities and how said constructions structure how people think and classify (including how they differentiate between 'good' and 'evil,' and 'us' and 'them'), then there may well be a future for us. That future, unlike many of the issues raised in the two other subquestions, is ultimately in our hands. It seems to me that either we can chose to be relevant and show others (in the Humanities, among other places) just what we have learned from our investigations and understanding of religion as a social formation, or we can be in the business of trying to articulate that which is inarticulable (to wit, the so-called sacred).

Within this context, *Religion in Five Minutes* has successfully presented answers to some of the major questions that we have about religion. It should also be clear that there are many of us that opt for studying religion as a historical and social phenomenon as opposed to a timeless manifestation of the sacred.

In the final analysis, whatever we may think of it, howsoever we may define it, and how we choose to study it, 'religion'—no matter how it is constructed, imagined, studied, or undermined—does not seem to be going away anytime soon.

About the author

Aaron W. Hughes is the Philip S. Bernstein Chair in the Department of Religion and Classics at the University of Rochester.

Suggestions for further reading

In this book

See also Chapter 80 (future of 'religion').

Elsewhere

Arnal, William and Russell T. McCutcheon. *The Sacred Is the Profane: The Political Nature of 'Religion.'* New York: Oxford University Press, 2013.

Smith, Jonathan Z. *Relating Religion: Essays in the Study of Religion.* Chicago, IL: University of Chicago Press, 2004.

Index

CPSIA information can be obtained
at www.ICGtesting.com
Printed in the USA
LVHW080602281120
672719LV00001B/1

9 781781 794654